T0330033

Trade Specialisation, Technology and Economic Growth

NEW HORIZONS IN THE ECONOMICS OF INNOVATION

General Editor: Christopher Freeman, *Emeritus Professor of Science Policy, SPRU – Science and Technology Policy Research, University of Sussex, UK*

Technical innovation is vital to the competitive performance of firms and of nations and for the sustained growth of the world economy. The economics of innovation is an area that has expanded dramatically in recent years and this major series, edited by one of the most distinguished scholars in the field, contributes to the debate and advances in research in this most important area.

The main emphasis is on the development and application of new ideas. The series provides a forum for original research in technology, innovation systems and management, industrial organization, technological collaboration, knowledge and innovation, research and development, evolutionary theory and industrial strategy. International in its approach, the series includes some of the best theoretical and empirical work from both well-established researchers and the new generation of scholars.

Titles in the series include:

The Economics of Knowledge Production
Funding and the Structure of University Research
Aldo Geuna

Innovation and Research Policies
An International Comparative Analysis
Paul Diederen, Paul Stoneman, Otto Toivanen and Arjan Wolters

Learning and Knowledge Management in the Firm
From Knowledge Accumulation to Strategic Capabilities
Gabriela Dutrénit

Knowledge Spillovers and Economic Growth
Regional Growth Differentials across Europe
M.C.J. Caniëls

Successful Innovation
Towards a New Theory for the Management of Small and Medium Sized Enterprises
Jan Cobbenhagen

Industrial Diversification and Innovation
An International Study of the Aerospace Industry
François Texier

Trade Specialisation, Technology and Economic Growth
Theory and Evidence from Advanced Countries
Keld Laursen

Firm Size, Innovation and Market Structure
The Evolution of Industry Concentration and Instability
Mariana Mazzucato

Knowledge Flows in National Systems of Innovation
A Comparative Analysis of Sociotechnical Constituencies
in Europe and Latin America
Edited by Roberto Lopez Martinez and Andrea Piccaluga

Trade Specialisation, Technology and Economic Growth

Theory and Evidence from Advanced Countries

Keld Laursen

PhD, Assistant Professor, Department of Industrial Economics and Strategy, Copenhagen Business School, Denmark

NEW HORIZONS IN THE ECONOMICS OF INNOVATION

Edward Elgar
Cheltenham, UK • Northampton, MA, USA

Published by
Edward Elgar Publishing Limited
Glensanda House
Montpellier Parade
Cheltenham
Glos GL50 1UA
UK

Edward Elgar Publishing, Inc.
136 West Street
Suite 202
Northampton
Massachusetts 01060
USA

A catalogue record for this book
is available from the British Library

Library of Congress Cataloguing in Publication Data

Laursen, Keld, 1967–
    Trade specialisation, technology and economic growth : theory and evidence
from advanced countries / Keld Laursen.
    (New horizons in the economics of innovation)
    Includes bibliographical references and index.
    1. Technological innovations—Economic aspects. 2. Economic development.
3. International division of labor. I. Title. II. Series.

    HC79.T4 L375 2000
    338.9–dc21
                                                                    00–039370
ISBN 1 84064 385 4

Printed and bound in Great Britain by Bookcraft (Bath) Ltd.

Contents

PART V   CONCLUSION

Tables

Acknowledgements

This book is based on my PhD thesis carried out at Aalborg University in Denmark. The editing of the manuscript was carried out at the Department of Industrial Economics and Strategy, Copenhagen Business School. Bent Dalum supervised the thesis, and I would like to thank him for good supervision, encouragement and for allowing me to 'plug into' his large international network. To this end, the book has been created while I was a part of a number of international networks from which I have benefited greatly. First, I have gained a lot from taking part in the ETIC (Economics of Technical and Institutional Change) PhD programme, sponsored by the European Commission, not only from the lecturers, but also from my fellow students at the various ETIC courses. Furthermore, I have participated in a European Commission TSER (Targeted Socio-Economic Research) project on 'Technology, Economic Integration and Social Cohesion' (TEIS), co-ordinated by MERIT (Bart Verspagen and Luc Soete), in the period from 1996 to 1998. The research concerned the sub-theme 'Specialisation, Growth and Technology'. During the existence of this project I have profited greatly from having been given the opportunity of presenting my work at the accompanying conferences in Rome, Vienna, Maastricht, Naples and Göteborg in front of some of the best specialists in the field of international specialisation, growth and technology. In this context I wish to thank especially Bart Verspagen, but also Paolo Guerrieri, Daniele Archibugi and Mario Pianta for valuable inputs. Furthermore, I wish to thank the commentators on my work in connection with conferences of DRUID (Danish Research Unit for Industrial Dynamics).

I would like to thank the members of my thesis committee: Bengt-Åke Lundvall, Jan Fagerberg and Keith Pavitt. Other people have also given comments on individual chapters of the book. They include Esben Sloth Andersen, Pekka Ylä Antilla, John Cantwell, Bo Carlsson, Giovanni Dosi, Ina Drejer, Valentina Meliciani, David Mowery and Gert Villumsen. Their comments have been a valuable source of inspiration. Bent Vestergaard also deserves thanks for assistance in programming one of the models (in GAUSS), estimated in Chapter 5 of this book.

On a more personal note I wish to thank system administrator Lars Anderson and secretary Dorte Køster as well as my PhD colleagues in Aalborg, Anna, Frank, Ina, Marco, Mette and Søren together with my PhD colleagues in Sussex (SPRU), Amal-Lee, Andrea, Ammon, Chaisung, Eugenia, Jon, Orietta, Stefano, Patrizia, Tiago and Valentina for having provided good support throughout the process of creating the book.

PART I

Introduction

1. The Theme

> ...nor is this evolutionary character [of economic change] due to a quasi-automatic increase in population and capital or to vagaries of monetary systems of which exactly the same thing holds true. The fundamental impulse that sets and keeps the capitalist engine in motion comes from the new consumers' goods, the new methods of production or transportation, the new markets, the new forms of industrial organization that capitalist enterprise creates. (Schumpeter, 1942, pp. 82-3).

The aim of this book is to examine the role of international Ricardian specialisation in economic development processes. In this context Ricardian specialisation refers to *specific activities* (such as e.g. specialisation in electronics or in agricultural products), as opposed to Smithian specialisation, which concerns benefits arising due to the *depth* of specialisation, as a result of the division of labour, irrespective of the type of activity. In particular, it is argued in this book, not only does ('aggregate') technological change make a contribution to economic development (as well as do other more 'standard' factors); also specialisation in particular sectors offering differences in technological opportunities and/or differences in income elasticities of demand matter. In this way, the importance of sectoral differences is the centre of rotation of this book.

The book builds on Schumpeter's basic insights stating that technical change is the driving force of economic development and that this change is not evenly distributed over time, countries and sectors. Nevertheless, even though this view is underlying throughout the entire book the label 'neo-Schumpeterian'[1] was chosen, as we do not share the view of Schumpeter that economic development has to do with radical change only (argued forcefully in Schumpeter, 1912, in particular). Rather the Schumpeterian view should be combined with a Marshallian view emphasising that economic development for long periods of time undergoes incremental and path-dependent change, based on economies of scale (Marshall, 1890).[2]

The importance of sectoral differences in exports is demonstrated in Figure 1.1, which illustrates clearly that sectors of exports differ greatly in their growth rates over the period 1970-91.[3] High-tech sectors such as office machines and computers grew more than five times faster than some of the slow-growing sectors, over the period. However, it is also important to note that the sectors are not of equal size, hence increases in markets shares in for instance 'motor

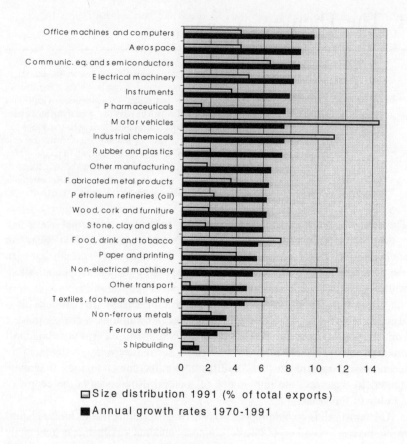

Office machines and computers
Aerospace
Communic. eq. and semiconductors
Electrical machinery
Instruments
Pharmaceuticals
Motor vehicles
Industrial chemicals
Rubber and plastics
Other manufacturing
Fabricated metal products
Petroleum refineries (oil)
Wood, cork and furniture
Stone, clay and glass
Food, drink and tobacco
Paper and printing
Non-electrical machinery
Other transport
Textiles, footwear and leather
Non-ferrous metals
Ferrous metals
Shipbuilding

0 2 4 6 8 10 12 14

☐ Size distribution 1991 (% of total exports)
■ Annual growth rates 1970-1991

Source: Calculations based on the OECD STAN data base, 1995 edition.

Figure 1.1 Annual growth rates of sectoral exports, by an aggregate of 18 OECD countries, 1970-91

vehicles' is of greater economic importance than an equal percentage increase in for instance 'instruments'.

Beside the observed differences between sectors, another motivation for writing this empirically oriented book, exploring the role of specialisation and structural change in the economy, has been the recent and rapid emergence of formal theoretical models looking at the same topic. Within the neoclassical framework Lucas (1988), Krugman (1987) and Grossman and Helpman, (1991a) can be mentioned, while Verspagen (1993) and Dosi *et al.* (1994) are some of the influential evolutionary theoretical contributions in this field.[4]

1.1. RESEARCH QUESTIONS

With the rapid development of theoretical models in the evolutionary tradition, as well as in some models in the neoclassical tradition (giving a prominent role to Ricardian specialisation in economic development), as a starting point, the research question to be addressed in this book can be posed: *How does Ricardian specialisation affect economic development in relatively advanced countries?*

The author is aware of the fact that this broad question can lead in many directions. Thus it is important to confine the focus of the book further. Firstly, we confine ourselves to the OECD countries, as being the 'relatively advanced countries', mentioned above. Secondly, the study is further focused by means of breaking down the question into three sub-questions:

A. Do countries converge or diverge in terms of their specialisation patterns over time? In this context we address the question of the degree to which trade (and technological) specialisation patterns are stable across both countries and sectors, as well as the question of whether countries tend to become more or less specialised over time. This is the most explorative part of the book, although we start from a hypothesis asserting that trade and technological specialisation patterns are path-dependent over time, and a hypothesis stating that 'OECD catch-up countries' are the countries experiencing the highest degree of structural change.

B. How does technology enter as an explanation of the direction of trade specialisation of countries? This question concerns firstly, the inducement mechanisms to innovation and the role of (horizontal) technological diversification as a determinant of trade specialisation. Secondly, the concern is the relative importance of 'own' sector technological effort *vis-á-vis* the importance of technological inter-sectoral linkages to other sectors. The basic hypothesis is in this context that 'own' sector effort is relatively more important for science based sectors, while linkages are relatively more important for production intensive sectors (scale intensive and specialised supplier sectors).[5]

C. Do international specialisation patterns (and changes therein) matter for growth? The question deals firstly with whether technological specialisation (and change therein) matters for trade growth at the level of the country. The second way of addressing the question is by examining whether trade specialisation matters for economic growth. The hypothesis is that specialisation and structural change are important factors in explaining growth both in terms of market shares as well as in terms of economic growth.

It should be pointed out that the contribution of this book is mainly empirical. It should also be stressed that the purpose of the book is not to discriminate between different theoretical approaches. Instead we test hypotheses based on theoretical *issues,* and in each case discuss what different theoretical approaches (under different labels be they 'appreciative'[6], neoclassical, post-Keynesian or evolutionary) have to say about the issue in question.

Another methodological issue to be dealt with is the fact that the unit of analysis is the nation state (in addition to the sector and industry). This choice is dictated by the belief that nations are still relevant units of analysis, for studying processes of economic development. However, in the light of increasing internationalisation, or even 'globalisation', such a view might be seen as increasingly controversial. Nevertheless, the author shares the view that institutions such as firm organisation; technological support systems; education systems; financial systems; and university systems are still national, and affect countries' technological and economic performance (Nelson, 1993). Empirical analyses, such as Hicks *et al.* (1994) have shown that publications produced by Japanese companies (basic research) tend to over-cite the national science system by approximately 30 per cent, which in turn suggests that the economic benefits of university research are to some extent geographically and linguistically localised, since they are embodied in persons and institutions, and thus mainly transmitted through personal contacts. Similar findings have been made by Narin and Olivastro (1992) showing that national patents cite national science and vice versa. Another piece of empirical evidence supporting the view that nations still matter, is provided by Patel and Pavitt (1991). They show that the 400 largest companies in the world, on average and in the period 1981-86, took out more than 80 per cent of their US patents in their perceived home country. Moreover, the type of activity a country attracts in the international division of labour, depends to some extent on the country's specific natural endowments, capabilities and institutions. Hence, national differences might in fact be reinforced by the locational decisions of multinational corporations (Cantwell and Janne, 1999).

1.2. OUTLINE

The book is split into five parts. However, the main contribution is to be found in the three analytical Parts (II-IV). Each of the three parts corresponds to one of the three sub-questions, described in the section above.

The present chapter is the first chapter in the introductory Part I of the book (Chapters 1-3). Part I proceeds in *Chapter 2*, with a survey of the theoretical literature, classified according to the three analytical parts of the book (Parts II-IV). The chapter discusses 'appreciative theories', neoclassical theories, post-Keynesian approaches and evolutionary approaches in relation to each of the (three) issues, dealt with in the three analytical parts. Each of the three sections in Chapter 2 end up in the formulation of a set of theoretical 'propositions'. These propositions will then be used as a starting point in each of the seven analytical chapters in Parts II-IV of the book. All analytical chapters relate in the conclusions to the relevant propositions set up in Chapter 2.

Chapter 3 is a comparison of different measures of specialisation, as applied in the empirical trade literature. However, the chapter gives firstly a description of how countries are specialised using the 'revealed comparative advantage' (*RCA*) as the measure of specialisation. Secondly, it is argued that the *RCA* is asymmetric around its neutral value. Hence, the *RCA* should be modified in such a way that it becomes symmetric around its neutral value. Finally, the (symmetric) *RCA* is compared to four other types of measures of specialisation. The nature of the differences between the measures is discussed from a theoretical perspective, and subsequently the measures are also compared on the basis of 'real numbers'. The latter analysis reveals that the different alternatives do in fact correlate with the *RCA*, rather strongly. The main contribution of the chapter lies in the analysis of the properties of the *RCA* index, as well as in the systematic comparison between the *RCA* measure, and the alternatives.

Part II of the book (Chapters 4 and 5) addresses sub-question A, as it deals with different aspects of the development of international specialisation patterns over the last 2-3 decades.

Chapter 4 examines whether or not the group of OECD countries are characterised by a high degree of stability of their *export* specialisation patterns at the country level. Furthermore we test whether countries have become more or less specialised. In this context we make a new distinction between specialisation (or de-specialisation) in trade patterns on the one hand, and divergence (or on the contrary convergence) on the other. A specialisation process refers to a process in which specialisation *intra-country* becomes more dispersed (and vice versa for de-specialisation). In contrast, a divergence process refers to a process in which countries become more different in terms of specialisation in a particular sector, *across countries* (and vice versa for convergence). We examine the sensitivity for the level of aggregation, and we apply a period of nearly three decades from 1965 to 1992. Twenty OECD countries are considered.

The *intra-country* results show that national specialisation patterns are rather sticky, although there is a tendency for countries to de-specialise in the medium to long term. The *sector-wise* results display convergence both in terms of β- and σ-convergence. Our results also confirm the hypothesis that the OECD catching up countries (Japan, Finland, Greece, Ireland, Italy, Portugal, Spain and Turkey) on average experience the highest degree of structural change in their specialisation patterns, over the period in question. In conclusion we discuss the general results of the chapter (de-specialisation in particular) in the context of economic integration.

As mentioned above, Chapter 4 shows that there is a general tendency for OECD countries to de-specialise in terms of export specialisation over the last 20-25 years. This finding is in contrast to findings made by other authors, working on technological specialisation. These authors found increasing technological specialisation from the late 1970s to the early 1980s measured as specialisation in US patents. Hence, the first aim of *Chapter 5* is to investigate whether these contradictory findings are due to a 'real world' phenomenon, or whether the explanation is purely technical, by comparing the development of export specialisation to specialisation in terms of US patents, using the same methodology, and level of aggregation. The second aim is to analyse the extent to which countries and sectors display stable specialisation patterns over time, also both in terms of exports and in terms of technology. The latter analysis is a novelty in the sense that it is conducted by means of the application of an empirical model, allowing for the analysis of the development of specialisation patterns for what concerns both sectors and countries, in one single model.

Chapter 5 confirms that the OECD countries did in general de-specialise in terms of export specialisation. The evidence is less conclusive with regard to technological specialisation, as the results are mixed in the sense that just about half of the countries tend to increase in terms of the level of specialisation, while the other half tend to engage in de-specialisation. In terms of country and sectoral stability of specialisation patterns, it can be concluded that both trade specialisation and technological specialisation patterns are path-dependent in the sense that all country and sectoral patterns are correlated over time (i.e. over seven three year intervals), within the period in question. In comparison however, trade specialisation patterns are found to be more stable than are technological specialisation patterns.

Among the countries, Australia, Finland, France, West Germany, Greece, Italy, Portugal, Spain, Sweden and the United Kingdom display the highest degree of turbulence in the specialisation patterns, across sectors and time. The criterion is whether or not the hypothesis of an unchanged pattern can be rejected for both types of specialisation. Concerning the hypothesis of OECD catching up countries experiencing the highest degree of turbulence in the specialisation patterns, the results are not as clear-cut as they were in Chapter 4, although for the OECD 'catch-up countries' in the period in question

(Finland, Greece, Italy, Spain and Portugal) we do find that the specialisation patterns of these countries (Spain and Portugal in particular) belong to the group of countries experiencing the highest degree of turbulence, both in terms of trade and technology. The difference in results has to do with the time periods considered, as Chapter 4 considers a period starting in 1965, while Chapter 5 starts in 1971. In this way it appears that e.g. Japan encountered a high degree of structural change in the 1960s, while this process stopped from the 1970s onwards.

After having dealt with the development of specialisations patterns over time, the next sequential step is to deal with the determinants of the direction of international trade specialisation, in order to address sub-question B. This is done in Part III of the book (Chapters 6-7).

Chapter 6 takes as its starting point the importance of advanced users in home markets as an inducement to technological innovation, providing an explanation for parts of international export specialisation. In this context, upstream-downstream interaction has been made the generic micro-foundation of theories of national systems of innovation. However, Chapter 6 argues that user-producer interaction is not the only (country-specific) inducement mechanism to innovation. Rather, the finding of Chapter 6 is in line with the proposition that when firms are science-based, linkages tend to be horizontal rather than vertical. The chapter mobilises historical and bibliometric methods to trace the long term development of technology in the Danish pharmaceutical company Novo Nordisk, and its links with the local (particularly university) environment. Chapter 6 demonstrates the importance of science-based competencies in moving from natural resource based technologies to those of greater sophistication, thereby influencing trade specialisation of advanced countries.

Whereas Chapter 6 looks at inducement mechanisms to trade specialisation in a science based sector, *Chapter 7* takes a more general approach in being a statistical analysis of several inducement mechanisms. Within the 'technology gap' approach there has been one tradition which has applied cumulativeness in technological change as an explanation, while another tradition has emphasised the role of inter-sectoral linkages (the so-called home market effect). However, given that the sources of innovation (inducements mechanisms) differ between firms according to principal sector of activity, different variables should not be expected to be of equal importance across industrial sectors. Thus, using the Pavitt taxonomy as a starting point, Chapter 7 statistically investigates the importance of a set of variables reflecting different inducement mechanisms, across 9 OECD countries. The main novelty of the chapter is the combination of the two technology based explanations for international trade specialisation, into one single empirical model. The chapter concludes that the two types of technological activities, namely technological activities in the 'own' sector, and inter-sectoral linkages are both important in the determination of national export specialisation patterns. However, the importance differs according to the mode of innovation in each type of sector.

After having dealt with the direction of trade specialisation, Part IV (Chapters 8-10), looks at whether the direction of specialisation has any impact on the rate of economic development in order to take up sub-question C.

Thus, *Chapter 8* examines whether the degree to which countries are specialised in initially, or move into, sectors with above average technological opportunities, has any impact on growth in aggregate market shares of exports, using constant market share (CMS) analysis. CMS analysis decomposes the aggregate growth rate of exports of a country into various components, based on the sectoral composition of the exports performed by that country, and then compares the vector of exports by that country to an average of all countries included in the analysis. One novelty of this chapter is the application of CMS analysis on patent data, rather than on the usual trade data. The components from the analysis are subsequently entered into a regression analysis, taken together with other variables.

The results of Chapter 8 demonstrate that there is a positive relationship between trade performance and the individual countries' ability to move (faster than average) into technological sectors offering above average technological opportunities.

Chapter 9 moves on from the issue of trade performance dealt with in Chapter 8 to the (controversial) question of to what extent the growth performance of an economy is determined by its external relations. Several types of theoretical literature on the topic of trade, growth and specialisation, including neoclassical approaches, post-Keynesian literature and some models in evolutionary economics, have shown that it is possible to enjoy higher rates of economic growth, given the presence of certain sectors in the economy, be they high-tech or fast-growing sectors. The chapter applies a data set on growth and trade in 11 manufacturing sectors, for the period 1965-1988, for the OECD area. The main novelty in the database is the assignment of these 75 products in the trade data to the 11 industrial sectors. The relationship between growth and specialisation is tested by running a regression with the sectoral growth of value added as the dependent variable, and several variables, including some measuring specialisation as well as other factors, as the independent variables. A novelty of the chapter is the application of principal components analysis in order to compress the abundant information on intra-sectoral specialisation.

The regression results presented in Chapter 9 indicate that specialisation does indeed matter for economic growth. However, this impact seems to be gradually wearing off during the 1980s, as is the case for other factors included in the regression analysis.

Chapter 10 extends the previous chapter by resting on the same theoretical discussion and by exploring a very similar research question, namely whether Ricardian specialisation matters for growth. However, whereas Chapter 9 examined whether intra-industry specialisation matters for growth at the level of the industry, Chapter 10 is an analysis of the effect of inter-industry specialisation on macro economic growth. Basically the idea is to conduct a constant market share (CMS) analysis (as in Chapter 8, but in this chapter based on trade data), and afterwards include the obtained effects in regression models, using panel data techniques.

The dependent variable is annual data on economic growth (18 OECD countries), over the period 1972-90. The independent variables are CMS effects mentioned above, as well as the initial level of income relative to the US (a catching up variable); growth in terms of technology, based on number of US patents held by the firms of the country in question; and growth in terms of capital stock.

The growth adaptation effect (measuring whether the country in question has actively - more than the average country - moved into slow or fast growing sectors) is the only significant variable (positive sign) of the CMS effects. Hence, it is concluded that a certain dynamism in terms of structural *change* is required by countries in order to achieve high levels of economic growth at the macro level. The final part of Chapter 10 deals with the question of whether the fast-growing sectors (as measured in the CMS analysis) are high-tech or not. Based on a comparison between the OECD growth vector from the CMS analysis, on the one hand, and R&D intensities in the 22 sectors (for the 1970s and for the 1980s), on the other, it is concluded that the fast-growing sectors are in general also high-tech sectors.

Finally, Part V *(Chapter 11)* contains the conclusion of the book. First the results of the book are briefly summed up. Second, policy implications of the results are discussed. The policy implications concern the importance of acknowledging sectoral differences, when implementing policy. Furthermore, the possibility and difficulties for enhancing economic growth through a policy effort, attempting to influence specialisation patterns are discussed. Finally, some directions for future research, based on the book, are presented and discussed.

1.3. MAIN LIMITATIONS

This book has two main limitations, given its aim. The first, and most serious limitation concerns the fact that the analysis of specialisation and structural change is confined to the manufacturing sector. In fact, the private service sector makes up the same proportion of the economy, as does manufacturing in many developed countries. In addition to being a growing sector in most advanced countries, the service sector has also become more innovative in recent years (Tidd, Bessant and Pavitt, 1997). However, the exclusion of the service sector is due to severe data limitations, and hence the inclusion of services (preferably broken down into industries) in analysis of this type, is left for future research. The second limitation concerns the fact that all chapters apply export data. Thus, production sold for domestic consumption is not included in the analysis. Again the exclusion is due to lack of available data.

NOTES

1. In fact 'post-Schumpeterian' would have been a better label. However, in order to position the book in the tradition of Nelson and Winter (1982), Fagerberg (1988), Dosi, Pavitt and Soete (1990), and Verspagen (1993) the term 'neo-Schumpeterian' has been maintained.

2. See Andersen (1994) for a discussion of the need to reconcile the Schumpeterian with the Marshallian point of view on the nature of technical change.

3. As no deflator was available for all 22 sectors over the entire period, the annual growth rates in exports for the OECD countries were deflated in a very rough way, as the OECD US GDP deflator was applied. However, since the purpose of Figure 1.1 is to give a broad overview of sectoral differences, the rough approximation can be justified.

4. Although not belonging to any of the two schools referred to here, Pasinetti's (1981) post-Keynesian model of structural change should be mentioned as another important source of inspiration for this book.

5. For a description of science based, scale intensive, and specialised supplier sectors, see Pavitt (1984). A description of the Pavitt sectors can also be found in Chapter 2 of this book.

6. Nelson and Winter (1982, p. 46) depicts appreciative theorising as being non-formal theorising defining the economic variables and the relationships that are important to understand, giving a language for discussing these, and providing a mode of acceptable explanation.

2. A Survey of the Theoretical Literature on Trade and Growth

This chapter surveys theories of the development, determinants and economic effects of international trade specialisation. In the spirit of this book, the chapter is organised according to the issues dealt with in the three empirical parts of the book (Parts II-IV), rather than according to different streams of literature[1], as it is done in many surveys of this type. It should also be noted in this context, that this chapter is not a survey of the entire literature on trade and growth; it is a survey of the theoretical literature relevant for the empirical parts of the book. Accordingly, the chapter is structured as follows. Section 2.1 is devoted to the discussion of theorising on the development of international trade specialisation patterns. In other words, the section discusses the mechanisms which might affect the specialisation patterns of relatively developed countries, in terms of convergence or divergence. Section 2.2 deals with the classical question of the determinants of international specialisation patterns. Finally, Section 2.3 addresses the theoretical discussion of how and the extent to which trade specialisation and growth are interrelated. Each of the three sections will end up by forming a set of propositions, which will be used as a point of departure in each of the chapters in Parts II-IV of the book.

2.1. THE DEVELOPMENT OF INTERNATIONAL SPECIALISATION PATTERNS

This section is an attempt to highlight the first research question of this book concerning whether countries converge or diverge in terms of their specialisation patterns over time, from a theoretical point of view. Hence this section is closely connected to Part II of the book, dealing with this question from an empirical point of view. First a discussion on the common forces which might change or preserve technological and trade specialisation over time will be carried out (Sub-section 2.1.1). Second, a discussion on mechanisms which can lead to a divergence between technological and trade specialisation patterns, can be found in Sub-section 2.1.2.

2.1.1. Structural Change and Patterns of Specialisation

Persistence in specialisation patterns

In the evolutionary literature it is recognised that important aspects of technology are mainly specific and tacit in nature, since it is to a large extent embodied in persons and in institutions, in addition to being cumulative over time (Dosi, Pavitt and Soete, 1990, p. 8). In this model, firms are not likely to improve their technology, by making a survey of the complete stock of knowledge, before making technical choices. Rather, given the differentiated nature of technology, firms will try to improve and diversify their technology by searching in zones that enable them to build on the firms' existing technology base. Thus, technological and organisational change is a cumulative process, constraining firms in the possibilities of what they can do, by what they have done in the past (i.e. path dependency). When such a perception of technology is recognised, its development over time ceases to be random, but is constrained by the set of existing activities (ibid). Thus, given that firms make up most of the exports (and technology) of a country, one should expect that specialisation patterns remain stable over long time periods.

Furthermore and from a neoclassical point of view, Krugman (1987) presents a model which predicts stability in the specialisation pattern of countries, given the presence of economies of scale. In the model the productivity of resources in each sector, in each country, depends on an index of cumulative experience ('learning-by-doing'), creating economies of scale at the level of the industry. Thus, once a pattern of specialisation is established (e.g. by chance) in the model, it remains unchanged with changes in relative productivity acting to further lock the pattern in.

Structural change

Dosi, Pavit and Soete (1990) describes how divergence/convergence in trade specialisation patterns might be related to overall growth performance. The basic idea is that, if divergence in overall growth performance prevails, this is seen as a result of cumulative innovation, being reflected in divergence in trade specialisation patterns. If, on the other hand, convergence in growth performance is the dominant feature, then this is mainly the result of diffusion of technology, which is in turn reflected in converging trade specialisation patterns.

If cumulativeness in technological progress is not only present at the company level, but also at the level of the country, virtuous and vicious circles might arise in the pattern of international advantages and disadvantages in trade, which in turn might affect national economic performance. Thus, in this situation, economic and technological forces interact in a cumulative way.

However, despite the forces in international trade which tend to reinforce strength and weaknesses in terms of growth and trade performance, there are forces enabling backward countries to catch up. According to Dosi, Pavitt and Soete (1990, p. 129) the following channels of technology transfer tend to induce convergence and the international diffusion of technology:
1) the 'free' international diffusion of codified knowledge, e.g. patents and publications, 2) processes of technological imitation, e.g. reverse engineering by late-coming companies and countries, 3) traded transfers of technology (licensing, transfer of know-how etc.), 4) foreign direct investment in late-coming countries, by companies which own, among their company-specific advantages, differential technological capabilities, and 5) international trade in capital goods and intermediate components.

However, while these are all channels of knowledge and rent spillovers, which might assist in explaining catching up, the catching up is not unconditional, since also an absorptive capacity is required. Such a capacity has been termed 'social capability' by Abramowitz (1986), and can be described as the level of education and institutions created for the purpose of absorbing knowledge diffused internationally. Thus rather than automatically capturing technology spillovers, countries have to invest in the capacity to do so.

Beelen and Verspagen (1994) suggest that the catching up process involves (at least) two different, but complementary, modes. The first is by means of the mechanism of knowledge spillovers, while the other is by means of structural change. While the first mechanism is pretty straightforward, the latter deserves further description. The latter mechanism reverses the arguments of Pasinetti (1981), who argued that the extent to which the specialisation structure of a country is similar to that of the countries operating at the technological frontier, determines the degree to which this country can catch up. The reverse argument states that in order to catch up, a country must change its production structure in order to become more adapted to catch technology spillovers. Furthermore, high-tech industries (or alternatively the areas of specialisation of the leading countries) generally seem to yield higher value added per unit of production. Thus, there is an incentive for followers to develop activities in high-tech sectors. From the demand-side, Pasinetti shows that fundamental structural change is unavoidable for an economy with increasing per capita income, since income elasticities change with the value of per capita income itself. With the level of per capita income growing, the importance of luxury goods becomes greater, and thus there will be an incentive for the firms of catching up countries to produce these goods domestically rather than to import them.

Thus, in relation to research of this book, one would expect trade specialisation patterns to converge in the OECD countries, given that convergence in per capita income has been a dominant feature in the postwar period, until 1973. However, since 1973 convergence has slowed down and has now nearly stopped. Nevertheless, Beelen and Verspagen (1994) argue that convergence in trade patterns will not slow down as fast as levels of per capita income, since the two modes of catching up are not likely to be synchronised in time. Accordingly, the follower country must first catch up in terms of competitiveness before convergence in patterns of specialisation can take place. Therefore, the authors argue that technology spillovers are likely to be most important initially. Once the catching up process has gained momentum, a convergence trend with regard to specialisation structures sets in.

From the supply-side, and based on the Dixit and Stiglitz (1977) model of monopolistic competition and expanding product variety, Krugman (1989) made a neoclassical model portraying the role of structural change in growth processes. The idea is that countries expand their product variety as they grow, and thus face favourable income elasticities at the aggregate level. Hence, we should also expect the fastest degree of structural change among catching-up countries, from this point of view.

Concerning the relationship between structural change and the types of products/technologies, it can be argued that more sophisticated products are more difficult to transfer across borders, as production techniques for these products are complex and hence hard to codify (Dosi, Pavitt and Soete, 1990). Therefore, we would expect high-tech products to be more stable across national borders, when compared to other more low-tech products. This idea is consistent with the so-called product-life-cycle theories (Vernon, 1966; Grossman and Helpman, 1991b) in which high-tech products are developed in the home country, while more mature products spread out to be produced abroad (in less sophisticated countries).

The main prediction of the Heckscher-Ohlin-Samuelson (HOS) model is that a country will export those goods which use most intensively the country's more abundant factors of production (for more detail, see Sub-section 2.2.1, below). However, the model also has implications in the context of this sub-section, as the model predicts increasing specialisation as well - all other things being equal - if trade barriers are being reduced, given different factor endowments in various countries. In this context it can be noted that European integration has been on-going throughout the period in question (for documentation of growing intra EU trade, see Ben-David, 1991). It should be stressed that the prediction is the same from more recent models of 'dynamic' comparative advantage (e.g. Grossman, 1992).

Nevertheless, countries might not (only) specialise inter-industry, they might also specialise intra-industry, due to product differentiation. In this context a distinction between horizontal and vertical product differentiation has been made. Horizontal product differentiation occurs when there is import and export between two countries, in basically the same products of similar quality, but with different characteristics, while vertical product differentiation refers to two-way trade in similar products of varying quality. The theoretical basis for the former type of product differentiation was developed by Lancaster (1980); Krugman (1981) and Helpman (1981), and more recently by Bergstrand (1990). These models suggest that the more similar countries are in terms of their endowments and incomes, the greater the share of horizontal intra-industry trade.

Theoretical models of the latter type of product differentiation was developed by Falvey (1981) and by Flam and Helpman (1987). In the Flam and Helpman model, the share of bilateral intra-industry trade between the North and the South is systematically related to differences in product quality in products produced and exported in each 'region'. The North is assumed to export higher quality products, while the South produces lower quality products. Two-way trade occurs when the quality range being produced does not exactly match the product versions being demanded.

2.1.2. The Relationship Between Trade and Technological Specialisation

The previous section discussed the relationship between growth processes on the one hand, and change in specialisation patterns on the other. This section will discuss the mechanisms which might make technological specialisation and trade specialisation patterns move in the same direction, or make these patterns move in different directions. In this context it can be noted that the direction of trade and technological specialisation will be examined empirically in Chapter 5 of the book. The discussion in this section will be carried out in terms of *technology as a determinant of trade*, (natural resource) *endowments*, the role and properties of *knowledge* in relation to localisation of business activities, and finally in terms of *measurement* problems.

Technology as a determinant of trade. Under the label of 'technology gap theory' Posner (1961) introduced the idea that temporary monopoly profits can be appropriated, based on a technological lead, in an international trade context. Hence trade flows can (partly) be explained by technological differences between countries within sectors (see Section 2.2 below, for a more detailed exposition).

Endowments. As will be argued below (in Section 2.2), the Heckscher-Ohlin-Samuelson model has been unable to explain the pattern of trade in general. Nevertheless, there are a number of commodities for which the model does work. For instance, it is clear that natural resource based commodities are in general exported from countries endowed with the relevant natural resources (e.g. agricultural products are exported from countries with abundant arable land). Given that some commodities are 'bound' to their natural resource endowment-base, we should expect that physical commodities are going to be more 'sticky' in relation to transfer of production across national borders, when compared to the corresponding technology class.

Knowledge and localisation. The general framework now used in the standard textbook for the analysis of the multinational enterprise (MNE) is due to Dunning (see e.g. Dunning, 1988), and offers a three part explanation of the existence of multinationals (known as the *OLI* paradigm). Multinationals can be explained by the *ownership* advantages enjoyed by the firm, the *location* advantages of foreign operation, and the *internalisation* advantages of keeping kinds of transactions within the firm. Foreign direct investment by, say, Nissan in the UK might be explained by the attraction of European consumers to particular qualities of Nissan's cars, the need to produce some of these products in Europe to avoid protectionist barriers to imports from Japan, or to encourage quicker corporate responses to local market needs. Formal models with the aim of incorporating some of these insights into trade theory have been developed by e.g. Markusen (1984) and Ethier (1986). These models allow the spatial separation of 'headquarter services' in terms of management and R&D on the one side, and production on the other. Given that a spatial separation (over national borders) between production and R&D exists, we cannot expect the evolution of technological specialisation and trade specialisation to be perfectly congruent.

Measurement. One possible cause of divergence between the development of technological and trade specialisation patterns is that trade specialisation might be determined by factors other than technology. In this way Posner (1961) argued that technology is an important determinant of trade in some sectors, but not in others. One of the reasons for technology not being so important for trade in some sectors, might be that production technology flows more easily across national borders in these sectors. Another potential measurement problem has to do with so-called 'multi-technological' characteristics of products. Granstrand and Sjölander (1990) point out that the product-technology relationship in firms is not of a one-to-one kind. Given the complexity of products, firms are often characterised as 'multi-technological'. That is, the development, production and use of a product usually involve more than one technology and each component can be applied in more than one product. As a consequence, firms require the ability to orchestrate several technologies. A somewhat extreme case in this context is the evidence provided by Patel and Pavitt (1994b). They show that among 440 of the world's largest firms, companies situated in the industry 'motor vehicles' only take out 28.8 per cent of their patents in the technology class 'transport'. Given that one of the ingredients in gaining competitiveness in automobiles is the application of electronics it is not surprising that 20.7 per cent of the patents taken out in the US by companies in 'motor vehicles', were situated in the patents class 'electrical equipment' (including electronics). However, this line of argument should not be stressed too far, since the evidence provided by Patel and Pavitt also displays a broad concordance between the technologies used by the firm and the firm's principal product group (sector). The problem should be kept in mind, but as we are applying data sets in this book at a relatively high level of aggregation, the problem is to some extent alleviated.

Summing up on the development of international specialisation patterns
This section has surveyed the literature on the development of international specialisation patterns. It is admittedly not an area which is fully understood from a theoretical point of view. Nevertheless, the discussion found in Sub-section 2.1.1 can lead to a number of propositions: (a) patterns of specialisation will display persistence over long time periods; (b) catching up countries will experience the fastest rate of change in the patterns of specialisation; (c) low tech products will be more footloose than high-tech products; and finally (d) when economic integration is a central feature of development, specialisation patterns of countries will diverge (or put differently the level of specialisation will increase).

Additionally, the discussion found in Sub-section 2.1.2 can lead to two propositions: (e) technological specialisation is less 'sticky' than is trade specialisation; (f) although several mechanisms, leading trade and technological specialisation to diverge from each other, can be identified, trade and technological specialisation will tend to co-evolve. These propositions [(a)-(f)], will be put under scrutiny in Chapters 4 and 5 of the book.

2.2. THE DETERMINANTS OF INTERNATIONAL SPECIALISATION

This section is an attempt to focus on the second research question of this book, concerning how technology enters as an explanation of the direction of trade specialisation of countries, from a theoretical point of view. Hence this section is closely connected to Part III of the book, dealing with this question mainly from an empirical point of view.

The explanation for international trade specialisation has been a central research topic in economics, at least since Ricardo's *Principles of Political Economy and Taxation* (1817). But whereas Ricardo applied differences in labour productivity across nations as the explanation, the standard explanation for international export specialisation has, in contemporary economics, relied on particular endowments of countries (Ohlin, 1933; Heckscher, 1949). Hence, Sub-section 2.2.1 discusses the Heckscher-Ohlin-Samuelson model of international trade specialisation, while Sub-section 2.2.2 is devoted to discussing approaches explicitly incorporating technology ('own' sector or 'own' country efforts) as an explanation for trade specialisation patterns. Sub-section 2.2.3 deals with the home market hypothesis as an explanatory factor, while Sub-section 2.2.4 makes an attempt to reconcile the three approaches, using the Pavitt taxonomy, and in addition discusses briefly 'national systems of innovation' approaches.

2.2.1. Heckscher-Ohlin

The Heckscher-Ohlin-Samuelson (HOS) model states that comparative advantage is determined by the interaction between nations' resources (the relative abundance of factors of production) and the technology of production (which influences the relative intensity with which different factors of production are used in the production of different products). Hence the prediction is that a country will export those goods which use most intensively the country's more abundant factor of production. The setting of the HOS model is a two-good, two-factor, two-country model, where the two factors considered are labour and capital. Hence, the exports of countries should reflect their relative endowment of labour and capital, by being either labour or capital intensive. Nevertheless, in order to arrive at that prediction, a number of assumptions have to be imposed. One assumption concerns technology, which is assumed to be identical across all countries. Other assumptions are perfect competition and perfect mobility of factors within a country, but complete immobility of factors between countries. Furthermore, demand is assumed to be identical in the two countries; i.e. the relative preferences for each good are identical, when faced with the same relative price for the two goods.

However, the factor proportions theory was first challenged by what became known as the 'Leontief-paradox' (1953), stating that the exports of the US ('endowed' with an internationally high K-L ratio), were slightly less capital-intensive than its imports. The finding spurred a hot debate on the empirical validity of the theory, ranging (at least) into the 1980s. However, Leamer (1980) shows that Leontief's findings do not reveal relative abundance of capital and labour in a multi-factor world, among a set of criticisms. Probably the most comprehensive test of the *n-factor case* of the Heckscher-Ohlin model, also known as the Heckscher-Ohlin-Vanek (HOV) theorem (Vanek, 1968), was conducted by Bowen, Leamer and Sveikauskas (1987). The study calculated the factor content of each of 12 factors embodied in net exports of 27 countries in

1967, using a US matrix of total input requirements for that year. These data were contrasted with national endowment data on the same 12 factors. Rank correlations were made both 'factor-wise' and 'country-wise'. For what concerns the factor-wise (across countries) results, only in four out of the twelve cases, were the variables positively and significantly related. The country-wise (across factors) results displayed only eight out of 27 positive and significant rank correlations. In addition, Trefler (1995) empirically rejected HOV in favour of a modification that allows for home bias in consumption and international technology differences. In the words of Paul Krugman:

> While nobody would deny that there must be some relationship between a country's resources and the resource content of its trade pattern, the effort to explain trade solely on the basis of such resources - in other words without making allowances for differences in national production functions - is generally seen as having, at long last, failed. (1996b, p. 345).

2.2.2. The Importance of Technology for Specialisation

The idea that temporary monopoly profits could be appropriated, based on a technological lead dates back to Schumpeter (1912). This idea was applied by Posner (1961) in an international trade context under the label of 'technology gap theory'. Given the assumption that technology is not a free and universally available good, Posner argued that while technology might be important for trade in some sectors, and not in others, innovations made in one country (in technology intensive sectors) would benefit that country as long as the lead could be kept. That is, a country will have ample first-mover advantages, until other countries have imitated the innovation. In the original formulation, once imitation has taken place, more traditional factors of adjustment and specialisation would take over and determine trade flows. However, as argued by Dosi and Soete (1988), there is not necessarily anything impermanent about the importance of technology in determining trade flows, since static and dynamic scale economies flowing from the initial breakthrough acts to prolong the lead. Coupled with new product innovations, these scale economies might well secure a continuous trade flow.[2]

An example of a formalised neoclassical treatment of the idea is found in Krugman (1985). In the model, technology differs between (two) countries in terms of level, but also goods can be ranked by technology-intensity. The trade pattern reflects an interaction between countries and goods; technologically advanced countries have a comparative advantage in technology-intensive goods (but an absolute advantage in all sectors). One of the outcomes of the model is that technical progress in an advanced country, which widens the technological gap, opens up greater opportunity to trade, which in turn raises real income levels in both countries, whereas 'catch up' by a follower tends to hurt the leader by elimination of gains from trade. An interesting (but implicit) feature of these experiments is that the technological level is not treated as a given resource (an 'endowment'). Rather, it can be constructed by means of human action, even though it might not (necessarily) be the result of deliberate actions at the level of the country. Another type of neoclassical 'technology gap' models is the 'stickiness models', as pioneered by Krugman (1987), and mentioned in the previous section. In Krugman's model comparative advantage is the outcome of history (which might have been created by means of a technological lead), as dynamic economies of scale are present, in which cumulative past output determines current productivity. Other models of this kind include Grossman and Helpman (1991a, Chapter 8) and Hansen (1997).

In 'evolutionary' ('technology gap') literature on international trade (Dosi, Pavitt and Soete, 1990; Verspagen, 1993; Dosi *et al.*, 1994), international trade specialisation is the outcome of country- and sector-specific (technological) learning processes. In this framework, the mechanism of transmission secures a certain degree of stability in trade specialisation, because of limited computational capabilities of the agents in question.

2.2.3. The 'Home Market Effect'

The idea that inter-sectoral linkages in the domestic economy have an impact on competitiveness has its most important roots in development economics. In this context Hirschman (1958) distinguishes between backward and forward linkages. Backward linkage effects are related to derived demand, i.e. the provision of input for a given activity. Forward linkage effects are related to output-utilisation, i.e. the outputs from a given activity will induce attempts to use this output as inputs in some new activities (Hirschman, 1958, p. 100). Hirschman generalises the linkage concept to the observation that:

> ...ongoing activities because of their characteristics, push or, more modestly, invite some operators to take up new activities. Whenever that is the case, a linkage exists between the ongoing and the new activity. (Hirschman, 1958, p. 80).

These 'new activities' emerging as a consequence of the supply and demand effects of ongoing activities could be perceived as induced innovations. In other words, if a relatively strong domestic upstream producer is present, it might in turn improve the comparative advantage of (or the competitiveness of) domestic users. But the positive effects of upstream and downstream linkages are not automatic; variables such as technological 'strangeness' or 'alienness' of the new economic activities in relation to the ongoing ones, play an important role for the effectiveness of linkages. Also obstacles in form of the need of large amounts of capital due to scale requirements and the lack of marketing access and knowledge are important for the effectiveness of linkages (Hirschman, 1977, pp. 77-8). These factors are somewhat parallel to the concepts of 'absorptive capacity' (Cohen and Levinthal, 1989) or 'technological relevance' (Fikkert, 1997) in the spillover literature; a certain degree of technological proximity is presumably necessary for the linkage to have an actual effect.

The importance of domestic linkages (the 'home-market effect') in a trade theory context, was suggested by the Swedish economist Linder (1961). The basic idea is that a country's domestic market may act as a 'kindergarten' for new products, before exports to foreign markets are initiated. One possible interpretation of Linder has been formalised by Krugman (1980). The model is based on imperfect competition, and allows for economies of scale and transportation costs. In a two country, two industry, setting the model demonstrates that when the two countries trade, each will be specialising (although not necessarily perfect specialisation, depending on the relative importance of transportation costs *vis-á-vis* economies of scale) in the industry for whose products it has the *relatively* larger demand. The reason for this is that there will be an incentive to concentrate the production of a good near its largest market, in order to reap economies of scale, while minimising transportation costs.

However, it should be pointed out that Linder was primarily concerned with the quality, rather than the mere size of demand. In other words, the original formulation made by Linder concerned the conditions for learning on the (national) home-market. Lundvall (1988) has further developed this idea by means of the *organised market,* which refers to close, and sometimes face-to-face interaction between sellers and buyers as a fertile environment for innovation. The interaction may take the form of mutual exchange of information, but may also involve direct co-operation between users and producers of technology. Two properties of the user-producer relationship are important in a 'home market' context. Firstly, because it is time-consuming and costly to develop efficient channels of communication and codes of conduct (often tacit) between users and producers, the relationships are likely to be durable and selective. Secondly, when technology is sophisticated and changing rapidly, proximity in terms of space and culture is seen to be conducive to innovation and thereby to competitiveness (Lundvall, 1988, p. 355). Thus, such localised and durable linkages give rise to dynamic increasing returns at the level of the country (or region). In the context of increasing returns, it should be pointed out that we are dealing with interaction between firms, situated in different industries (Young, 1928), rather than activities internal to the firm.

As pointed out by Fagerberg (1995), given the tacit nature of the user-producer interaction, such relationships are not only ways of increasing localised learning and innovation, but also act as a means of appropriating returns from learning and innovation, at least in the shorter run. Thus, localised vertical linkages might create/reinforce competitiveness or specialisation of both users (an upstream linkage) and producers (a downstream linkage), making sectors co-evolve at the national level (Andersen, Dalum and Villumsen, 1981).

2.2.4. Sector- and Country-specific Learning Processes

The Pavitt-taxonomy in a trade context
Given that the principal sources of technological change (inducement mechanisms) differ between firms according to principal sector of activity, different explanations should not be expected to be of equal importance across industrial sectors. Hence, the three types of explanations for trade specialisation found in the previous sub-sections of this section might not be general theories on their own. Instead the theories can be seen to complement each other, as different explanations apply to different types of sectors.

Pavitt (1984) identifies differences in the importance of different sources of innovation according to which broad sector the individual firm belongs. The taxonomy of firms, according to principal activity, emerged out of a statistical analysis of more than 2000 postwar innovations in Britain and was explained by the sources of technology; the nature of users' needs; and means of appropriation. Four types of firms were identified accordingly, namely supplier dominated firms, scale-intensive firms, specialised suppliers and science-based firms. *Supplier dominated* firms are typically small and found in manufacturing and non-manufacturing sectors. Most technology comes from suppliers of equipment and material (see Figure 2.1 for a description of the main external technological sources of different types of firms). *Scale intensive* firms are found in bulk materials and assembly. Their internal sources of technology are production engineering and R&D departments. External sources of technology include mainly interactive learning with specialised suppliers, but also inputs from science-based firms are of some importance. *Specialised suppliers* are small firms, which are producers of production equipment and control instrumentation. Their main internal sources are primarily design and development. External sources are users (science-based and scale-intensive firms). *Science-based firms* are found in the chemical and electronic sectors. Their main internal sources of technology are internal R&D and production engineering. Important external sources of technology include universities, but also specialised suppliers.

Even though the taxonomy was devised at the level of the firm, it has

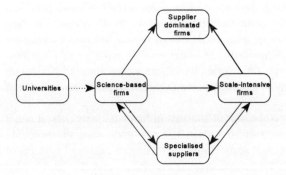

Figure 2.1 The main technological linkages amongst different categories of firms and universities (cf. Pavitt, 1984, p. 364)

implications at the level of the industry, as we would expect the broad sectoral regularities of firms to be reflected in the aggregate behaviour of the sector. Thus, given the above description of the taxonomy, one would expect internal R&D to be most important for specialisation in science-based sectors, while upstream and downstream linkages should be expected to be more important in the case of specialised suppliers. For scale intensive sectors, investment and inter-sectoral linkages - but also to some extent R&D - should be of importance, while supplier dominated sectors should to some extent be expected to be determined by upstream linkages. But as we are dealing with sectors of traditional manufacturing in this case, more traditional factors (resource endowments) might be particularly important for these sectors.

National trajectories and systems of innovation
Following Bell and Pavitt (1993), it can be said more generally, that technological accumulation along country-specific technological trajectories (cf. Dosi, 1982, pp. 227-8), in developed countries, has led to the acquisition of personal, organisational and institutional competencies, which have enabled countries to adopt and develop product and processes technologies of increasing sophistication.

Accordingly, Bell and Pavitt identify three types of mechanisms, which seem to have been particularly important in influencing such trajectories in their rate and direction: (i) factor endowments; (ii) inter-sectoral linkages; and (iii) the cumulative mastery of core technologies. The first mechanism has to do with the innovative response to alleviate particular scarce factor endowments of countries. The second mechanism has to do with inter-sectoral linkages, sometimes starting off with the exploitation of abundant raw materials, then later creating a base for competitiveness in downstream sectors. In turn (national) upstream sectors are reinforced through vertical linkages, making the sectors co-evolve (in other words the home market hypothesis). The third mechanism has to do with trajectories which are traced through horizontal technological diversification, based on an R&D base (in other words the role of technology).

Although the country is the unit of analysis in many trade models, it is not uncontroversial that countries should matter for trade specialisation and performance *per se*. However, appreciative theorising on 'national systems of innovation' (Lundvall, 1992; Nelson, 1993; Patel and Pavitt, 1994a) contemplates that nations make a difference in this context in terms of the institutional set-up of particular countries (e.g. country differences in firm organisation; strength of inter-sectoral linkages; technological support systems; education systems; financial systems; and university systems). This view is supported by the fact that in much empirical work on international trade (as well as by the evidence presented in Chapter 1, Section 1.2), country-specific dummies turn out to be significant (e.g. Magnier and Toujas-Bernate, 1994; Amable and Verspagen, 1995; Verspagen and Wakelin, 1997).

Summing up on the determinants of international specialisation
This section has surveyed an important part of the theoretical literature on the determinants of international trade specialisation. The first part of the section focused on the limitations of the standard HOS explanation for trade specialisation.

Subsequently two types of 'technology based' (technology gap) explanations for trade specialisation were given. The first type of explanation (associated with Schumpeter and Posner, among others) had to do with the partly tacit, and hence localised nature of technological change, leading to exports from one sector situated in one country, without the immediate underlying technological knowledge 'spills over' to other sectors and countries. Hence, the technological effort by a sector in a country should cause exports by that sector in that country. The other type of literature (associated with Hirshman and Linder, among others) emphasises the effect of linkages to other sectors in the domestic economy. Hence, the interaction with technologically strong actors of either upstream sectors (to suppliers) or downstream (to customers) sectors has an effect on the relative strength of the sector in question.

However, this chapter argued that the Pavitt (1984) taxonomy can in fact reconcile the two positions, as the two types of inducement mechanisms should not be expected to be of equal importance across industrial sectors. Hence we can formulate a number of propositions: (g) *internal technological activity* is most important for specialisation in science-based sectors, but is also expected to be of some importance for scale intensive sectors; (h) *upstream and downstream linkages* are more important in the case of specialised suppliers, but should also be of importance in the case of scale intensive sectors. Downstream linkages should be of importance for supplier dominated sectors; (i) it is anticipated that investment will be important in the case of scale intensive sectors; while (j) low *labour costs* are predicted to be an important determinant of specialisation in the case of supplier dominated types of sectors. The empirical examination of this set of propositions [(g)-(j)], is to be found in Chapters 6 and 7 of this book.

2.3. EFFECTS OF INTERNATIONAL SPECIALISATION

This section is an attempt to highlight the third research question of this book, concerning whether international specialisation patterns (and changes therein) matter for growth, from a theoretical point of view. Hence this section is closely connected to Part IV of the book, dealing with this question from an empirical point of view mainly. The first part of this section (2.3.1) discusses the notion of technological opportunities, while the second part of this section (2.3.2) discusses how such differences might affect growth performance across countries.

2.3.1. Differences in Technological Opportunity Amongst Sectors

In their seminal book on evolutionary economics, Nelson and Winter (1982, pp. 258-9) introduced the notion of 'technological regimes' as determinants of the patterns of innovative activities across industries. The idea has later on been further developed by Malerba and Orsenigo (1990), in such a way that a technological regime is viewed as a particular combination of some fundamental properties of technologies. These properties are; opportunity and appropriability conditions; degrees of cumulativeness of technological knowledge; and finally characteristics of the relevant knowledge-base.

Since a central focus of this book is on technological opportunity[3], opportunity conditions will be discussed a bit further. Basically, opportunity conditions reflect the easiness of innovating, given an amount invested in technological search. In evolutionary economic theory of R&D activity - which analogises R&D to drawing a ball from an urn - technological opportunity describes the distribution of values of the balls in the urn. When technological opportunity is 'high' the distribution of draws has a higher mean than when the opportunity is low (Klevorick *et al.*, 1995, p. 188).

According to Malerba and Orsenigo (1990) four basic dimensions of opportunity can be identified; *level, pervasiveness, sources* and *variety*. A high *level* of opportunities provide strong incentives to the undertaking of innovative activities and denotes the probability of innovating for a given amount of resources devoted to search. Therefore, high opportunities are to be found in an environment that is not functionally constrained by scarcity. In the case of high *pervasiveness*, new knowledge may be applied to several products and markets, while in the case of low pervasiveness new knowledge applies to only a few products and markets. The *sources* of technological opportunities differ amongst technologies and industries, as shown by Klevorick *et al.*(1995). In some industries opportunity conditions are closely related to scientific advance made at universities. In other sectors internal R&D and endogenous learning is the most dominant source of innovation, yet in other sectors users or suppliers seem to the most important source (Pavitt, 1984). In some cases, high levels of technological opportunity are associated with a potentially rich *variety* of technological solutions, approaches and activities. This might especially be the case in the early stage of an industry life-cycle (Abernathy and Utterback, 1975). At a later stage - when a dominant design has emerged - technical change may proceed along more specific trajectories, where the variety between technical solutions is reduced.

2.3.2. The Interdependencies Between Trade Specialisation and Growth

In the field of economic growth, a major question concerns differences in growth performance between nations. Traditionally, i.e. in the neoclassical growth model due to Solow (1956), growth was viewed as determined by a country's resources. Technological change was seen as exogenous and equally available to all countries. Thus, in this framework, growth only depends on the availability of labour and capital. In the long run, all countries converge to an identical steady state, but in the short run growth rate differentials may arise due to so-called transitory dynamics.

In recent so-called 'new' growth models, e.g. Romer (1990) and Lucas (1988), the purely resource based point of view is abandoned in favour of technological change as an endogenous phenomenon. Although the extent to which countries invest in technology is still also determined by its resources (in this case human capital), parameters such as technological opportunities and efficiency of the R&D process now enter the analysis. Moreover, a very important role is played in these models by increasing returns to scale due to Marshallian externalities in the R&D process. A third point of view on economic growth argues that growth is to an important extent determined by the external relations of a country. This idea is a controversial one. For example, Krugman (1994) has forcefully argued that the issue of competitiveness, which underlies the idea that growth is determined by the performance in international product markets, does not make sense from a theoretical point of view. Growth models in the 'Solow-tradition', as well as the so-called 'new growth' models, take a production function as the main determinant of economic growth. Because of the (implicit) assumption of full utilisation of factors such as labour and capital, and given the functional form of the production function, growth of production is simply the result of the growth rate of inputs (labour and capital) and their productivity increases. This rather straightforward explanation of economic growth is best illustrated by the 'art' of growth accounting, as pioneered by Tinbergen (1943).

Obviously, the supply of production factors such as labour and capital mostly results from domestic sources. Factors related to the supply of foreign labour, such as migration, often do not have a straightforward economic interpretation, although theory exists on the relation between economic growth and migration (see e.g. Blanchard and Katz, 1992). International capital flows, for example in the form of foreign direct investment (FDI), do have an obvious economic interpretation, but the (neoclassical) theory on the impact of FDI on growth is still ill-developed. Under the 'normal' assumption of homogeneity of domestically produced goods and imports, trade, in the form of imports of capital and intermediate goods, is also not related to any of the traditional production factors, and therefore does not enter the neoclassical growth models directly.

As summarised in Dowrick (1997), the impact of trade in the traditional models is thus mainly an indirect one, related to the issues of allocation and factor prices. The idea here is that an economy that is opened up to international trade, can benefit from a more efficient allocation of its production factors (along the lines of the HOS theory), and the resulting lower consumer prices. Thus, welfare is higher in an open economy as compared to a situation where domestic markets are protected by tariffs or quota. However, typically, these welfare effects are relatively small (Dowrick, 1997).[4]

As mentioned in Chapter 1, Dowrick (1997) distinguishes between two approaches within the more recent so-called new growth theory: the Smithian approach and the Ricardian approach. The Smithian approach, with authors such as Rivera-Batiz and Romer (1991) and Rivera-Batiz and Xie (1993), stresses the importance of 'learning-by-doing' or increasing returns to scale. Opening up to trade enables individual countries to specialise in a narrow range of goods, and thus exploit these increasing returns. The difference relative to the traditional models discussed above is that, due to the endogenous growth nature of the models in the Smithian tradition, there will be a lasting effect on growth rates, rather than just a level effect in terms of welfare. In the Ricardian type models, different activities are characterised by different rates of growth of productivity, e.g., due to differences in technological opportunities. Thus, countries specialising in activities with higher rates of productivity growth are in a better position to achieve fast overall growth.

Krugman (1987) showed that in a model in which technical progress results from learning-by-doing (over time), and at the level of the industry, it is possible for a predatory trade policy to raise one country's relative wage and perhaps its living standard at other countries' expense. However, Krugman did not specify differences in terms of learning opportunities (or level of increasing returns) between sectors. Hansen (1997) has extended the model of Krugman to incorporate such a feature. While the paper of Hansen accentuates the endogenous character of comparative advantage, as modelled by Krugman, it also has something to say about the industrial structure in an open economy. The point is that if one country is initially the stronger one in the 'dynamic' sectors, there will only be room for 'dynamic' sectors when the economy is opened up to free trade in that country. The disadvantaged country could, in contrast, end up with a mixed structure consisting both of 'dynamic' and 'non-dynamic' sectors. It should be pointed out however, that the models of Krugman and Hansen are basically both trade models and not growth models.

Grossman and Helpman (1991a, Chapters 7 and 8 in particular) is an example of a Ricardian growth model.[5] Grossman and Helpman construct a two-country, two-sector growth model. The model encompasses a manufacturing sector that offers no prospect for technological change ('the traditional sector'), while in another manufacturing sector new goods are continuously being introduced ('the high technology sector'). The main idea is to answer the question of what the characteristics are of a country that makes a contribution to comparative advantage in a high-technology sector (the answer is that it depends on the nature of spillovers). However, the model implies that for a country, specialised in the high-technology sector, real output growth is faster, compared to the other country, as the overall growth rate is a weighted average of the growth rate of the two sectors. However, it should be pointed out that the fast growing country does not, in the long run equilibrium, experience a higher growth rate of real consumption. The reason for this is that consumers enjoy benefits from innovation through the purchase of traded goods. Hence, the deteriorating terms of trade offsets the faster growth of output by the country specialised in 'high-tech', in the long run.

As acknowledged by Dowrick (1997), the idea of a relation between trade and growth is not new. The dynamic analysis of Keynesian models, long before new growth theory, established the idea that trade matters for growth. As in the recent neo-classical models discussed above, the argument comes in two flavours here (see e.g. McCombie and Thirlwall, 1995). First, there is the export-led growth theory, which, following Kaldor (1966; 1970), argues that the economy is not constrained by supply-side factors, because the main production factor, capital, must be seen as an endogenous factor. Should capital constrain economic growth in the short run, so it is argued, increased profits will solve this constraint in the medium- to long-run. Thus, only natural resources (which are indeed exogenous) are accepted as a possible supply-side factor constraining economic growth (McCombie and Thirlwall, 1995, p. 392).[6] Seen in this way, the only truly exogenous factor to the domestic economy is foreign demand (domestic demand is endogenous to the extent that it is determined by savings behaviour and wages).

Kaldor (1970) argued that dynamic increasing returns to scale play an important role in the process of economic growth. The argument goes back at least to Young (1928), and states that when production expands, new ways of doing things (*learning-by-doing*) are discovered, which makes productivity increase. The functional form Kaldor used to illustrate his argument is the so-called Verdoorn-law, which argues that production growth causes productivity growth. Naturally, increased productivity may, in its turn, lead to increased growth (as Kaldor argued, by means of increasing exports), which opens up possibilities for self-reinforcing mechanisms. Cumulative causation and virtuous growth cycles thus play an important role in the Kaldorian export-led growth theory. Dixon and Thirlwall (1975) have expressed the Kaldor-Verdoorn theory in a dynamic model of export-led growth, and present conclusions with regard to under which conditions growth rate differentials between regions or nations will converge to a stable value.

The second variety of the post-Keynesian theory on trade and growth is mainly due to Thirlwall. Thirlwall (1979), although operating in the same post-Keynesian theoretical framework as Kaldor, argued that the 'simple' export-led growth theory does not take into account the role of the balance of payments. For example, in the model by Dixon and Thirlwall (1975), export growth, and thus output growth, is not constrained at all, even if the balance of payments, which is not explicitly modelled, grows without bounds. Viewed from the balance of payments point of view, demand elements (domestic demand for imports as a fraction of domestic GDP, and domestic exports as a function of foreign GDP) are again the main determinants of growth.

McCombie and Thirlwall (1995, pp. 234-7) set out the 'model' of balance of payments restricted growth as follows. Denote the respective price changes of imports and exports (both in domestic currency, so the price of imports includes the exchange rate as well as foreign prices) by p_m and p_x. The price and income elasticities of imports are denoted e_{pm} and e_{ym} (both negative), respectively, and accordingly define e_{px} and e_{yx} (both positive). For balance of payments equilibrium to hold, nominal exports must grow at a rate equal to nominal imports, or

$$p_m + e_{pm}(p_m - p_x) + e_{ym}y = p_x - e_{px}(p_m - p_x) + e_{yx}y^*,$$ (2.1)

where y and y^* are the growth rates of real GDP of the domestic and foreign economies, respectively. The above equation can easily be rearranged to yield

$$y = \frac{(1 + e_{pm} + e_{px})(p_x - p_m) + e_{yx}y^*}{e_{ym}}.$$ (2.2)

This implies that a non-zero growth rate differential between the domestic economy and the rest of the world may arise as a result of long-run differences in the rate of inflation, as well as differences in the income elasticities of demand. The proposition made by Thirlwall (1979) is that the long-run effect of differences in inflation is small (in other words, that $p_x = p_m$ in the long run), so that differences in the income elasticities of demand are the main reason for growth rate differentials.

As was argued by Fagerberg (1988), the main problem with Thirlwall's theory is that it does not provide an endogenous explanation of the differences between the two income elasticities. Fagerberg argued that one might explain these differences by factors such as product quality and R&D efforts. He thus builds a bridge between the post-Keynesian literature and 'evolutionary' inspired theories of growth. In the 'evolutionary' literature on economic growth, (stochastic) technological change plays an important role. From an evolutionary perspective Verspagen (1993, Chapter 8) for example constructed a model inspired by the post-Keynesian tradition. Thus, growth is basically driven by growth of exports (determined by competitiveness, argued to be mainly determined by technological factors), under a balance-of-payments constraint. In the model a 'domestic' country competes with a 'foreign' country (the rest of the world) in a number of sectors. If the competitiveness of a country in a given sector is higher than average, the country expands its market share in that sector and thus - all other things being equal - expands its aggregate market share, as the sum of the individual sectors add up to the country aggregate (there are no spillovers in the model). An important aspect of the model, is that both supply side factors (non-symmetric learning rates across sectors) as well as demand side factors (non-symmetric consumption structures) cause differences in growth rates among countries. Such differential rates of growth of the total market size in different sectors, under the influence of income elasticities, as in Pasinetti (1981), imply that different sectors grow at different rates, such that specialisation matters for growth. A similar model is presented by Dosi *et al.* (1994).

Boggio (1996) rightfully argues that the evolutionary models, in many important respects, resemble the early and later post-Keynesian models that were discussed above. He argues, however, against a strict interpretation of the concept of balance of payments constrained growth, and shows that in models of national growth partly based on 'evolutionary notions', trade balance disequilibrium may indeed be related to rapid growth in a Kaldor-Verdoorn framework. One important difference between the 'evolutionary' growth model by Verspagen (1993) and the work in the post-Keynesian tradition outlined in this section, however, is that the latter does not attach much importance to the issue of specialisation. In the export-led growth theory, specialisation does not play a large role, as is illustrated, for example, by Dixon and Thirlwall (1975), who present a one-sector model, which by definition excludes specialisation from the analysis. In the balance of payments constrained growth literature, specialisation patterns may be seen as entering the growth equation indirectly, through the elasticities of imports and exports. But this is at best only one of the many interpretations that can be given to the differences in elasticities, and a more elaborate empirical analysis, as done by Fagerberg (1988) with respect to product quality and technological factors, is necessary to establish the empirical importance of this argument.

How does all this relate to the question of the relationship between economic growth and specialisation? The common conclusion from the literature discussed in this section seems to be that this relationship takes two forms. First, as is argued by both the new growth theorists ('Smithians') and the Kaldorian export-led theory, specialisation, by opening up possibilities for increased specialisation, leads to higher productivity growth in the form of learning. In this argument, the emphasis is not so much on what a country specialises in, but rather whether it specialises, irrespective of the nature of the specialisation.

Second, some activities might provide larger growth opportunities than others, and therefore it matters in which activities a country is specialised (the 'Ricardian' view). The reasons for this might be supply side related (e.g. differential technological opportunities between activities) or demand side related (e.g. differential income elasticities between activities). In the neo-classical (or new growth) version of this argument, an additional complication is formed by the interrelatedness of the economy in the form of general equilibrium. An exact modelling of the result of specialisation on growth thus not only requires the modelling of learning, but also of the evolution of factor prices and the resulting allocation.

Summing up on the effects of international specialisation

It has been the traditional view in standard economics (i.e. in the neoclassical growth model due to Solow1956), that growth was determined by a country's resources in terms of capital and labour. However, some part of new growth theory under the label of 'Ricardian models' does not only allocate a role to the resources of countries for explaining economic growth, but also attributes a role to being specialised in activities associated with higher growth rates in terms of productivity, in explaining economic growth.

The post-Keynesian theory has given a role to trade in explaining economic growth as well. In fact one of the possible interpretations of the differences in terms of differences in elasticities with respect to demand, is that it reflects disparities in technological opportunities across sectors. However, also some parts of evolutionary theory are Ricardian in assigning a (however more explicit) role to differences in demand structures as well as to differences in technological opportunities, across sectors, in explaining economic growth.

This book adopts the Ricardian proposition (k) that the growth rate of an economy depends, at least partly, on what it the country is specialised in and how the specialisation pattern changes over time. This proposition will be dealt with in particular in Chapters 8, 9 and 10 of this book.

NOTES

1. For a good survey, organised in such a way, see Wakelin (1997, Chapter 2).
2. Freeman (1963) found that, for the plastics industry, technological progress could give leadership in productions by 10 to 15 years, through a combination of patents and secrecy. In a study of 48 product innovations, Mansfield, Schwartz and Wagner (1981) found that on average it took four years to 'get around' 60 per cent of the patents in question. In addition, the study showed that imitation is not a costless activity; the cost of conducting the imitation was approximately 65 per cent of the cost of the original innovation.
3. In this book the terms 'technological opportunities' and 'learning opportunities' will be used interchangeably.
4. The welfare gains are generally larger in situations where increasing returns to scale characterise the production process, possibly in combination with product differentiation.
5. Other well-known examples of such a model, with similar predictions, are to be found in Lucas (1988, model II), and in Young (1991).

6. Kaldor (1966) also forcefully argued that labour must be seen as an endogenous factor, due to labour reserves contained in the primary sector of the economy, which, by the nature of industrialisation, is contracting, and therefore 'hides' labour available for industry.

3. A Comparison of Measures of International Specialisation

This chapter describes and compares different measures of international export specialisation. The chapter is organised as follows. Firstly, in Section 3.1, figures on international specialisation of 19 OECD countries will be described in order to give the reader a feel for how countries are specialised. The measure to be used is the 'revealed comparative advantage' (*RCA*) developed by Balassa (1965), more than 30 years ago. Since then the measure has been applied in numerous reports (e.g. UNIDO, 1986; World Bank, 1994) and in academic publications (e.g. Aquino, 1981; Crafts and Thomas, 1986; van Hulst, Mulder and Soete, 1991; Lim, 1997; Laursen and Drejer, 1999). This measure will be applied throughout the book (in Chapters 4, 5, 6, 7 and 9). In Section 3.2, it will be argued that when using the *RCA*, it should always (at least in regression analysis) be adjusted in such a way that it becomes symmetric. Section 3.3 compares the adjusted *RCA* (labelled the 'revealed symmetric comparative advantage' or '*RSCA*' in short) to other measures of international trade specialisation, used in the literature. These measures include the Michaely index, the chi square measure, and the 'specialisation vector' from constant market share analysis (constant market share analysis is applied in Chapters 8 and 10 of this book). Finally, Section 3.4 sums up.

3.1. TRADE SPECIALISATION OF COUNTRIES

The measure chosen (the arguments for choosing this measure can be found in Section 3.3) for mapping international trade specialisation is the Revealed Comparative Advantage (Balassa, 1965):

$$RCA_{ij} = \frac{X_{ij} / \sum_i X_{ij}}{\sum_j X_{ij} / \sum_i \sum_j X_{ij}}. \tag{3.1}$$

The numerator represents the percentage share of a given sector in national exports - X_{ij} are exports of sector i from country j. The denominator represents the percentage share of a given sector in OECD exports. The *RCA* index thus contains a comparison of national export structure (the numerator) with the

Table 3.1 Export specialisation figures (RSCAs), for 1990 for 19 OECD countries and the 22 STAN sectors

	Australia	Austria	Belgium	Canada	Denmark	Finland	France	Germany	Greece	Italy	Japan	Netherl.	New Ze.	Norway	Portugal	Spain	Sweden	UK	US
Food, drink and tobacco	0.65	-0.43	0.10	-0.14	0.58	-0.52	0.23	-0.23	0.52	-0.15	-0.86	0.44	0.77	0.13	-0.04	0.12	-0.57	-0.04	0.01
Textiles, footw. and leather	0.17	0.21	0.13	-0.73	-0.05	-0.29	0.04	-0.06	0.70	0.51	-0.48	-0.03	0.25	-0.62	0.73	0.14	-0.50	-0.06	-0.30
Wood, cork and furniture	-0.76	0.46	-0.03	0.56	0.48	0.58	-0.21	-0.15	-0.52	0.26	-0.86	-0.27	0.16	0.13	0.54	-0.09	0.46	-0.55	-0.13
Paper and printing	-0.48	0.28	-0.18	0.54	-0.22	0.77	-0.14	-0.14	-0.59	-0.34	-0.66	-0.07	0.29	0.34	0.20	-0.12	0.57	-0.15	-0.05
Industrial chemicals	-0.40	-0.14	0.15	-0.22	-0.27	-0.27	0.10	0.08	-0.41	-0.26	-0.19	0.26	-0.54	0.01	-0.36	-0.13	-0.33	0.08	0.05
Pharmaceuticals	-0.10	0.12	0.09	-0.72	0.51	-0.43	0.20	0.04	-0.13	-0.16	-0.61	-0.02	-0.48	-0.48	-0.40	0.01	0.29	0.29	-0.02
Petroleum refineries (oil)	0.43	-0.67	0.21	0.16	-0.10	-0.22	-0.19	-0.39	0.54	-0.06	-0.66	0.55	0.06	0.62	0.22	0.41	0.08	0.08	-0.06
Rubber and plastics	-0.51	0.15	0.05	-0.11	0.15	-0.32	0.14	0.05	-0.33	0.13	-0.11	0.05	-0.31	-0.30	-0.30	0.21	-0.12	-0.01	-0.17
Stone, clay and glass	-0.42	0.28	0.20	-0.38	0.01	-0.24	0.10	-0.02	0.48	0.40	-0.20	-0.15	-0.64	-0.18	0.42	0.34	-0.30	-0.12	-0.31
Ferrous metals	0.08	0.28	0.38	-0.29	-0.36	0.15	0.12	0.02	0.24	-0.03	0.08	-0.14	-0.25	0.20	-0.57	0.18	0.23	-0.07	-0.55
Non-ferrous metals	0.77	0.04	0.19	0.46	-0.58	0.15	-0.06	-0.09	0.46	-0.34	-0.47	-0.08	0.45	0.75	-0.72	-0.10	-0.08	0.03	-0.12
Fabricated metal products	-0.27	0.24	-0.01	-0.19	0.22	0.02	0.04	0.12	-0.39	0.24	-0.21	-0.02	-0.38	-0.08	-0.20	0.05	0.11	-0.07	-0.19
Non-electrical machinery	-0.52	0.11	-0.35	-0.42	0.05	0.04	-0.15	0.15	-0.75	0.17	0.05	-0.27	-0.69	-0.28	-0.56	-0.23	0.13	0.01	0.01
Office mach. and computers	-0.52	-0.49	-0.59	-0.28	-0.46	-0.51	-0.20	-0.28	-0.96	-0.22	0.28	0.02	-0.97	-0.38	-0.75	-0.35	-0.23	0.22	0.28
Electrical machinery	-0.51	0.11	-0.31	-0.46	-0.10	-0.14	0.01	0.11	-0.41	0.02	0.17	-0.21	-0.40	-0.37	0.04	-0.05	-0.06	-0.05	-0.02
Communic. eq.and semicon.	-0.63	0.01	-0.43	-0.16	-0.20	-0.10	-0.22	-0.22	-0.84	-0.42	0.43	-0.19	-0.87	-0.49	-0.28	-0.57	-0.04	-0.02	0.14
Shipbuilding	0.01	-0.67	-0.84	-0.73	0.50	0.60	-0.21	-0.21	-0.60	-0.42	0.44	-0.25	-0.73	0.84	-0.18	0.31	0.06	-0.48	-0.27
Other transport	-0.67	0.13	-0.39	0.24	-0.63	0.11	-0.09	-0.22	-0.94	0.21	0.46	-0.29	-0.95	-0.58	-0.33	-0.36	-0.31	-0.40	-0.26
Motor vehicles	-0.55	-0.21	0.07	0.34	-0.68	-0.60	-0.02	0.12	-0.93	-0.27	0.24	-0.53	-0.93	-0.75	-0.35	0.22	-0.01	-0.23	-0.18
Aerospace	-0.60	-0.91	-0.68	-0.05	-0.41	-0.92	0.11	-0.23	-0.84	-0.30	-0.89	-0.29	-0.93	-0.47	-0.80	-0.28	-0.42	0.34	0.48
Instruments	-0.38	-0.19	-0.55	-0.54	0.02	-0.39	-0.11	0.03	-0.81	-0.30	0.26	0.01	-0.76	-0.34	-0.66	-0.58	-0.10	0.09	0.16
Other manufacturing	-0.13	0.03	0.61	-0.65	-0.51	-0.53	-0.16	-0.25	-0.66	0.28	-0.07	-0.44	-0.55	-0.65	-0.30	-0.28	-0.54	0.32	-0.19

OECD export structure (the denominator). When *RCA* equals 1 for a given sector in a given country, the percentage share of that sector is identical with the OECD average. Where *RCA* is above 1 the country is said to be specialised in that sector and vice versa where *RCA* is below 1. However, since the *RCA* turns out to produce an output which cannot be compared on both sides of 1^1, the index is made symmetric, obtained as *(RCA-1)/(RCA+1)*; this measure ranges from -1 to +1. The measure is labelled 'Revealed Symmetric Comparative Advantage' (*RSCA*).

Table 3.1 contains specialisation figures among 19 OECD countries for 1990, based on calculations on the OECD STAN database (1995 edition). Figures comparing the specialisation of countries in 1970 and in 1990 can be found in Table A3.1 of this chapter. The table can serve as a 'map' when the reader of the book wishes to inspect the data that underlies the (mainly econometric) analysis, to be found in the analytical chapters (Chapters 4-10).

From Table 3.1, it can be seen that among *OECD catching-up countries* Spain is specialised in (among other things) petroleum refineries; stone, clay and glass; shipbuilding; and motor vehicles. Areas of under-specialisation include office machinery and computers; communication equipment and semiconductors; and instruments. Among *small high-income countries* it can for instance be seen that Denmark is specialised in food, drink & tobacco; wood, cork and furniture; and in pharmaceuticals. Areas of relative weakness include motor vehicles; and office machinery. Among the *large high-income countries*, Germany has a relative strength in machinery (electrical and non-electrical), as well as in motor vehicles. Areas of relative weakness include petroleum refineries, and sectors producing information and communication technology goods, more generally. The US is, on the other hand, specialised in office machinery and computers, as well as in aerospace, while areas of relative weaknesses include textiles, footwear and leather; stone, clay and glass; and shipbuilding.

3.2. THE SYMMETRIC RCA

In the previous section the *RCA* index was made symmetric, although not much explanation was given for following this procedure. However, this section will argue that the index should always be made symmetric (when used in regression analysis)[2], because the 'pure' *RCA* is basically not comparable on both sides of unity, as the index ranges from zero to one, if a country is said not to be specialised in a given sector, while the value of the index ranges from one to infinity, if a country is said to be specialised. Vollrath (1991) suggests taking the logarithm to the *RCA*, as a solution to this problem. However, in the case that a country exports zero in a sector, the index is not defined.

This section will illustrate the issue by discussing it in the context of the question of whether countries tend to decrease or increase the level of specialisation. This issue is to be analysed in depth in Chapters 4 and 5. Hence, the methodology will only be presented briefly in this chapter, while the reader can consult Chapter 4 in particular (or Cantwell, 1991), for further detail. Stability (and specialisation trends) is tested by means of the following regression equation (country bý country):

$$RSCA_{ij}^{t_2} = \alpha_j + \beta_j RSCA_{ij}^{t_1} + \epsilon_{ij}. \tag{3.2}$$

The superscripts t_1 and t_2 refer to the initial year and the final year, respectively. The dependent variable, *RSCA* at time t_2 for sector i, is tested against the independent variable which is the value of the *RSCA* in the previous year t_1. α and β are standard linear regression parameters and ϵ is a residual term. Basically, the size of $\hat{\beta}$ measures how stable the specialisation pattern of a country has been, between the two periods. If $\hat{\beta}$ is low, one can talk about a high degree of turbulence, while the pattern can be said to be unchanged, if $\hat{\beta}$ is not significantly different from one. $\hat{\beta}/\hat{R}$ ($\hat{R}$ is the correlation coefficient from the regression) measures whether the level of specialisation has gone up or down between the two periods (an increase or a fall in dispersion of specialisation). If $\hat{\beta}/\hat{R} > 1$, specialisation increases, while specialisation decreases, if $\hat{\beta}/\hat{R} < 1$.

However, if the non-adjusted *RCA* is used in estimating Equation 3.2, one can obtain biased estimates. Examples of applications of the unadjusted *RCA* in regression analysis include Crafts and Thomas (1986), Cantwell (1989), Amendola, Guerrieri and Padoan (1992), Dollar and Wolff (1993), and Patel and Pavitt (1994c). One way of expressing the problem is that the Balassa measure has the disadvantage of an inherent risk of lack of normality because it takes values between zero and infinity with a (weighted) average of 1.0. A skewed distribution violates the assumption of normality of the error term in regression analysis, thus not producing reliable *t*-statistics. Another way of putting the problem is that the use of the non-adjusted *RCA* in regression analysis gives much more weight to values above one, when compared to observations below one. The problem can be illustrated by an example. If, for instance, a country increases its *RCA* value from 1/2 to 1, between two periods (as in Table 3.2), specialisation in this sector has increased by factor two. Similarly, if the *RCA* value goes up from 1 to 2, specialisation has increased by

Table 3.2 An example of the effect of RCA vs. RSCA

	RCA_{t-1}	RCA_t	$RSCA_{t-1}$	$RSCA_t$	Specialisation/ de-specialisation
Automobiles	8	4	7/9	3/5	D
Aeroplanes	1/4	1/8	-3/5	-7/9	S
Computers	1	2	0	1/3	S
Chemicals	1/2	1	1/3	0	D
Result for all sectors	De-specialisation		Neutral		

factor two. However, the absolute differences are 1/2 and 1, respectively.

Table 3.2 displays the problem in the context of an increased or decreased level of specialisation, between two periods (*t-1* and *t*). In the example specialisation has gone up or down by exactly the same percentages, on both sides of unity. However, since the changes in the *RCAs* above one are numerically much larger than the values below one, the conclusion, when using the Balassa figures is that the country has de-specialised, when in fact it remained neutral.

Table 3.3[3] reproduces the results of the estimations based on Equation 3.2, both using the original Balassa figures, and by using the *RSCA*.[4] The results show that (at least in this case) the fall in specialisation between 1971-91 is less outspoken, when using the unadjusted *RCA*. The table also contains the results of the Jarque-Bera test for normality of the error terms. The hypothesis of normality of the error terms can be rejected for 2 out of 19 regressions (10 per cent level), when using the adjusted *RCA*, while the hypothesis can be rejected for 8 out of 19 regressions, when the standard Balassa figures are applied.

3.3. A COMPARISON OF FOUR MEASURES OF INTERNATIONAL TRADE SPECIALISATION

Although widely used, the *RCA* is not the only measure which has been applied for measuring international trade specialisation. Other measures include the Michaely index and the chi square measure, and although constant market share analysis is not an analysis of specialisation *per se*, it does contain a 'specialisation vector'.[5] The latter will be interpreted as the effect of specialisation in Chapters 8 and 10. This section will define the alternative and

Table 3.3 Differences between increased or decreased specialisation, using RCA and RSCA respectively, 1971-91 (n=19 sectors)

	RSCA			RCA		
	$\hat{\beta}$	$\hat{\beta}/\hat{R}$	Jarque-Bera test (*p*-value)	$\hat{\beta}$	$\hat{\beta}/\hat{R}$	Jarque-Bera test (*p*-value)
Australia	0.83*	0.97	0.1361	0.99*	1.20	0.0001
Austria	0.87*	0.95	0.3355	0.80*#	0.88	0.4875
Belgium	0.99*	1.06	0.5212	0.86*#	0.92	0.6226
Canada	0.80*	0.98	0.8990	0.80*#	0.86	0.3142
Denmark	0.89*	0.94	0.2970	1.04*	1.16	0.0001
Finland	0.74*#	0.91	0.2588	0.84*#	0.89	0.0001
France	0.63*#	0.94	0.6430	0.64*#	0.97	0.8434
Germany (West)	0.43*#	0.67	0.0524	0.58*#	0.77	0.0689
Greece	0.94*	1.04	0.5236	0.83*	1.05	0.0001
Italy	0.72*#	0.93	0.6375	0.69*#	0.96	0.9402
Japan	0.94*	1.01	0.4987	0.77*#	0.86	0.3432
The Netherlands	0.68*#	0.81	0.6720	0.84*#	0.88	0.6980
New Zealand	1.08*	1.20	0.7572	0.86*#	0.90	0.0001
Norway	0.83*	0.94	0.0163	1.44*#	1.58	0.0076
Portugal	0.60*#	0.87	0.9373	0.68*	1.05	0.1725
Spain	0.51*#	0.76	0.9591	0.55*#	0.83	0.4504
Sweden	0.65*#	0.85	0.4358	0.78*#	0.90	0.0800
United Kingdom	1.02*	1.35	0.5817	1.05*	1.28	0.5842
United States	0.81*#	0.87	0.7089	0.72*#	0.74	0.9748
Mean	0.79	0.95		0.83	0.98	

Notes:
* denotes significantly different from zero at the 10% level. # denotes significantly different from unity at the 10% level. For a description of the 19 sectors, see Table 5.4.

then compare each individual measure to the *RSCA*.

The Michaely index can be defined as:

$$MI_{ij} = X_{ij}/\sum_i X_{ij} - M_{ij}/\sum_i M_{ij}, \tag{3.3}$$

where X_{ij} are exports of sector *i* from country *j*, and M_{ij} are imports for sector *i* to country *j*. The first part of the formula (before the minus sign) represents the percentage share of a given sector in national exports, while the latter part represents the percentage share of a given sector in national imports. The measure ranges between [-1;1], with a neutral value of zero. If the value of the index is positive, a country is specialised in a sector, while given a negative value, a country is said to be under-specialised in a sector. The indicator was developed by Michael Michaely (1962/67), as an 'index of dissimilarity' for a country. In the original contribution, Michaely sums over the sectors for each country, so that the larger the value of the index, the less similar is the commodity composition of the country's exports and imports. The index takes the value of zero in the case of perfect 'similarity'. Nevertheless, since the original contribution of Michaely, a number of researchers, working on international trade e.g. Kol and Mennes (1985); and Webster and Gilroy (1995), has applied the index, as a measure of trade specialisation at the level of the sector.

Another *very* similar measure has been introduced by CEPII (1983), termed the Contribution to Trade Balance (*CTB*). The *CTB* can be defined as:

$$CTB_{ij} = \frac{X_{ij}-M_{ij}}{(\sum_i X_{ij}+\sum_i M_{ij})/2} * 100 - \frac{\sum_i X_{ij}-\sum_i M_{ij}}{(\sum_i X_{ij}+\sum_i M_{ij})/2} * \frac{X_{ij}+M_{ij}}{\sum_i X_{ij}+\sum_i M_{ij}} *100, \quad (3.4)$$

where the letters denote the same, as in Equation 3.3. The measure ranges between [-400; 400]. Values greater than zero (less than zero) of the *CTB* index identify those sectors which give a contribution higher (lower) than their percentage share in the country's total trade. The measure has been applied, for example, by Amendola, Guerrieri and Padoan (1992), Padoan and Pericoli (1993), Amable (1997) and by Guerrieri (1997). In this chapter we shall compare only the Michaely index to the *RSCA* index, since the *CTB* measure correlates strongly with the Michaely index by definition, leaving the pros and cons of the Michaely index and the *CTB* index alike. The two measures differ only if very large trade imbalances are present for a given country. Hence, in the real world the two measures are close to being identical.[6]

In comparison with the *RSCA*, the Michaely index is a measure of relative net export in a given sector. However, when comparing the *RSCA* to the Michaely index, the type and size of intra industry-trade becomes of importance. One advantage of the index is the elimination of re-export as a source of distortion, when calculating specialisation. However, when intra-industry trade is due to the fact that firms in other sectors purchase equipment not only domestically, but also by means of imports, the Michaely index will underestimate the comparative advantage of a country in a given sector. An example of this is given in Table 3.4, in the case of the Danish specialisation in shipbuilding. It can be seen that the value of the *RSCA* points to being (rather strongly) specialised in this sector, whereas the Michaely index points to being slightly under-specialised in this sector. The explanation is that Denmark has a strong shipping sector, not only buying ships from domestic shipyards. So in this case, this book will argue that the *RSCA* is the better measure of comparative advantage. In general it seems reasonable to argue that the benefit of avoiding problems, due to re-exports is smaller than the (to some extent arbitrary)[7] demand of other sectors in the economy. Another argument for using the *RSCA* in this book rather than the Michaely index, is that the *RSCA* can be applied in an analogous way on patent data (the '*RSTA*'), as well as on e.g. investment data. The Michaely index can be used on trade data only.

The χ^2 measures the sum of the squared difference between the export distribution of a given country and the total OECD divided by the OECD export distribution. The definition of the χ^2 measure can be set up as follows:

$$\chi^2 = [(X_{ij}/\sum_i X_{ij}) - (\sum_j X_{ij}/\sum_i \sum_j X_{ij})]^2 / (\sum_j X_{ij}/\sum_i \sum_j X_{ij}), \tag{3.5}$$

here the letters denote the same as in the definition of the *RCA*, in Equation 1. The χ^2 measures the squared difference between the export distribution of a given country and the total OECD divided by the OECD export distribution. The size of χ^2 is an indication of how strongly each country is specialised. The more a country differs from the OECD, the greater the value. In the original formulation, Archibugi and Pianta (1992) always sums over the sectors (i), in order to arrive at one single number for each country in such a way, that if a country has an export structure exactly similar to the OECD, the value of the indicator will be zero. However, since we want to compare directly to the *RSCA*, we have left out the summation. This procedure does of course not change the properties of the measure. However, a very important difference between the chi square measure and the *RSCA* is that the chi square is only devised to measure the level of specialisation, as it takes high values, both when a country is seen to be (much) less specialised than the average of the countries, and when the country is (much) more specialised in a commodity group as compared to the average of the countries. The measure ranges between [0;∞], although the index only takes the value of zero, if there is only one country in the world, producing everything. When compared to the *RSCA*, the index has a disadvantage of producing very large values, when one commodity class makes up a large percentage of total exports. An example of this phenomenon can be found in Table 3.4, where the chi square value for Denmark's export of food, drink & tobacco is 5.5, while the second largest value is only 0.95

Table 3.4 An example of differences between indices of specialisation: Denmark 1990

	RSCA	Michaely index	χ^2	CMS coefficient
Food, drink and tobacco	0.581	0.166	5.527	0.055
Textiles, footwear and leather	-0.049	-0.026	0.005	0.013
Wood, cork and furniture	0.484	0.023	0.703	0.042
Paper and printing	-0.219	-0.032	0.054	0.009
Industrial chemicals	-0.271	-0.061	0.204	0.008
Pharmaceuticals	0.508	0.022	0.530	0.044
Petroleum refineries (oil)	-0.104	-0.015	0.008	0.012
Rubber and plastics	0.149	0.000	0.024	0.020
Stone, clay and glass	0.011	0.002	0.000	0.015
Ferrous metals	-0.363	-0.032	0.106	0.007
Non-ferrous metals	-0.577	-0.012	0.127	0.004
Fabricated metal products	0.218	0.012	0.109	0.023
Non-electrical machinery	0.048	0.030	0.012	0.016
Office mach. and computers	-0.458	-0.031	0.165	0.005
Electrical machinery	-0.104	-0.008	0.017	0.012
Communic. eq. and semiconductors	-0.201	-0.001	0.069	0.010
Shipbuilding	0.502	-0.001	0.353	0.044
Other transport	-0.633	-0.004	0.030	0.003
Motor vehicles	-0.683	-0.034	0.951	0.003
Aerospace	-0.414	-0.008	0.130	0.006
Instruments	0.023	0.008	0.001	0.015
Other manufacturing	-0.514	-0.005	0.082	0.005

(indicating Danish under-specialisation in motor vehicles). Food, drink & tobacco made up 27 per cent of Danish exports in 1990. Compare this figure to e.g. Danish specialisation in non-electrical machinery (about 13 per cent of total Danish exports in 1990), where the chi square value is 0.012. A difference of no less than factor 461, while the difference between specialisation in the two sectors, using the *RSCA*, is (only) factor 12. One implication of the χ^2 measure bias is that the index is very sensitive to *changes* in the size of large commodity classes, over time.

The 'specialisation vector' from constant market share analysis is defined as:

$$x_{ij} = X_{ij}/\sum_{j} X_{ij},$$

(3.6)

where the letters denote the same, as in the case of the *RCA*. The measure expresses a country's share of a given sector in terms of exports. The measure ranges between [0;1]. It is important to know that the index is not truly an alternative to the *RSCA*, as it only expresses specialisation in an indirect way. The reason for including it in the present paper is that the measure is the 'vector of specialisation' from constant market share (CMS) analysis.

CMS analysis decomposes the aggregate growth rate of exports of a country into various components, based on the sectoral composition of the exports performed by that country, and in this context compares the vector of exports of that country to an average of all countries included in the analysis (cf. Fagerberg and Sollie, 1987). Hence, the growth rate of aggregate export can be decomposed into four components[8], namely first, a *market share effect* measuring the growth of exports by the country in question, assuming that sectors had grown at equal rates over the period. Second, one can identify a *structural market effect* measuring the effect of a country being specialised in the fast-growing (or slow-growing) sector in the initial year. Third, one can get a *market growth adaptation effect*, measuring whether the country in question has actively (more than the average country) moved into slow or fast growing sectors. Finally, one can identify a *market stagnation adaptation effect*, measuring the degree to which a country 'manages' to get out of slow growing sectors (or indeed moves into them).[9]

The specialisation vector can only be compared to the other measures, across the same country, as it is not normalised for country size, as are the other measures. However, this is not a problem given that the outcome of the CMS analysis (of which the specialisation vector is a part) is indeed normalised (expressed in percentage points). It should be pointed out strongly, that the aim of the CMS analysis is to measure *effects* of specialisation over time on performance, and that the aim is not to measure specialisation *per se*.

Nevertheless, it is important to examine whether the concept of specialisation used in Chapters 4, 5, 6, 7 and 9 is similar to the concept used in Chapters 8 and 10. Table 3.5 contains correlations between the *RSCA* index and the three other measures discussed in this chapter, for each individual country in the STAN database, across 22 sectors and 24 years. It can be seen that the CMS country vectors are indeed similar to the *RSCA* vectors for each country, as the average ρ equals 0.89 (all 19 correlations significant). Hence, it can be concluded that the two ways of measuring specialisation applied in this book are consistent, as should be expected given that measures are related per definition.

*Table 3.5 Correlations between the RSCA index, and other indices of
international trade specialisation; yearly observations 1970-93, across 22
sectors (n=528)*

	Michaely index	x^2	CMS-coefficient
Australia	0.76	0.68	0.84
Austria	0.62	0.76	0.93
Belgium	0.35	0.65	0.90
Canada	0.75	0.78	0.92
Denmark	0.57	0.52	0.90
Finland	0.68	0.60	0.84
France	0.47	0.76	0.97
Germany (West)	0.55	0.77	0.97
Greece	0.73	0.58	0.88
Italy	0.64	0.59	0.94
Japan	0.72	0.75	0.90
The Netherlands	0.77	0.77	0.89
New Zealand	0.68	0.58	0.78
Norway	0.73	0.66	0.81
Portugal	0.71	0.54	0.80
Spain	0.66	0.68	0.87
Sweden	0.71	0.66	0.87
United Kingdom	0.37	0.73	0.92
United States	0.37	0.73	0.91
Average	0.64	0.67	0.89

Note: All correlation coefficients differ from zero at the 1 per cent level.

For what concerns the χ^2 measure, it has been adjusted in Table 3.5, so that
the index can be directly compared to the other measures[10], as the numerator has
been multiplied by -1, if the 'non-squared' numerator was smaller than zero. As
already pointed out it should be stressed that the chi square measure has only
been used in the literature for measuring the level of specialisation (and hence
change in the level), while the other measures also capture the direction of
specialisation. However, as shown in Section 3.2 the *RSCA* can also be used for
measuring change in the level of specialisation. A question which arises is then:
do the *RSCA* regressions and the χ^2 measure generally point in the same
direction, when it comes to an increased or a decreased level of specialisation?
In order to investigate this question, we took the seven years[11], pooled in
Chapter 5 (Table 5.4), and examined whether specialisation went up or down
from year to year, using both types of indices (114 observations in total, given

six periods and 19 countries). As mentioned earlier, the condition for increased specialisation in the case of the *RSCA* is that $\hat{\beta}/\hat{R} > 1$ ($\hat{\beta}/\hat{R} < 1$ for de-specialisation), while the equivalent condition for the χ^2 measure is $\chi^2_{t2}/\chi^2_{t1} > 1$ ($\chi^2_{t2}/\chi^2_{t1} < 1$ for de-specialisation). The result of a correlation analysis displays a highly significant ρ, although the ρ equals 0.32 only. So the answer to the question posed above is that the two measures do in general point in the same direction, when it comes to an increased or decreased level of specialisation, but the two measures certainly do not always point in the same direction.

More generally, when looking at measures reflecting the direction of specialisation, however, it can be seen from Table 3.5 that although this chapter has stressed differences between the different measures of international specialisation, the measures do in fact correlate for all 19 countries. In this context, it should be stressed that the correlations between the *RSCA* on the one hand, and the CMS-coefficient and the chi square measure on the other, were to some extent expected, as the definitions of these three measures applies different combinations of basically the same components.

3.4. SUMMING UP

This chapter displayed figures on international specialisation of 19 OECD countries in order to give the reader a feel for how countries are specialised (Section 3.1), and can hence be used as a point of reference in the analytical chapters to follow. The measure used was the 'revealed comparative advantage' (*RCA*). In Section 3.2, it was argued that when using the *RCA*, it should always (at least in regression analysis) be adjusted in such a way that it becomes symmetric. The conclusion was based on a theoretical discussion of the properties of the measure, but also on convincing empirical evidence, based on the Jarque-Bera test of normality of the error terms from regressions, using both the *RCA* and the *RSCA*.

Section 3.3 compared the *RSCA* to other measures of international trade specialisation, used in the literature. These measures included the Michaely index (and the *CTB* measure), the chi square measure, and the 'specialisation vector' from constant market share analysis. The conclusion emerging from the analysis is that the *RSCA* is better at measuring changes in the *level* of specialisation, as compared to the chi square measure, given the heavy dependence on extreme values, when using the chi square measure. In relation to comparative advantage it was concluded that the *RSCA* is a better measure, when compared to the Michaely index (or to the *CTB*), since the *RSCA* measures the direction of specialisation, without taking into account aspects of performance, which is irrelevant to the issue of *comparative* advantage. Nevertheless, all the measures correlate rather strongly.

NOTES

1. A fuller discussion of this topic is present in Section 3.2.

2. Another and very similar measure to the *RSCA* has been applied by Hariolf Grupp in various publications (see e.g. Grupp, 1994; Grupp, 1998). The so-called *RPA* can be defined as:
    $RPA_{ij} = (RTA^2-1)/(RTA^2+1) * 100$,
    where *RPA* is short for 'Revealed Patent Advantage', and *RTA* is short for 'Revealed Technological Advantage', calculated in an analogous way to the *RCA* (see Equation 3.1), but based on US patent data.

3. The reason for only using 19 out of 22 possible sectors is that we want to compare export specialisation to technological specialisation in Chapter 5, from where the calculations are taken. When a concordance between exports and patents is made, one arrives at 19 comparable sectors.

4. The estimations based on the *RSCA* values, are taken from Chapter 5, Table 5.2.

5. Other measures include for example Bowen's (1983) *net trade index*. However, this particular index has been criticised for a number of reasons, including the underlying assumption of identical and homothetic preferences across countries (see Ballance, Forstner and Murray 1985).

6. In a correlation between the two measures across 24 years and 22 sectors (528 observations), for 19 countries, all countries displayed correlation coefficients of about 0.99.

7. It can be argued that e.g. the relative strength of the Danish shipyards is, at least partially, due to the strength of the shipping industry (and maybe vice versa). However, it would be awkward to argue that Denmark is not specialised in building ships and boats.

8. Other (and more) components can be identified, but this book (Chapters 8 and 10) uses the four components described in the present paragraph.

9. A formal description of the CMS methodology can be found in Chapter 8.

10. The problem is that - as mentioned earlier - that the χ^2 measure takes high values *both* if a country is (much) more specialised in a sector, *and* if a country is (much) less specialised in a sector.

11. The years: 1972, 1975, 1978, 1981, 1984, 1987 and 1990.

Table A3.1 Export specialisation figures (RSCAs) for 19 OECD countries and 22 STAN sectors

	Australia		Austria		Belgium		Canada		Denmark		Finland		France		Germany		Greece		Italy	
	1970	1990	1970	1990	1970	1990	1970	1990	1970	1990	1970	1990	1970	1990	1970	1990	1970	1990	1970	1990
Food, drink and tobacco	0.73	0.65	-0.46	-0.43	-0.12	0.10	-0.18	-0.14	0.62	0.58	-0.38	-0.52	0.14	0.23	-0.50	-0.23	0.50	0.52	-0.29	-0.15
Textiles, footw. and leather	-0.33	0.17	0.30	0.21	0.20	0.13	-0.68	-0.73	-0.06	-0.05	-0.10	-0.29	0.14	0.04	-0.10	-0.06	0.40	0.70	0.41	0.51
Wood, cork and furniture	-0.74	-0.76	0.59	0.46	-0.08	-0.03	0.53	0.56	0.25	0.48	0.78	0.58	-0.30	-0.21	-0.28	-0.15	-0.68	-0.52	-0.12	0.26
Paper and printing	-0.69	-0.48	0.22	0.28	-0.26	-0.18	0.56	0.54	-0.48	-0.22	0.80	0.77	-0.29	-0.14	-0.43	-0.14	-0.62	-0.59	-0.42	-0.34
Industrial chemicals	-0.14	-0.40	-0.23	-0.14	0.03	0.15	-0.30	-0.22	-0.22	-0.27	-0.50	-0.27	0.01	0.10	0.11	0.08	0.09	-0.41	-0.16	-0.26
Pharmaceuticals	-0.16	-0.10	-0.37	0.12	-0.17	0.09	-0.62	-0.72	0.33	0.51	-0.86	-0.43	0.13	0.20	0.14	0.04	-0.57	-0.13	0.06	-0.16
Petroleum refineries (oil)	-0.12	0.43	-0.73	-0.67	0.11	0.21	-0.68	0.16	-0.17	-0.10	-0.51	-0.22	-0.07	-0.19	-0.07	-0.39	-0.11	0.54	0.39	-0.06
Rubber and plastics	-0.44	-0.51	0.21	0.15	-0.08	0.05	-0.63	-0.11	0.12	0.15	-0.40	-0.32	0.22	0.14	-0.02	0.05	-0.12	-0.33	0.25	0.13
Stone, clay and glass	-0.64	-0.42	0.48	0.28	0.29	0.20	-0.59	-0.38	-0.10	0.01	-0.46	-0.24	0.10	0.10	0.08	-0.02	0.07	0.48	0.27	0.40
Ferrous metals	-0.22	0.08	0.26	0.28	0.43	0.38	-0.38	-0.29	-0.67	-0.36	-0.38	0.15	0.14	0.12	0.03	0.02	0.47	0.24	-0.34	-0.03
Non-ferrous metals	0.52	0.77	-0.16	0.04	0.41	0.19	0.52	0.46	-0.68	-0.58	-0.08	0.15	-0.21	-0.06	-0.26	-0.09	0.51	0.46	-0.54	-0.34
Fabricated metal products	-0.25	-0.27	0.15	0.24	-0.10	-0.01	-0.39	-0.19	-0.03	0.22	-0.33	0.02	0.00	0.04	0.15	0.12	-0.59	-0.39	0.08	0.24
Non-electrical machinery	-0.64	-0.52	-0.06	0.11	-0.37	-0.35	-0.30	-0.42	0.03	0.05	-0.35	0.04	-0.13	-0.15	0.18	0.15	-0.93	-0.75	0.15	0.17
Office mach. and computers	-0.93	-0.52	-0.76	-0.49	-0.68	-0.59	-0.36	-0.28	-0.54	-0.46	-0.95	-0.51	-0.04	-0.20	-0.03	-0.28	-1.00	-0.96	0.13	-0.22
Electrical machinery	-0.59	-0.51	0.18	0.11	-0.23	-0.31	-0.44	-0.46	0.02	-0.10	-0.37	-0.14	0.04	0.01	0.15	0.11	-0.67	-0.41	0.06	0.02
Communic. eq. and semicon.	-0.81	-0.63	0.01	0.01	-0.20	-0.43	-0.34	-0.16	-0.23	-0.20	-0.54	-0.10	-0.26	-0.22	-0.05	-0.22	-0.64	-0.84	-0.24	-0.42
Shipbuilding	-0.61	0.01	-0.41	-0.67	-0.55	-0.84	-0.33	-0.73	0.35	0.50	0.45	0.60	-0.30	-0.21	-0.22	-0.21	-0.86	-0.60	-0.50	-0.42
Other transport	-0.87	-0.67	0.33	0.13	-0.46	-0.39	0.27	0.24	-0.68	-0.63	-0.79	0.11	0.13	-0.09	-0.23	-0.22	-0.99	-0.94	0.05	0.21
Motor vehicles	-0.44	-0.55	-0.65	-0.21	-0.05	0.07	0.39	0.34	-0.74	-0.68	-0.85	-0.60	0.05	-0.02	0.16	0.12	-0.97	-0.93	-0.09	-0.27
Aerospace	-0.90	-0.60	-0.85	-0.91	-0.54	-0.68	0.10	-0.05	-0.65	-0.41	-0.98	-0.92	-0.07	0.11	-0.67	-0.23	-0.68	-0.84	-0.55	-0.30
Instruments	-0.65	-0.38	-0.30	-0.19	-0.73	-0.55	-0.40	-0.54	-0.01	0.02	-0.80	-0.39	-0.09	-0.11	0.15	0.03	-0.93	-0.81	-0.25	-0.30
Other manufacturing	-0.31	-0.13	0.34	0.03	0.26	0.61	-0.64	-0.65	-0.20	-0.51	-0.51	-0.53	-0.16	-0.16	-0.11	-0.25	-0.43	-0.66	0.17	0.28

[Table continues on next page]

	Japan		Netherl.		New Zea.		Norway		Portugal		Spain		Sweden		UK		US	
	1970	1990	1970	1990	1970	1990	1970	1990	1970	1990	1970	1990	1970	1990	1970	1990	1970	1990
Food, drink and tobacco	-0.50	-0.86	0.46	0.44	0.81	0.77	0.14	0.13	0.42	-0.04	0.49	0.12	-0.60	-0.57	-0.14	-0.04	-0.06	0.01
Textiles, footw. and leather	0.20	-0.48	0.09	-0.03	-0.01	0.25	-0.50	-0.62	0.56	0.73	0.25	0.14	-0.40	-0.50	0.02	-0.06	-0.52	-0.30
Wood, cork and furniture	-0.35	-0.86	-0.39	-0.27	-0.08	0.16	-0.14	0.13	0.68	0.54	0.21	-0.09	0.55	0.46	-0.62	-0.55	-0.30	-0.13
Paper and printing	-0.59	-0.66	-0.18	-0.07	-0.15	0.29	0.48	0.34	0.18	0.20	-0.03	-0.12	0.60	0.57	-0.31	-0.15	-0.06	-0.05
Industrial chemicals	-0.09	-0.19	0.22	0.26	-0.60	-0.54	-0.03	0.01	-0.16	-0.36	-0.16	-0.13	-0.38	-0.33	0.00	0.08	0.09	0.05
Pharmaceuticals	-0.55	-0.61	0.12	-0.02	-0.79	-0.48	-0.68	-0.48	0.17	-0.40	-0.32	0.01	-0.32	0.29	0.24	0.29	0.03	-0.02
Petroleum refineries (oil)	-0.79	-0.66	0.59	0.55	-0.62	0.06	-0.18	0.62	0.05	0.22	0.41	0.41	-0.39	0.08	0.04	0.08	-0.13	-0.06
Rubber and plastics	0.22	-0.11	-0.07	0.05	-0.75	-0.31	-0.19	-0.30	-0.08	-0.30	0.26	0.21	-0.12	-0.12	0.05	-0.01	-0.25	-0.17
Stone, clay and glass	0.03	-0.20	-0.21	-0.15	-0.71	-0.64	-0.29	-0.18	0.27	0.42	0.04	0.34	-0.33	-0.30	0.03	-0.12	-0.25	-0.31
Ferrous metals	0.34	0.08	-0.22	-0.14	-0.93	-0.25	0.04	0.20	-0.67	-0.57	-0.45	0.18	0.12	0.23	-0.21	-0.07	-0.33	-0.55
Non-ferrous metals	-0.48	-0.47	-0.32	-0.08	-0.80	0.45	0.69	0.75	-0.79	-0.72	-0.13	-0.10	-0.18	-0.08	0.11	0.03	-0.16	-0.12
Fabricated metal products	0.05	-0.21	-0.07	-0.02	-0.72	-0.38	-0.16	-0.08	-0.09	-0.20	0.11	0.05	0.06	0.11	0.11	-0.07	-0.12	-0.19
Non-electrical machinery	-0.26	0.05	-0.40	-0.27	-0.86	-0.69	-0.43	-0.28	-0.73	-0.56	-0.25	-0.23	0.08	0.13	0.10	0.01	0.15	0.01
Office mach. and computers	-0.11	0.28	-0.25	0.02	-1.00	-0.97	-0.81	-0.38	-0.62	-0.75	-0.37	-0.35	0.09	-0.23	-0.02	0.22	0.34	0.28
Electrical machinery	0.04	0.17	0.03	-0.21	-0.80	-0.40	-0.35	-0.37	-0.34	0.04	-0.11	-0.05	-0.07	-0.06	0.06	-0.05	-0.02	-0.02
Communic. eq. and semicon.	0.45	0.43	0.19	-0.19	-0.97	-0.87	-0.39	-0.49	-0.06	-0.28	-0.58	-0.57	0.01	-0.04	-0.14	-0.02	0.03	0.14
Shipbuilding	0.51	0.44	-0.05	-0.25	-0.93	-0.73	0.71	0.84	-0.84	-0.18	0.45	0.31	0.41	0.06	-0.18	-0.48	-0.30	-0.27
Other transport	0.56	0.46	-0.63	-0.29	-0.98	-0.95	-0.54	-0.58	-0.33	-0.33	0.17	-0.36	-0.27	-0.31	-0.09	-0.40	-0.53	-0.26
Motor vehicles	-0.16	0.24	-0.67	-0.53	-0.98	-0.93	-0.85	-0.75	-0.92	-0.35	-0.51	0.22	-0.07	-0.01	0.04	-0.23	0.00	-0.18
Aerospace	-0.87	-0.89	-0.29	-0.29	-0.98	-0.93	-0.76	-0.47	-0.98	-0.80	-0.92	-0.28	-0.71	-0.42	0.11	0.34	0.54	0.48
Instruments	0.17	0.26	-0.07	0.01	-0.92	-0.76	-0.67	-0.34	-0.79	-0.66	-0.62	-0.58	-0.33	-0.10	0.07	0.09	0.20	0.16
Other manufacturing	0.20	-0.07	-0.38	-0.44	-0.89	-0.55	-0.73	-0.65	0.43	-0.30	-0.23	-0.28	-0.51	-0.54	0.37	0.32	-0.16	-0.19

PART II

The Development of International Specialisation
Patterns

4. Structural Change in OECD Export Specialisation Patterns: De-specialisation and 'Stickiness'[1]

One of the main conclusions of the literature on convergence-divergence of growth patterns is that convergence has been the dominant feature among the OECD countries in the postwar period. In addition, Archibugi and Pianta (1992; 1994) found convergence in aggregate (national-level) science and technology (S&T) indicators such as R&D intensity, patent intensity and in bibliometric indicators, in their comprehensive study of international specialisation in S&T among the advanced countries. However, at the sectoral level they found increasing technological specialisation. Also Cantwell (1989; 1991) generally found increasing technological specialisation patterns among most of the countries examined.

This chapter examines three related issues which concern trade specialisation, rather than technological specialisation. Firstly, we want to assess whether the group of OECD countries are characterised by a high degree of stability of their *export* specialisation patterns at the country level. Secondly, we want to cast light on whether the 20 relatively advanced countries have become more or less specialised in terms of trade specialisation in the period in question. Finally, we want to analyse the extent to which export specialisation patterns tend to converge or diverge. The countries examined are 20 OECD countries during a period of nearly three decades from 1965 to 1992.

In this context we will distinguish between specialisation (or de-specialisation) in trade patterns on the one hand, and divergence (or convergence) in trade patterns on the other. A specialisation process refers to a process in which specialisation *intra-country* becomes more dispersed (and conversely for de-specialisation). On the other hand, a divergence process refers to a process in which countries become more different in terms of specialisation in a particular sector, *across countries* (and conversely for convergence). This distinction is an important one, since the two kinds of processes might not in all cases move in the same direction, and are probably going to take place at different speeds. Thus we will discuss these differences further - in the empirical section - and test for the rate and direction of both kinds of processes.

Section 4.1 deals with the statistical methodology involved in measuring stability of specialisation patterns and whether these tend to become more or less dispersed over time. Section 4.2 contains the core empirical part of the chapter in terms of our stability tests of export specialisation and Section 4.3

contains the conclusions, including a discussion of some implications for the issue of economic integration.

The contribution of this chapter is mainly empirical; thus we do not have exact expectations on all our results. Nevertheless, a number of theoretical propositions were made in Chapter 2 of this book. These propositions, along with the underlying theory will act as a tool for interpretation. The propositions to be tested in this chapter are: (a) patterns of specialisation will display persistence over long time periods; (b) catching up countries will experience the fastest rate of change in the patterns of specialisation; (c) low tech products will be more footloose than high-tech products; and finally (d) when economic integration is a central feature of development, specialisation patterns of countries will diverge (or put differently the level of specialisation will increase).

4.1. THE METHODOLOGY

As mentioned in Chapter 3, it can be concluded that most empirical studies of international specialisation patterns use as a central indicator Balassa's so-called Revealed Comparative Advantage index (Balassa, 1965), originally developed for analysis of specialisation in international trade, but later also used in studies of specialisation in S&T, based on R&D, bibliometric data or patents (the latter also known as *RTA*; relative technological advantage). In a trade context the algebra can be set up as in Chapter 3:

$$RCA_{ij} = \frac{X_{ij} / \sum_i X_{ij}}{\sum_j X_{ij} / \sum_i \sum_j X_{ij}}. \tag{4.1}$$

The numerator represents the percentage share of a given sector in national exports - X_{ij} are exports of sector i from country j. The denominator represents the percentage share of a given sector in OECD exports. The *RCA* index, thus, contains a comparison of national export structure (the numerator) with the OECD export structure (the denominator). When *RCA* equals 1 for a given sector in a given country, the percentage share of that sector is identical to the OECD average. Where *RCA* is above 1 the country is said to be specialised in that sector and vice versa where *RCA* is below 1.

The work of Pavitt (1989) paved the way for empirical studies of the stability characteristics of technological specialisation patterns at the country level. He found positive and significant correlations between the *RTA* distributions, country by country, in nine out of ten OECD countries - i.e. relative stability of the *RTA* patterns. Such stability is interpreted as the statistical reflection of the cumulative and path dependent character of technological change at the micro level. When firms have gained some kind of competitive advantage in one field they tend to strengthen that advantage further (or go bankrupt). For the same reasons diversification often occurs only in fields which are close to the core competence of firms.

In the present chapter we are going to present a statistical test of the stability of the national export specialisation patterns. Recall from Chapter 3 that the Balassa measure has, for testing purposes, the disadvantage of an inherent risk of lack of normality because it takes values between zero and infinity with a (weighted) average of 1.0. A skewed distribution violates the assumption of normality of the error term in regression analysis, thus not producing reliable *t*-statistics. In addition, the use of the *RCA* in regression analysis gives much more weight to values above one, when compared with observations below one. Cantwell (1989, pp. 31-2) solved the problem rather pragmatically by testing for skewness and kurtosis of his data sample. He found the distribution of the data set used to be approximately normal. However, it does not seem to hold for the export data sets used in this chapter. The null hypothesis that the residuals from the regressions below, are a random sample taken from a normal distribution, can be rejected for e.g. 7 out of 20 estimations for the long term period using the *RSCA* (($(RCA-1)/(RCA+1)$)), while this is the case for 18 estimations for the 'pure' *RCA*, according to the Jarque-Bera-test, and applying a 10 per cent level. Hence, we shall apply the *RSCA*.

The methodology for testing whether countries are stable across sectors and whether they tend to become more or less specialised intra-country *and* the test of whether countries tend to converge within the same sector are analogous. However, we will start off by describing the methodology to be used for the intra-country, cross sectoral analyses. We are going to employ a method first used in the context of specialisation, by John Cantwell (1989). His basic source of inspiration was a 'Galtonian' regression model presented by Hart and Prais (1956). Stability (and specialisation trends) is tested by means of the following regression equation (country by country), bearing in mind that nothing can be said on these grounds about the determinants of the initial export specialisation pattern:

$$RSCA_{ij}^{t_2} = \alpha_j + \beta_j RSCA_{ij}^{t_1} + \epsilon_{ij}. \qquad (4.2)$$

The superscripts t_1 and t_2 refer to the initial year and the final year, respectively. The dependent variable, *RSCA* at time t_2 for sector i, is tested against the independent variable which is the value of the *RSCA* in the previous year t_1. α and β are standard linear regression parameters and ϵ is a residual term. It should be pointed out that the method is one of comparing two cross-sections at two points in time; i.e. there is no element of time across the observations.

The idea behind the regression is that $\beta=1$ corresponds to an unchanged pattern from t_1 to t_2. If $\beta>1$ the country tends to become more specialised in sectors where it is already specialised, and less specialised where initial specialisation is low - i.e. the existing pattern of specialisation is strengthened. If one makes an analogy to the convergence literature, $\beta>1$ might be termed *β-specialisation*. Similarly, $0<\beta<1$ can be termed *β-de-specialisation*, i.e., *on average* sectors with initial low *RSCA*s increase over time while sectors with initial high *RSCA*s decrease their values. The magnitude of $(1-\beta)$ therefore measures the size of what has been termed as the 'regression effect', and this is the interpretation placed on the estimated coefficient of β in the present chapter. In the special case where $\beta<0$ the ranking of sectors has been reversed. Those *RSCA*s initially below the country average are in the final year above average and vica versa. Given the above listed line of reasoning, the test of cumulativeness (or 'stickiness') is whether $\hat{\beta}$ is significantly greater than zero. If $\hat{\beta} \leq 0$, it cannot be rejected that the development of the trade specialisation pattern of a country is either reversed or random, contrary to the hypothesis of cumulativeness.

Another feature emerging from the regression analysis is a test of whether the degree of specialisation changes. Following Cantwell (1989, pp. 31-2) it can be deduced that $\beta>1$ is not a necessary condition for an increase in the overall national specialisation pattern. With reference to Hart (1976) it can be shown that:

$$\sigma_j^{2\,t_2}/\sigma_j^{2\,t_1} = \beta_j^2/R_j^2. \tag{4.3}$$

Thus,

$$\sigma_j^{t_2}/\sigma_j^{t_1} = |\beta_j|/|R_j|. \tag{4.4}$$

It follows that the dispersion of a given distribution is unchanged when $\beta=R$. If $\beta>R$ (equivalent to an increase in the dispersion) the degree of specialisation has increased. Thus making the same kind of analogies as above, one might term this as *σ-specialisation*. If $\beta<R$ (equivalent to a decrease in the dispersion) the degree of specialisation has decreased. Likewise, such a situation can be

described as *σ-de-specialisation*. Whether countries tend to specialise or de-specialise is to our mind an empirical question. However, the outcome has important implications. We shall discuss these implications in the conclusion.

The estimated Pearson correlation coefficient is a measure of the mobility of sectors up and down the *RSCA* distribution. A high level of the coefficient indicates that the relative position of sectors is little changed, while a low value indicates that some sectors are moving closer together and others further apart, quite possibly to the extent that the ranking of sectors change. The value of (1-R) measures what has been described as the 'mobility effect'. It may well be that, even where the 'regression effect' (1-β) suggest a fall in the degree of specialisation due to a proportional change in sectors towards the average (β<1), this is outweighed by the mobility effect, due to changes in the proportional position between sectors (β>R). Following Cantwell's vocabulary we can also characterise an increase in the dispersion as a change towards a more 'narrow' specialisation pattern; and a decrease in the dispersion as a change towards a more 'broad' pattern.

The latter interpretation should, however, be treated with care. In general, the R^2 is a decomposition of the variance (σ^2) of the dependent variable, *RSCA* in the final year t_2, into the sum of the variance of the independent variables - i.e. the sum of the variance of the initial *RSCA* and the error term ϵ. The combination of β<1 and β>R, which is identical to an increased variance of the *RSCA*s over time, is thus to some extent caused by the variance of the residual term ϵ. The mechanism causing increased standard deviation (dispersion) of the final *RSCA*s, in the case of β<1, is the existence of a positive variance of the residual term - i.e. the increased standard deviation of the final *RSCA*s is partly caused by the residual and therefore not by a recognisable economic explanation (such as cumulativeness).[2] These problems of interpretation have their parallel in the discussion in 'new growth' analysis of β- versus σ-convergence of per capita incomes as introduced by Barro and Sala-i-Martin (1991).

We will now turn to the sector-wise methodology, which is used to test whether specialisation patterns tend to *converge* across countries, within the same sector:

$$RSCA_{ij}^{t_2} = \alpha_i + \beta_i RSCA_{ij}^{t_1} + \epsilon_{ij}. \tag{4.5}$$

As in the case of the country-wise analysis, the idea behind the regression is that β=1 corresponds to an unchanged pattern from t_1 to t_2. If β>1 the countries which are (heavily) specialised in the sector in question tend to become increasingly specialised in this sector, while countries which are under-specialised in the sector in question tend to become even less specialised in this sector. Such a movement can be termed *β-divergence* in trade patterns. If $0<\beta<1$ the existing specialisation pattern changes i.e., *on average* countries with initial low *RSCA*s increase over time, while countries with initial high *RSCA*s decrease their values. The situation in which $0<\beta<1$ can be termed *β-convergence*. In the special case where $\beta<0$ the ranking of countries has changed fundamentally, so that those *RSCA*s initially below the OECD average are in the final year above average and vica versa.

As in the case of specialisation/de-specialisation it can be shown for divergence/convergence that:

$$\sigma_i^{t_2}/\sigma_i^{t_1} = |\beta_i|/|R_i|. \tag{4.6}$$

From the above it follows that the dispersion of a given distribution is unchanged when $\beta=R$. If $\beta>R$ the degree of divergence has increased. Thus, one can term this situation as *σ-divergence*. If $\beta<R$ the countries have converged in their trade patterns, which in turn can be described as *σ-convergence*.

4.2. THE CHARACTERISTICS OF OECD EXPORT SPECIALISATION PATTERNS

4.2.1. The Country-wise Specialisation Patterns

In the country-wise category of studies of stability of export specialisation we are only aware of the study by Amendola, Guerrieri and Padoan (1992) and the study by Papagni (1992). Amendola, Guerrieri and Padoan follow Cantwell's methodology and compare the development of *RCA*s and *RTA*s for three periods. In slightly more than 50 per cent of their estimated equations the hypothesis of 'constant' specialisation ($\beta=1$) could not be rejected and the R^2s are generally high. On this basis they conclude that both trade and technological specialisation patterns have been remarkably stable in the medium term, although to a decreasing degree in the long term. The normality problem with the *RCA*s as well as the *RTA*s is, however, neglected.

The Papagni study confirms the stability of trade specialisation patterns for high-technology goods, using three-mode principal components analysis. However, the study only considers seven individual countries and a rather limited time-period (1981-87), and contains no analysis of the development of

Table 4.1 Country-wise stability and development of OECD export specialisation patterns in the long term

Country	1965-92				1965-79				1979-92			
	α̂	β̂	R̂	β̂/R̂	α̂	β̂	R̂	β̂/R̂	α̂	β̂	R̂	β̂/R̂
United States	-0.01	0.75 *#	0.74	1.01	-0.02	0.97 *#	0.80	1.21	0.00	0.79 *#	0.94	0.84
Japan	-0.12**	0.62 *	0.58	1.07	-0.05	0.77 *#	0.74	1.04	-0.04	0.95 *#	0.93	1.03
Germany	-0.02	0.52 *	0.73	0.70	-0.02	0.67 *#	0.85	0.79	-0.01	0.77 *#	0.86	0.89
France	-0.04	0.37 *	0.40	0.94	-0.03	0.60 *	0.63	0.94	-0.01	0.78 *#	0.78	1.00
Italy	-0.07***	0.59 *	0.55	1.06	-0.04	0.87 *#	0.84	1.04	-0.03	0.78 *#	0.76	1.02
United Kingdom	-0.03	0.57 *	0.71	0.80	-0.02	0.72 *#	0.87	0.84	-0.02	0.76 *#	0.80	0.95
Belgium-Lux	-0.02	0.66 *#	0.69	0.96	-0.04	0.68 *#	0.76	0.89	0.02	0.97 *#	0.91	1.07
Canada	-0.01	0.72 *#	0.82	0.88	-0.03	0.77 *#	0.84	0.92	-0.01	0.83 *#	0.87	0.96
Denmark	0.07**	0.78 *#	0.88	0.88	0.08*	0.89 *#	0.95	0.93	0.00	0.86 *#	0.91	0.94
Finland	0.07	0.61 *	0.68	0.90	0.08	0.79 *#	0.82	0.97	0.01	0.78 *#	0.84	0.93
Netherlands	-0.02	0.61 *	0.64	0.94	-0.04	0.79 *#	0.79	0.99	0.02	0.84 *#	0.89	0.94
Norway	-0.18*	0.74 *#	0.80	0.92	-0.10*	0.85 *#	0.89	0.95	-0.08*	0.91 *#	0.94	0.97
Austria	0.01	0.67 *#	0.76	0.89	0.00	0.69 *#	0.77	0.90	-0.02	0.79 *#	0.81	0.98
Switzerland	-0.02	0.86 *#	0.90	0.96	0.02	0.96 *#	0.95	1.01	-0.03***	0.92 *#	0.97	0.95
Sweden	0.01	0.70 *#	0.76	0.91	0.04	0.84 *#	0.90	0.94	-0.01	0.89 *#	0.91	0.97
Greece	0.04	0.63 *	0.58	1.10	0.01	0.71 *#	0.63	1.12	0.03	0.87 *#	0.89	0.98
Ireland	-0.05	0.37 *	0.39	0.95	0.00	0.46 *	0.50	0.93	-0.04	0.85 *#	0.84	1.02
Portugal	-0.10	0.54 *	0.64	0.84	-0.04	0.69 *#	0.73	0.94	-0.11**	0.64 *#	0.72	0.89
Spain	-0.06	0.29 *	0.51	0.57	0.01	0.52 *	0.68	0.77	-0.06**	0.59 *	0.79	0.74
Turkey	-0.15**	0.36 *	0.43	0.83	-0.11	0.72 *#	0.73	0.99	-0.02	0.64 *#	0.76	0.84
Mean (unweighted)		0.60	0.66	0.91		0.75	0.78	0.96		0.81	0.86	0.95

Notes:
*/**/*** denote significantly different from zero at the 1%; 5%; and 10% levels, respectively (t-test). # denotes higher and significantly different from 0.5 at the 10% level (t-test).

59

the specialisation patterns.

Our analysis is conducted across 60 sectors (described in Table A4.3) for 20 OECD countries. More detailed characteristics of the data set used are documented in the Appendix. It should be stressed that the selection criteria for the data has been a search for 'peak' years. The aim has been to avoid effects of short term fluctuations in trade patterns in the cross section analyses. Data for 1992 were chosen as well, since they were the most recent data available at the time of writing. The results of our tests are summarised in Table 4.1, which shows the values for $\hat{\beta}$, $\hat{R}$ and $\hat{\beta}/\hat{R}$ for the period 1965-92 ('long' term) and for two sub-periods 1965-79 and 1979-92 (both 'medium' term). In the long term perspective (1965-92), the results show a general decrease in the dispersion of export specialisation, implying a trend towards a decrease in specialisation (so-called σ-de-specialisation). The exceptions are Greece, Italy, Japan and US, which become more specialised.

The decomposition of the dispersion in a 'regression' effect $(1-\beta)$, and a 'mobility' effect $(1- R)$, reveals two features. On the one side, the $\hat{\beta}$-values are significantly different from zero and significantly below unity at the one per cent level for all the 20 countries, meaning that the hypothesis of a reverse or random pattern can be rejected. Trade patterns do not change 'overnight' and do not change fundamentally even over three decades. Put differently, this feature points to a general tendency to increases in industries where countries have been relatively less specialised and to decreases in industries where they have been highly specialised.

A few 'stylised' features in the specialisation patterns between various groups of countries seem to emerge from the analysis. The *catching up OECD countries* generally show high regression effects (low $\hat{\beta}$) and high mobility effects (low $\hat{R}$), implying a stronger tendency towards decrease in initially advantaged industries and increase in disadvantaged industries. Most of the small high-income countries show low regression effects (high $\hat{\beta}$) and low mobility effects (high $\hat{R}$). This point is illustrated by the fact that all catching up countries (Japan, Finland, Greece, Ireland, Italy, Portugal, Spain and Turkey) have $\hat{\beta}$ values either significantly lower than 0.5 (10 per cent level), or values not significantly different from 0.5, while nearly all *smaller high-income countries* have indeed very sticky specialisation patterns, in the sense that they all (Belgium, Canada, Denmark, Norway, Austria, Switzerland and Sweden), except the Netherlands, display $\hat{\beta}$ values significantly higher than 0.5. Also the United States displays a very stable pattern as the $\hat{\beta}$ value is significantly higher than 0.5. Furthermore there are some *high-income countries* (but slow growing in terms of economic growth) with relatively low $\hat{\beta}$ values, namely France, the UK, and the Netherlands. This might well imply that relatively low stability in terms of the export specialisation pattern is not associated with economic growth *per se* - especially not for initially rich countries. However, the third largest economic power in the OECD, Germany, has a $\hat{\beta}$ value not significantly different from 0.5, but this development has been associated with relatively strong 'broadening out' of the specialisation pattern, as measured by the relatively low $\hat{\beta}/\hat{R}$. In this context, an example may be useful. A comparison of Japan and Germany shows that both countries have high regression effects, but Japan clearly has a higher mobility effect. In fact, the mobility effect has outweighed the regression effect in the Japanese case - in 1992 the dispersion of export specialisation was slightly higher compared to 1965. A high mobility in relation to an unchanged or even an increased dispersion indicates a shift in the pattern of export specialisation. In 1965 Japan was highly specialised in fish, textile fabrics, clothing, consumer electronics, and ships. In 1992 the highly specialised industries were consumer electronics, semiconductors, telecommunications equipment, ships, and photographical, optical goods & watches. Thus, an important change in the ranking has taken place without changing the dispersion of the *RSCA*s. In contrast Germany displays no radical change despite the relatively low $\hat{\beta}$ value. Germany remains specialised in sectors which were already strong (but to a smaller degree), such as various chemical products as well as in different types of machinery. In addition Germany tends to increase specialisation in areas of initial weakness (but despite this, Germany remains weak in these areas), such as meat products; cereals & cereal preparations; beverages & tobacco; and clothing.

Concerning the medium term of 1965-79 and 1979-92, it should be noted that the unweighted mean of the dispersions increase slightly, with $\hat{\beta}/\hat{R}$ equal to 0.91 in 1965-79 and 0.96 in 1979-92, indicating a stronger σ-de-specialisation in the first period. During 1965-79 σ-specialisation can be found in five countries - the same as in 1979-92. The unweighted β-de-specialisation measure was 0.75 and 0.74, respectively - indicating a lower degree of ('explained') β-de-specialisation compared to the long term period 1961-92. The estimated 'regression' effects $(1-\hat{\beta})$ as well as the 'mobility' effects $(1-\hat{R})$ are, thus, generally lower (equivalent to larger values of $\hat{\beta}$ and $\hat{R}$) for the two medium term sub-periods implying the long term changes have evolved gradually.

How sensible are the data with respect to the level and kind of aggregation? And does the inclusion of primary goods influence the results? In order to answer these questions we did a similar analysis based on the categorical aggregation - at the 2-digit and 3-digit SITC levels, respectively. However, the levels of aggregation do not seem to affect our conclusion based on the 60-sectors aggregation. On average, both for 2 and 3-digit SITC the same kind of slow trend towards de-specialisation appears. Only three countries show $\hat{\beta}/\hat{R}$-values above unity. Secondly, concerning the scope of the analysis, it could be argued that the inclusion of primary goods would automatically produce lower $\hat{\beta}/\hat{R}$-values since the process of industrialisation is followed by a broadening in the production and export structure. In fact our conclusions would not change if we limit the analysis to manufacturing. In this case only five countries (compared to four for the whole economy) seem to become more specialised (Italy, Switzerland, Japan, UK and US). And the unweighted mean for $\hat{\beta}/\hat{R}$ 1965-92 is slightly smaller (0.89 vs. 0.91).

The picture of de-specialisation as well as path-dependent change is further underlined by the data for the six 'short' term periods presented in Table A4.1. Compared to the medium term periods, the short term $\hat{\beta}$- and $\hat{R}$-values are generally found to be at a higher level, as it would be expected. Only in the case of the US in 1969-73, could statistically significant β-specialisation be registered.

4.2.2. The Sector-wise Specialisation Patterns

The empirical results reported in the literature of the sector-wise category of studies point in different directions. Soete and Verspagen (1992) analysed a sample of 22 manufacturing industries across countries in the period 1970-90. The specification was similar to our sector-wise specification (β-convergence), the only difference being that they estimated a restricted model assuming no intercept. Soete and Verspagen concluded that convergence was predominant in every sector except food (non-significant convergence) and textiles (significant divergence).

Dollar and Wolff (1993, Chapter 7) report, however, that the trade specialisation patterns of 11 OECD countries 1970-86 did not become more similar, also based on a sector-wise approach. They use a slightly simpler methodology based on comparing coefficients of variation of the *RCA*s over time; six sectors show increasing dispersion and the other six show a decrease. But the study, however, uses the non-modified *RCA*s and does not take the problems of normality into account.

The general results from Table 4.2 have much in common with the country-wise findings of Table 4.1. For all sectors we find β-convergence and in all cases $\hat{\beta}$ is significantly below unity (and above 0). Further, we find σ-convergence for all sectors except five; i.e. the dispersion of specialisation in almost all sectors has decreased. Put differently, the countries which have been under-specialised in given sectors tend to increase specialisation in these sectors and/or countries which are specialised in given sectors tend to decrease specialisation in these sectors. This β-convergence appears marginally stronger compared to the country-wise σ-de-specialisation when the level of disaggregation shown in Table A4.3 is used.

Table 4.2 Sector-wise stability and development of OECD export specialisation patterns in the long term (1965-92)

No.	Sector	1965-92 $\hat{\alpha}$	$\hat{\beta}$	$\hat{R}$	$\hat{\beta}/\hat{R}$	No.	Sector	1965-92 $\hat{\alpha}$	$\hat{\beta}$	$\hat{R}$	$\hat{\beta}/\hat{R}$
1	Meat & meat preparations	-0.07	0.82 * #	0.85	0.96	31	Agricul. & food proces. mach.	0.07	0.57 *	0.69	0.83
2	Dairy products	-0.13	0.70 *	0.75	0.94	32	Textile & sewing machines	-0.08	0.83 * #	0.88	0.94
3	Fish & fish preparations	-0.04	0.65 *	0.79	0.82	33	Paper & pulp machinery	0.10 **	0.87 * #	0.94	0.93
4	Cereals & cereal preparations	0.17	0.65 *	0.62	1.04	34	Mach. for other spec. industries/processes	0.08	0.81 * #	0.83	0.99
5	Feeding-stuff for animals	-0.19 ***	0.35 **	0.45	0.77	35	Heating & cooling equipment	0.00	0.45 *	0.68	0.67
6	Other food products	0.01	0.72 * #	0.88	0.83	36	Metalworking machinery	0.00	0.77 * #	0.87	0.89
7	Beverages & tobacco	-0.05	0.70 * #	0.90	0.79	37	Power generating machinery	-0.01	0.58 *	0.69	0.85
8	Animal & vegetable oil & fats	0.05	0.84 * #	0.76	1.10	38	Pumps & centrifuges	-0.01	0.63 *	0.85	0.74
9	Cut flowers, bulbs, & oth. plants	-0.24 *	0.62 *	0.73	0.86	39	Typewriters & office mach.	-0.08	0.57 **	0.55	1.04
10	Seeds & spores for planting	-0.14 ***	0.73 * #	0.83	0.89	40	Computers & peripherals	-0.21	0.20	0.23	0.87
11	Skins & leather manufactures	-0.08	0.51 **	0.53	0.97	41	Semiconductors	-0.18	0.54 *	0.64	0.84
12	Wood & wood manufactures	0.02	0.76 * #	0.84	0.91	42	Telecommunications equipment	-0.09	0.40 **	0.53	0.76
13	Pulp & paper	0.11	0.69 * #	0.90	0.77	43	Mach. for prod. & dist. of electricity	-0.02	0.24 ***	0.39	0.60
14	Textile fibers	-0.18	0.58 *	0.74	0.79	44	Consumer electronics	-0.19	0.39 ***	0.41	0.96
15	Textile yarn, fabrics, etc.	0.03 **	0.48 **	0.56	0.87	45	Domestic electrical equipment	-0.02	0.36 **	0.48	0.75
16	Iron ore	-0.27 *	0.82 * #	0.90	0.91	46	Electromedical equipment	-0.10	0.58 *	0.65	0.89
17	Iron, steel & ferro-alloys	0.06 *	0.33 **	0.44	0.76	47	Non-elec. medical equipment	0.04	0.54 *	0.61	0.89
18	Aluminium	0.04	0.48 *	0.62	0.77	48	Measuring & control. instrum.	-0.03	0.60 *	0.78	0.77
19	Non-ferrous ores & metals	0.04	0.58 *	0.76	0.77	49	Photographic & optical goods, watches	0.01	0.73 * #	0.90	0.81
20	Crude fertilizers, crude minerals & coal	-0.12 **	0.63 *	0.78	0.80	50	Railway vehicles	-0.06	0.53 *	0.60	0.88
21	Non-metallic minerals	0.05	0.40 **	0.50	0.81	51	Road motor vehicles	0.01	0.69 *	0.73	0.95
22	Rest: rubber; electr. energy	-0.06	0.37 **	0.50	0.75	52	Aircraft	-0.13	0.67 *	0.70	0.95
23	Oil & gas	-0.09	0.32	0.30	1.10	53	Ships & boats (& oilrigs)	-0.03	0.60 *	0.72	0.84
24	Organic chemicals	0.00	0.46 *	0.58	0.80	54	Other non-electrical equipm.	0.03	0.72 * #	0.90	0.80
25	Inorganic chemicals	-0.03	0.22	0.33	0.65	55	Other electrical equipment	0.00	0.73 * #	0.90	0.81
26	Dyestuffs, colouring materials	0.03	0.57 *	0.75	0.76	56	Manufactures of metal	0.03	0.37 *	0.57	0.66
27	Pharmaceuticals	0.06	0.69 *	0.73	0.94	57	Furniture	-0.02	0.52 *	0.62	0.83
28	Fertilizers, manufactured	-0.07	0.20	0.28	0.69	58	Clothing	-0.04	0.05	0.04	1.18
29	Plastic materials	-0.01	0.34 *	0.59	0.57	59	Orthopaed. eq. & hearing aids	0.00	0.60 *	0.68	0.88
30	Other chemicals	-0.05	0.42 **	0.56	0.76	60	Industrial products, n.e.s.	0.01	0.63 *	0.78	0.81
	Mean (unweighted)							0.56	0.56	0.66	0.85

Notes:
*/**/*** denote significantly different from zero at the 1%; 5%; and 10% levels, respectively. # denotes higher and significantly different from 0.5 at the 10% level (t-test).

63

While Section 4.2.1 above showed that the overall de-specialisation trends were not sensitive to the different levels of disaggregation tested, the interpretation of the detailed sector-wise results of Table 4.2 demands some further comments on the specific kind of disaggregation used. Besides the inherent problems of missing values in foreign trade data, mainly at the 4 and 5 digit SITC levels, the basic idea behind the chosen list of 60 sectors - aggregated to 5 main sectors - is to get a slightly more richly faceted division than the standard two main sectors of manufacturing versus 'raw materials'. The first main sector (so-called natural resource based products) consists of raw materials and highly resource based semi-manufactures. Oil & gas is treated as a main sector of its own, while chemicals is identical to SITC 5. The main sector of 'other industrial products' (or 'traditional industries') contains the more labour intensive (and low skilled) parts of manufacturing, while the fourth main sector contains engineering, electronics & transport equipment. In a non-rigorously defined sense the natural resource based main sector, and of course also oil & gas, to a certain extent reflect the natural endowments of a country. On the other hand the 'traditional industries' appears to be pretty well characterised as labour intensive (low-skilled) sectors. Chemicals and engineering, electronics & transport equipment contain the more R&D and/or capital intensive areas.

Sectors with low $\hat{\beta}$s usually reveal a high mobility effect $(1-\hat{R})$ indicating a major shift in the ranking of the country specialisation in the specific sector. However, Table 4.2 points at important differences in the level of $\hat{\beta}$ (and $\hat{R}$) across sectors. As should be somehow expected, the components of the natural resource based main sector (no. 1-22) have generally high $\hat{\beta}$s (many significantly higher than 0.5) and low mobility.[3] The 'traditional industries' (no. 56-60) show high β-convergence and high mobility consistent with a conception of these areas as characterized by the importance of relative factor intensities, more in line with the standard Heckscher-Ohlin type of explanation.

Within chemicals as well as in engineering, electronics & transport equipment there are quite evident differences in the degree of β-convergence. The machinery oriented sectors (no. 31-38: agricultural & food processing machinery; textile & sewing machines; paper & pulp machinery; metalworking machinery; machinery for other special industries and processes; power generating machinery; and pumps & centrifuges) all display mobility below the average (the unweighted mean). This observation is further underlined by the fact that four of these industries show a $\hat{\beta}$ significantly higher than 0.5. On the other hand, sectors like computers; consumer electronics; telecommunications equipment; and domestic electrical equipment show much stronger β-convergence and a much higher mobility. These sectors may be argued to a certain degree to be dominated by multinational companies capable of exploiting economies of scale and scope world-wide in their production and foreign trade pattern (but not necessarily so in their technological development patterns). Other parts of electronics, such as semiconductors; electromedical equipment; and measuring & control instruments display lower than average β-convergence, indicating that these fields are less 'footloose' in their foreign trade pattern.

These more intuitive and preliminary indications of potentially systematic sector specificities in the stability characteristics of international specialisation may act as a complement to the more widespread analyses of country-wise patterns (see also Yeats, 1985). The country-wise and sector-wise results are more or less by definition two sides of the same coin. Countries with relative high $\hat{\beta}$s in their country-wise specialisation patterns tend to be specialised in those sectors that display a fairly low degree of β-convergence (high $\hat{\beta}$s) in their sector-wise patterns.

4.3. CONCLUSION AND DISCUSSION

In the present chapter we have made a distinction between the two concepts of β- and σ-specialisation/de-specialisation on the one hand and β- and σ-convergence/divergence on the other; the latter introduced to the growth literature by Barro and Sala-i-Martin (1991). We shall deal with the analysis of the results using the concepts in turn.

In terms of the *stability* of each of the national export specialisation patterns the long term perspective of 1965-92 shows that the hypothesis of a reverse or random patterns can be rejected. Since the $\hat{\beta}$-values are significantly smaller than one (and significantly greater than zero), the development can be characterised as β-de-specialisation, i.e., *on average* sectors with initial low *RSCAs* increase over time while sectors with initial high *RSCAs* decrease their values, for each country. From this observation, it can also be concluded that national export specialisation patterns are quite stubborn or sticky. Put differently, proposition (a) stating that patterns of specialisation will display persistence over long time periods, is confirmed. These findings are in line with evolutionary theorising, as well as the neoclassical model by Krugman (1987). However, it should be mentioned that Krugman's model cannot (endogenously) account for the observed incremental changes of the specialisation patterns.

In terms of the process of *specialisation versus de-specialisation* (measured by σ-specialisation) the results display a process of de-specialisation. The unweighted mean for $\hat{\beta}/\hat{R}$ 1965-92 is 0.91. β-de-specialisation has apparently been more outspoken than σ-de-specialisation. It should be noted that the results were not *in general* sensitive to the level of aggregation used. Furthermore, a few 'stylised' features in the specialisation patterns between various groups of countries should be noted. The less developed 'catching up' OECD countries generally show high regression effects (low $\hat{\beta}$) and high mobility effects (low $\hat{R}$) whereas most of the small high-income countries show low regression effects (high $\hat{\beta}$) and low mobility effects (high $\hat{R}$). Slow growing high-income countries usually show higher regression effects (lower $\hat{\beta}$-values) implying a stronger tendency towards decrease in initially advantaged industries and increase in disadvantaged industries. This finding is in line with proposition (b), stating that catching up countries will experience the fastest rate of change in the patterns of specialisation.

In the sector-wise (i.e. *convergence versus divergence*) results we find for all sectors β-convergence and in all cases $\hat{\beta}$ is significantly below unity (and above 0). Further, we find σ-convergence for all sectors except five; i.e. the dispersion of specialisation in almost all sectors has decreased. Concerning proposition (c), asserting that low tech products will be more footloose than high-tech products, we found that the picture is (a lot) more complicated than is indicated by the low-tech versus high-tech dichotomy. For what concerns low-tech, we found that for a group of natural resource based industries, shifts in specialisation across countries are very slow. On the other hand for the group of 'traditional industries' shifts in specialisation across countries can be characterised as being 'footloose'. In contrast, medium-tech, 'machinery oriented' industries overall display rather stable patterns of specialisation. The opposite goes for some high-tech industries, as some parts of electronics (computers; consumer electronics; telecommunications equipment; and domestic electrical machinery) were found to be rather 'footloose'. Nevertheless, other high-tech sectors which include semiconductors; electromedical equipment; measuring and control instruments; as well as pharmaceuticals, display neither a high degree of turbulence nor a remarkable degree of stability in the change of specialisation patterns across countries.

An observation emerging from this chapter is that, while European integration has been on-going throughout the period (for documentation of growing intra EU trade, see Ben-David, 1991), there has been a tendency for European countries to de-specialise and across the OECD countries (among which the EU countries dominate in numbers) a tendency to converge in the same sectors. Standard trade theory (Heckscher-Ohlin) would predict increasing specialisation - all other things being equal - if trade barriers are being reduced, given different factor endowments in various countries. Seen in that light our findings may appear as surprising and contradict proposition (d), stating that when economic integration is a central feature of development, specialisation patterns of countries will diverge (or put differently the level of specialisation will increase). However, it appears to be a fact that intra-industry trade grows in a period of economic integration (Stone and Lee, 1995; OECD, 1997). This observation appears to be true even at a quite detailed level of aggregation (182 industries).

Hence, the findings are more in line with theoretical models allowing for increasing returns and differentiated products, such as the model made by Grossman and Helpman (1989). It can be noted that the model of Grossman and Helpman concerns horizontally differentiated products, which might be more important for trade between developed countries, while vertically differentiated (possibly imitated) products - as analysed by Flam and Helpman (1987) - might be more important for what concerns catching up countries. The main point is that such models allow countries to specialise increasingly according to consumer preferences (within the same industries), rather than specialising increasingly in different industries. It should however be pointed out, from a theoretical point of view, that the structural *change* associated with catching up processes is not well understood, as the only explanation appears to be a (exogenous) change in the stock of human capital.

This chapter has shown that it is a stylised fact that international trade specialisation in the OECD countries has decreased slightly in the near 30 year period 1965-92 as opposed to the general findings concerning technological specialisation. The next chapter is concerned with exploring this apparent contradiction, by means of making a comparison of the development of trade and technological specialisation, using the same methodology and the same level of aggregation.

NOTES

1. This chapter draws on Dalum, Laursen and Villumsen (1998).
2. We are grateful to Bart Verspagen who pointed this out.
3. The low β and the low mobility for oil & gas may be a reflection of the geographical division between oil drilling and oil refinery which may cross national borders.

APPENDIX A4.1: THE IKE TRADE DATABASE

The trade data are based on the taped version of OECD's *Trade by Commodities, Series C*, which has been published annually since 1961. The data consist of trade by 'visible' goods in current US $. Trade in services ('invisibles') are not included. The OECD tapes consist of exports from and imports to 23 OECD countries. The data are delivered at their most detailed level according to the Standard International Trade Classification (SITC).

The IKE trade database at the Department of Business Studies, Aalborg University was initiated in the early 1980s for studies of long term structural features of OECD trade. Construction of comparable time series data has been the major analytical aim from the beginning. The database contains a selection of years between 1961 and 1992. As far as possible, the selection criterion has been 'peak years' in world trade/'average' OECD business cycles. The following years have been used in the present chapter (1961), 1965, 1969, 1973, 1979, 1984, 1988 and 1992. Given the long term focus mentioned, all data have been converted from the two more recent versions of the SITC to SITC, Revision 1. In 1961-77 the OECD reported the data in Revision 1. But in 1978-87 the data have been published according to SITC, Revision 2. The latter has been converted to the previous classification in order to construct comparable time series. From 1988 the data are published according to SITC, Revision 3.

The first step in handling the data consists of aggregating the 'raw' tapes to country matrices with 625 rows (the number of commodity groups at the 4-digit SITC, Revision 1 level) and 33 columns (23 OECD countries, the World, OECD, the Nordic countries and 7 groups of non-OECD countries, including e.g. the former Soviet Union, the OPEC countries, and a group of Newly Industrialised Countries). Then follows several steps of checking for confidentiality clauses in the tapes, whether at the commodity or the country level. The tapes, thus, contain a large amount of so-called alphanumeric codes (instead of the usual numeric SITC codes) for which the trade information is omitted *at the given level of disaggregation*. This information is, however, included in the SITC codes at a more aggregate level.

The data have then been aggregated to 60 commodity groups and then further to 5 main sectors as shown in Table A4.1. The data for Japan and Finland for 1961 are not available in the OECD tapes and have been reconstructed from national statistical sources - with some approximation for Finland, but rather precise for Japan.

Table A4.1 *Country-wise stability and development of OECD export specialisation patterns (six sub-periods)*

	1965-69			1969-73			1973-79			1979-84			1984-88			1988-92		
	β	R	β/R	β	R	β/R	β	R	β/R	β	R	β/R	β	R	β/R	β	R	β/R
United States	0.09	0.91	0.98	**1.12**	0.95	1.17	0.91	0.93	0.98	0.97	0.97	1.00	0.92	0.95	0.97	**0.82**	0.96	0.86
Japan	**0.87**	0.93	0.94	1.02	0.93	1.09	0.97	0.95	1.03	1.02	0.97	1.05	0.96	0.98	0.98	0.98	0.98	1.00
Germany	**0.89**	0.94	0.94	0.94	0.97	0.97	**0.85**	0.94	0.90	**0.91**	0.94	0.97	**0.86**	0.97	0.98	**0.90**	0.96	0.94
France	0.90	0.91	0.99	**0.83**	0.90	0.92	0.89	0.88	1.01	0.99	0.91	1.09	**0.86**	0.91	0.95	0.92	0.95	0.97
Italy	0.91	0.92	1.00	0.98	0.96	1.02	0.92	0.92	1.00	0.95	0.93	1.03	**0.87**	0.95	0.92	0.98	0.91	1.08
United Kingdom	0.98	0.97	1.01	**0.86**	0.95	0.91	**0.84**	0.93	0.91	0.94	0.93	1.01	**0.89**	0.90	0.99	**0.81**	0.85	0.95
Belgium-Lux	0.92	0.94	0.98	**0.88**	0.93	0.95	**0.87**	0.92	0.94	1.01	0.92	1.10	0.94	0.96	0.98	0.98	0.99	0.99
Canada	**0.91**	0.95	0.96	0.95	0.97	0.98	0.90	0.92	0.98	**0.89**	0.95	0.94	0.98	0.93	1.05	0.95	0.97	0.98
Denmark	0.95	0.93	1.02	0.99	0.97	1.01	**0.91**	0.97	0.95	0.95	0.96	0.99	0.94	0.98	0.96	0.96	0.97	0.99
Finland	**0.85**	0.85	1.00	0.91	0.92	0.99	0.97	0.95	1.01	0.93	0.96	0.97	0.94	0.91	1.03	**0.82**	0.88	0.93
Netherlands	**0.91**	0.94	0.97	0.92	0.95	0.97	0.96	0.93	1.03	0.94	0.91	1.03	**0.89**	0.96	0.92	0.98	0.98	1.00
Norway	0.93	0.94	0.99	0.95	0.97	0.98	0.90	0.92	0.98	**0.94**	0.98	0.96	0.98	0.98	1.00	0.98	0.98	1.00
Austria	0.97	0.97	1.01	0.94	0.95	0.99	**0.79**	0.83	0.96	0.96	0.95	1.01	**0.84**	0.87	0.97	0.96	0.95	1.01
Switzerland	0.97	0.97	0.99	1.02	0.97	1.05	0.94	0.96	0.98	0.99	0.98	1.00	**0.96**	0.99	0.97	**0.96**	0.99	0.97
Sweden	0.92	0.92	0.99	0.96	0.97	0.99	0.91	0.94	0.98	**0.90**	0.96	0.93	0.97	0.95	1.02	1.00	0.97	1.02
Greece	0.94	0.88	1.07	0.91	0.90	1.02	**0.84**	0.87	0.97	1.00	0.97	1.03	**0.90**	0.93	0.97	0.92	0.94	0.99
Ireland	**0.91**	0.87	1.04	**0.62**	0.72	0.85	0.94	0.90	1.04	**0.86**	0.88	0.98	**0.91**	0.93	0.98	0.96	0.91	1.06
Portugal	0.93	0.93	0.99	0.92	0.91	1.01	**0.86**	0.89	0.96	**0.81**	0.85	0.95	**0.81**	0.86	0.94	0.93	0.93	1.00
Spain	0.84	0.85	0.98	**0.77**	0.87	0.89	**0.76**	0.85	0.89	**0.79**	0.78	1.01	**0.70**	0.84	0.83	**0.78**	0.89	0.88
Turkey	0.96	0.94	1.02	0.87	0.90	0.97	0.89	0.88	1.01	0.73	0.82	0.90	**0.84**	0.85	0.99	**0.80**	0.85	0.94
Mean (unweighted)	0.92	0.92	0.99	0.92	0.93	0.99	0.89	0.91	0.98	0.92	0.93	1.00	0.90	0.93	0.97	0.92	0.94	0.98

Notes:
Bold types indicate β-*values* significantly different from unity at the 5% level. All β-*values* differ from zero at the 1% level.

69

Table A4.2 Sector-wise stability and development of OECD export specialisation patterns for six sub-periods

	1965-69		1969-73		1973-79		1979-84		1984-88		1988-92	
	β	β/R	β	β/R	β	β/R	β	β/R	β	β/R	β	β/R
Meat & meat preparations	0.97	1.01	0.97	0.99	1.00	1.01	0.98	1.01	0.96	0.99	0.93	0.96
Dairy products	0.96	0.99	1.00	1.05	0.97	0.98	0.86	0.94	0.84	0.93	1.03	1.04
Fish & fish preparations	0.96	0.97	0.94	0.95	0.94	0.96	0.93	0.93	0.96	0.99	1.00	1.01
Cereals & cereal preparations	0.87	1.00	0.79	0.97	0.87	1.08	0.94	0.99	0.89	1.03	0.94	0.97
Feeding-stuff for animals	0.93	0.97	0.93	0.98	0.69	0.93	0.70	0.94	0.69	0.85	1.02	1.09
Other food products	0.91	0.92	0.94	0.95	1.00	1.03	0.94	0.95	1.01	1.01	0.95	0.95
Beverages & tobacco	0.97	0.98	0.92	0.94	0.91	0.93	0.92	0.94	1.03	1.03	0.92	0.94
Animal & vegetable oil & fats	1.02	1.07	0.92	0.97	0.92	0.94	0.94	1.06	0.88	0.96	1.03	1.10
Cut flowers, bulbs, & oth. plants	0.99	1.00	0.85	0.89	0.96	1.01	0.93	0.99	0.98	1.01	0.94	0.96
Seeds & spores for planting	0.96	0.98	0.88	0.97	0.96	1.02	0.95	0.98	0.96	0.99	0.91	0.95
Skins & leather manufactures	0.96	0.98	0.86	0.91	0.95	1.05	0.97	1.03	0.93	0.99	0.96	1.02
Wood & wood manufactures	0.97	0.98	0.93	0.97	1.00	1.04	0.90	0.94	0.97	0.99	0.97	0.98
Pulp & paper	0.93	0.94	0.96	0.97	0.90	0.92	0.95	0.98	0.98	0.99	0.94	0.95
Textile fibers	0.98	1.00	0.97	1.00	0.83	0.88	0.95	1.01	0.88	0.90	0.87	0.98
Textile yarn, fabrics, etc.	0.85	0.89	0.89	0.99	1.02	1.07	1.06	1.08	0.92	0.93	0.91	0.92
Iron ore	1.02	1.03	0.89	0.92	0.98	1.00	0.94	0.94	1.01	1.09	0.87	0.93
Iron, steel & ferro-alloys	0.83	0.95	0.89	0.95	0.84	0.89	0.82	0.98	0.96	1.03	0.91	0.93
Aluminium	0.73	0.99	0.80	0.89	0.80	0.84	1.02	1.10	0.90	0.95	0.96	0.99
Non-ferrous ores & metals	0.84	1.00	0.96	1.02	0.73	0.77	0.97	1.04	0.87	0.98	0.87	0.97
Crude ferti., crude minerals & coal	0.94	0.98	0.88	0.93	1.00	1.08	0.90	0.94	0.93	0.99	0.85	0.88
Non-metallic minerals	0.94	0.97	0.75	0.84	0.84	1.06	0.99	1.02	0.90	0.92	0.97	1.00
Rest: rubber; electr. energy	0.79	0.91	0.93	1.06	0.87	0.94	0.73	0.87	0.83	0.89	0.96	1.07
Oil & gas	0.84	0.92	0.92	1.23	0.78	1.11	0.71	0.84	1.02	1.04	0.93	1.00
Organic chemicals	0.94	1.01	0.87	0.98	0.86	0.94	0.85	0.92	0.76	0.84	1.05	1.12
Inorganic chemicals	0.48	0.79	0.79	0.86	0.70	0.97	0.72	0.99	0.97	1.13	0.79	0.87
Dyestuffs, colouring materials	0.84	0.94	1.01	1.03	0.90	0.94	0.94	0.97	0.85	0.93	0.89	0.93
Pharmaceuticals	0.98	1.01	0.89	0.93	0.87	0.92	1.00	1.02	0.93	0.96	1.03	1.11
Fertilizers, manufactured	0.80	0.86	0.90	1.00	0.65	0.99	0.58	0.79	0.93	1.10	0.83	0.94
Plastic materials	0.90	0.95	0.89	0.94	0.90	0.96	0.81	0.89	0.67	0.77	0.87	0.97
Other chemicals	0.86	0.92	0.91	0.94	0.84	0.96	0.96	1.02	0.84	0.97	0.89	0.93

Agricul. & food proces. mach.	0.97	1.00	0.92	0.95	0.90	0.93	0.83	0.94	1.03	1.08	0.91	0.93
Textile & sewing machines	0.98	1.03	0.91	0.94	0.97	0.98	0.97	1.00	0.88	1.00	0.91	0.99
Paper & pulp machinery	0.95	0.98	0.81	0.93	0.95	1.02	0.98	1.02	0.95	0.99	0.98	0.99
Mach. for other spec. indu./proces.	0.98	1.00	0.92	0.93	1.00	1.04	1.00	1.02	0.98	0.99	0.99	1.01
Heating & cooling equipment	0.96	0.99	0.87	0.92	0.87	0.96	0.95	0.98	0.84	0.86	0.84	0.91
Metalworking machinery	1.00	1.01	0.96	0.97	0.96	0.99	0.94	0.96	0.94	0.96	0.97	0.99
Power generating machinery	1.03	1.07	0.96	0.98	0.93	0.95	0.70	0.87	0.90	0.98	0.97	1.01
Pumps & centrifuges	0.91	0.94	0.93	0.97	0.89	0.93	0.93	0.94	0.88	0.94	0.97	0.99
Typewriters & office mach.	0.91	0.96	0.79	0.92	0.82	1.11	0.70	1.00	0.78	0.95	0.92	1.12
Computers & peripherals	0.95	1.00	0.77	0.92	0.85	0.98	0.92	0.99	0.95	1.01	0.91	0.96
Semiconductors	0.71	1.00	0.84	0.94	0.93	1.02	0.95	0.99	0.87	0.92	0.91	0.97
Telecommunications equipment	0.75	0.81	0.83	0.91	0.93	1.02	0.87	1.01	0.99	1.07	0.90	0.94
Mach. for prod. & dist. of electricity	0.90	0.94	0.88	0.92	0.79	0.92	0.71	0.85	0.83	0.89	0.91	0.99
Consumer electronics	0.76	0.90	0.95	1.05	0.81	0.94	0.96	1.00	0.80	0.96	1.04	1.14
Domestic electrical equipment	0.90	1.01	0.88	0.95	0.87	0.93	0.90	0.97	0.82	0.86	0.92	1.01
Electromedical equipment	0.94	0.98	0.92	0.95	0.93	0.98	0.97	1.06	0.90	0.95	0.94	0.95
Non-elec. medical equipment	0.96	0.98	0.79	1.09	0.86	0.93	0.95	1.00	0.92	0.95	0.94	0.95
Measuring & control. instrum.	0.95	0.97	0.98	0.99	0.92	0.96	0.94	1.00	0.95	0.98	0.82	0.85
Photogr. & optical goods, watches	0.97	0.98	0.83	0.93	0.93	0.95	0.99	1.00	0.94	0.96	0.96	0.98
Railway vehicles	0.90	1.03	0.78	0.97	0.78	0.98	0.62	0.79	0.42	1.21	0.51	0.94
Road motor vehicles	0.98	1.04	0.96	0.99	0.90	0.93	1.00	1.01	0.97	0.99	0.98	0.99
Aircraft	0.91	0.96	0.95	0.98	0.95	1.02	0.92	1.02	0.87	0.96	0.99	1.01
Ships and boats (& oilrigs)	1.00	1.03	0.85	0.90	0.92	1.03	0.94	1.00	0.85	0.97	0.67	0.92
Other non-electrical equipm.	0.88	0.90	0.97	0.99	0.88	0.92	0.97	0.99	0.91	0.93	1.04	1.06
Other electrical equipment	0.88	0.90	0.98	1.03	0.99	1.01	0.91	0.94	0.89	0.92	0.98	1.01
Manufactures of metal	0.86	0.92	0.84	0.86	0.94	1.01	0.80	0.87	0.83	0.93	0.99	1.02
Furniture	0.92	0.96	1.08	1.12	0.84	0.89	0.84	0.94	0.91	0.99	0.90	0.93
Clothing	0.74	0.88	0.67	1.00	1.07	1.14	1.10	1.13	1.01	1.03	0.98	1.01
Orthopaed. eq. & hearing aids	0.90	0.94	0.81	0.94	1.04	1.18	0.86	0.93	0.90	0.92	0.91	0.99
Industrial products, n.e.s.	0.92	0.95	0.92	0.96	0.93	0.99	0.93	0.96	0.79	0.88	1.02	1.06
Mean (unweighted)	*0.91*	*0.97*	*0.89*	*0.96*	*0.90*	*0.98*	*0.90*	*0.97*	*0.90*	*0.97*	*0.93*	*0.98*

Note:
All *β-values* significantly differ from zero at the 1% level.

Table A4.3 Sectoral classification

Products based on natural resources	
1 Meat & meat preparations	00, 01, 091.3, 411.3
2 Dairy products	2
3 Fish & fish preparations	03, 411.1
4 Cereals & cereal preparations	4
5 Feeding-stuff for animals	8
6 Other food products	05, 06, 07, 091.4, 099
7 Beverages & tobacco	11, 12
8 Animal & vegetable oil & fats	22, 42, 43
9 Cut flowers, bulbs & oth. plants	292.1-4, 292.6-9
10 Seeds & spores for planting	292.5
11 Skins & leather manufactures	21, 61, 291
12 Wood & wood manufactures	24, 63
13 Pulp & paper	25, 64
14 Textile fibers	26
15 Textile yarn, fabrics, etc.	65
16 Iron ore	281
17 Iron, steel & ferro-alloys	67
18 Aluminium	684
19 Non-ferrous ores & metals	282-86, 681-83, 685-89
20 Crude fertilizers, crude minerals & coal	27, 32
21 Non-metallic minerals (cement, ceramics, glass, etc.)	66
22 Rest: rubber; electr. energy	23, 62, 35
Oil and gas	
23 Oil & gas	33, 34
Chemicals	
24 Organic chemicals	512
25 Inorganic chemicals	513, 514
26 Dyestuffs, colouring materials	53
27 Pharmaceuticals	54
28 Fertilizers, manufactured	56
29 Plastic materials	581.1, 581.2
30 Other chemicals	515, 52, 55, 57, 581.3, 581.9, 59

Engineering, electronics and transport equipm.	
31 Agricul. & food proces. mach.	712, 718.3
32 Textile & sewing machines	717.1, 717.3
33 Paper & pulp machinery	718.1
34 Machinery for other special industries or processes	717.2, 718.2, 718.4-5,
35 Heating & cooling equipment	719.1
36 Metalworking machinery	715
37 Power generating machinery	711
38 Pumps & centrifuges	719.2
39 Typewriters & office mach.	714.1, 714.9
40 Computers & peripherals	714.2, 714.3
41 Semiconductors	729.3
42 Telecommunications equipment	724.9
43 Machinery for production & distribution of electricity	722, 723
44 Consumer electronics	724.1, 724.2, 891.1
45 Domestic electrical equipment	725
46 Electromedical equipment	726
47 Non-elec. medical equipment	861.7
48 Measuring & control. instrum.	729.5
49 Photographic & optical goods, watches	861.1-6, 861.8-9,
50 Railway vehicles	731
51 Road motor vehicles	732
52 Aircraft	734
53 Ships and boats (& oilrigs)	735
54 Other non-electrical equipm.	719.6-7, 719.9, 733
55 Other electrical equipment	729.1-2, 729.4, 729.6-7, 729.9
Other industrial products ('traditional industries')	
56 Manufactures of metal	69, 719.4, 812.1, 812.3
57 Furniture	82
58 Clothing	84
59 Orthopaed. eq. & hearing aids	899.6
60 Industrial products, n.e.s.	812.2, 812.4, 83, 85, 863, 891.2-9, 892-97, 899.1-5, 899.9, 9

5. Do Export and Technological Specialisation Patterns Co-evolve in Terms of Convergence or Divergence?

In the previous chapter it was shown that there has been a general tendency for 20 OECD countries to de-specialise in the period from 1965 to 1992 for what concerns export specialisation. This finding is in contrast to findings made by other authors working on technological specialisation (Cantwell, 1989; Cantwell, 1991; Archibugi and Pianta, 1992; Archibugi and Pianta, 1994), who found increasing technological specialisation from the late 1970s to the early 1980s measured as specialisation in US patents. The first aim of this chapter is to investigate whether these seemingly contradictory findings are due to a 'real world' phenomenon, or whether the explanation is purely technical, by comparing the development of export specialisation to specialisation in terms of US patents, using the same methodology. By a 'real world phenomenon' we mean that there is some economic explanation underlying the observed differences, while a 'technical explanation' refers to differences in ways of measuring specialisation, found in the literature. The second aim is to analyse the extent to which countries and sectors display stable specialisation patterns over time, also both in terms of export and technology.

One of the contributions made in Chapter 4, was the distinction made between specialisation (or de-specialisation) in trade patterns on the one hand, and divergence (or convergence) on the other. A specialisation process refers to a process in which specialisation *intra-country* becomes more dispersed (and conversely for de-specialisation). In contrast, a divergence process refers to a process in which countries become more different in terms of specialisation in a particular sector, *across countries* (and conversely for convergence). However the estimations made in Chapter 4 were made making separate estimations for countries and sectors, respectively. In this chapter, the stability characteristics of both trade and technological specialisation patterns will (respectively) be estimated for both countries and sectors, in one single model.

The following theoretical propositions from Chapter 2 are relevant in the case of the present chapter: (a) patterns of specialisation will display persistence over long time periods; (b) catching up countries will experience the fastest rate of change in the patterns of specialisation; (c) low tech products will be more footloose than high-tech products; and finally (d) when economic integration is a central feature of development, specialisation patterns of countries will diverge (or put differently the level of specialisation will increase).

Furthermore, (e) technological specialisation is less 'sticky' than is trade specialisation; (f) although several mechanisms, leading trade and technological specialisation to diverge from each other, can be identified, trade and technological specialisation will tend to co-evolve.

This chapter is structured as follows. Section 5.1 contains the empirical analysis. Sub-section 5.1.1 contains a description of the data to be applied, while Sub-section 5.1.2 deals with the question of whether countries tend to become more or less specialised over time in terms of export- and technological specialisation. Sub-section 5.1.3 deals with the stability issue in an empirical model, looking both across sectors and across countries in a single model. The conclusion of the chapter can be found in Section 5.2.

5.1. EMPIRICAL ANALYSIS

5.1.1. The Data

The export data are taken from the OECD STAN database (1995 edition), in which data are available from 1970 and onwards. The patent data are taken from the US patent office, and concern patent grants, dated by the year of grant. The attribution of patents to countries and industrial sectors is done by the patent office. In this context it should be pointed out that such an attribution of technical patents to economic sectors necessarily involves some degree of approximation. However, the measure does correlate with other measures of technology at the sectoral level, such as R&D statistics (a technology input measure). Furthermore, we argue that patent data are the best available measure of technology output, partly because the data are available on a yearly basis, over a long time span. Whenever a patent is attributed to more than one, say m sectors, the patent is counted as $1/m$ in each of these. Hence we follow Verspagen (1997) and argue that the secondary assignments of patents contain useful knowledge, relevant for economic activity (in many studies of technological development, only the first reference on the patent is used, e.g. in Patel and Pavitt, 1994b; Patel and Pavitt, 1997). In Chapter 2 it was pointed out that the product-technology relationship is not always one-to-one. When a patent contains more than one reference to a product class, this can be said to reflect the fact that technologies can be applied in several products, and by assigning patents to all relevant product classes we further alleviate the potential 'multi-technology' problem. It was decided to work with US patents because, rather than patent statistics from each of the national patent offices, US patents are subject to a common institutional system (novelty requirements etc.), and moreover, the US, for most of the period under consideration, constituted the largest 'technology market' in the world.

The variable chosen for measuring specialisation is as in Chapter 4, the Revealed Comparative Advantage (Balassa, 1965):

$$RCA_{ij} = \frac{X_{ij}/\sum_i X_{ij}}{\sum_j X_{ij}/\sum_i \sum_j X_{ij}}. \tag{5.1}$$

The numerator represents the percentage share of a given sector in national exports - X_{ij} are exports of sector i from country j. The denominator represents the percentage share of a given sector in OECD exports. For further detail on the measure, the reader is referred to Chapter 3. The index is made symmetric, in the same manner as in the two preceding chapters. The measure is labelled 'Revealed Symmetric Comparative Advantage' (*RSCA*). The calculation of technological specialisation (US patents) is analogous, and hence termed 'Revealed Symmetric Technological Advantage' (*RSTA*).

In order to avoid the problem of small numbers, the patent data were aggregated over three years, so that the midyear for the patents corresponds to the year chosen for exports. In this way the patents in the first set of observations is the sum of the patents 1971-73, while the corresponding export figures are taken from 1972. The second set of observations in terms of patents is the sum of US patents 1974-76, corresponding to export figures from 1975, and so on.

5.1.2. Are Countries Becoming More or Less Specialised in Trade and Technology?

In order to test for whether countries are stable across sectors and whether they tend to become more or less specialised intra-country, we are going to employ the same method applied in the previous chapter. In this way, stability (and specialisation trends) is tested by means of the following regression equation (country by country):

$$RSCA_{ij}^{t_2} = \alpha_j + \beta_j RSCA_{ij}^{t_1} + \epsilon_{ij}. \tag{5.2}$$

The superscripts t_1 and t_2 refer to the initial year and the final year, respectively. The dependent variable, *RSCA* at time t_2 for sector i, is tested against the independent variable which is the value of the *RSCA* in the previous year t_1. α and β are standard linear regression parameters and ϵ is a residual term.

Recall from the previous chapter, that the idea behind the regression is that $\beta=1$ corresponds to an unchanged pattern from t_1 to t_2. If $\beta>1$ the country tends to become more specialised in sectors where it is already specialised, and less specialised where initial specialisation is low - i.e. the existing pattern of specialisation is strengthened. If one makes an analogy to the convergence literature, $\beta>1$ might be termed *β-specialisation*. Similarly, $0<\beta<1$ can be termed *β-de-specialisation*, i.e., *on average* sectors with initial low *RSCAs* increase over time while sectors with initial high *RSCAs* decrease their values. The magnitude of $(1-\beta)$ therefore measures the size of what has been termed as the 'regression effect', and this is the interpretation placed on the estimated coefficient of β in the present chapter. In the special case where $\beta<0$ the ranking of sectors has been reversed. Those *RSCAs* initially below the country average are in the final year above average and vice versa. Given the above listed line of reasoning, the test of cumulativeness (or 'stickiness') is whether $\hat{\beta}$ is significantly greater than zero. If $\hat{\beta} \leq 0$, it cannot be rejected that the development of the trade specialisation pattern of a country is either reversed or random, contrary to the hypothesis of cumulativeness.

Another feature emerging from the regression analysis is a test of whether the degree of specialisation changes. Following Cantwell (1989, pp. 31-2) it can be deduced that $\beta>1$ is not a necessary condition for an increase in the overall national specialisation pattern. It this context it can be shown that:

$$\sigma_j^{2\,t_2}/\sigma_j^{2\,t_1} = \beta_j^2/R_j^2. \tag{5.3}$$

Thus,

$$\sigma_j^{t_2}/\sigma_j^{t_1} = |\beta_j/R_j|. \tag{5.4}$$

It follows that the dispersion of a given distribution is unchanged when $\beta=R$. If $\beta>R$ (equivalent to an increase in the dispersion) the degree of specialisation has increased. Thus making the same kind of analogies as above, one might term this as *σ-specialisation*. If $\beta<R$ (equivalent to a decrease in the dispersion) the degree of specialisation has decreased. Likewise, such a situation can be described as *σ-de-specialisation*.

The estimated Pearson correlation coefficient is a measure of the mobility of sectors up and down the *RSCA* distribution. A high level of the coefficient indicates that the relative position of sectors is little changed, while a low value indicates that some sectors are moving closer together and others further apart,

Table 5.1 The standard deviation for export and trade specialisation patterns 1971-73 for 19 OECD countries in descending order (n=19 sectors)

Country	Exports	Patents
Greece	0.52	0.65
Norway	0.49	0.44
Australia	0.45	0.30
Finland	0.45	0.42
Japan	0.44	0.20
New Zealand	0.42	0.55
Denmark	0.40	0.46
Portugal	0.40	0.69
Spain	0.39	0.44
Austria	0.38	0.30
Canada	0.37	0.19
Belgium	0.33	0.36
The Netherlands	0.32	0.29
Sweden	0.32	0.31
United States	0.26	0.04
Italy	0.26	0.19
Germany (West)	0.25	0.21
France	0.16	0.22
United Kingdom	0.15	0.13

Note: For a description of the 19 sectors, see Table 5.4.

quite possibly to the extent that the ranking of sectors changes. The value of $(1-R)$ measures what has been described as the 'mobility effect'. It may well be that, even where the 'regression effect' $(1-\beta)$ suggests a fall in the degree of specialisation due to a proportional change in sectors towards the average $(\beta<1)$, this is outweighed by the mobility effect, due to changes in the proportional position between sectors $(\beta>R)$. Thus, we can characterise an increase in the dispersion as a change towards a more 'narrow' specialisation pattern; and a decrease in the dispersion as a change towards a more 'broad' pattern.

In order to compare our results to e.g. the results of Archibugi and Pianta (1992; 1994), and their studies of technological specialisation, we have included results, based on the χ^2 measure of specialisation (in Tables 5.2 and 5.3). Recall from Chapter 3 that the χ^2 measures the sum of the squared difference between

Table 5.2 The development of trade specialisation patterns 1971-91 for 19 OECD countries (n=19 sectors)

	1989-91 on 1971-73			1980-82 on 1971-73			1989-91 on 1980-82		
	$\hat{\beta}$	$\hat{\beta}/R$	χ^2_{c2}/χ^2_{t1}	$\hat{\beta}$	$\hat{\beta}/R$	χ^2_{c2}/χ^2_{t1}	$\hat{\beta}$	$\hat{\beta}/R$	χ^2_{c2}/χ^2_{t1}
Australia	0.83 *#	0.97	0.77	0.87 *	0.98	0.94	0.96 *	0.98	0.81
Austria	0.87 *	0.95	0.63	0.96 *	1.05	1.01	0.87 *#	0.91	0.62
Belgium	0.99 *	1.06	1.20	1.03 *	1.10	1.12	0.93 *	0.97	1.08
Canada	0.80 *#	0.98	0.67	0.78 *#	0.89	0.68	1.01 *	1.10	0.98
Denmark	0.89 *	0.94	0.89	0.96 *	0.98	1.08	0.93 *	0.96	0.83
Finland	0.74 *#	0.91	0.63	0.93 *	0.99	0.69	0.72 *	0.92	0.91
France	0.63 *#	0.94	0.95	0.76 *#	0.88	0.76	0.83 *	1.06	1.24
Germany (West)	0.43 *#	0.67	0.60	0.45 *#	0.65	0.51	0.93 *	1.04	1.18
Greece	0.94 *	1.04	1.59	0.95 *	1.04	1.05	0.97 *	1.00	1.51
Italy	0.72 *#	0.93	1.46	0.88 *	0.99	1.16	0.86 *	0.94	1.26
Japan	0.94 *	1.01	0.93	1.06 *#	1.09	1.15	0.89 *#	0.93	0.81
The Netherlands	0.68 *#	0.81	0.88	0.91 *	0.95	1.52	0.79 *#	0.85	0.58
New Zealand	1.08 *	1.20	0.65	1.03 *	1.12	0.69	0.99 *	1.07	0.94
Norway	0.83 *#	0.94	1.18	0.89 *#	0.95	0.72	0.94 *	0.99	1.64
Portugal	0.60 *#	0.87	1.65	0.87 *	0.95	1.28	0.71 *#	0.92	1.29
Spain	0.51 *#	0.76	0.48	0.63 *#	0.81	0.52	0.78 *#	0.94	0.91
Sweden	0.65 *#	0.85	0.76	0.98 *	1.05	0.92	0.71 *#	0.81	0.83
United Kingdom	1.02 *	1.35	1.03	1.16 *#	1.27	0.88	0.93 *	1.07	1.18
United States	0.81 *#	0.87	0.70	1.03 *	1.05	0.84	0.75 *#	0.83	0.83
Mean (unweighted)	0.79	0.95	0.93	0.90	0.99	0.92	0.87	0.96	1.02

Notes:
* denotes significantly different from zero at the 10% level. # denotes significantly different from unity at the 10% level (t-statistics calculated on the basis of White's heteroscedasticity consistent standard errors). For a description of the 19 sectors, see Table 5.4.

Table 5.3 The development of technological specialisation patterns 1971-91 for 19 OECD countries (n=19 sectors)

	1989-91 on 1971-73			1980-82 on 1971-73			1989-91 on 1980-82		
	$\hat{\beta}$	$\hat{\beta}/R$	χ^2_{12}/χ^2_{11}	$\hat{\beta}$	$\hat{\beta}/R$	χ^2_{12}/χ^2_{11}	$\hat{\beta}$	$\hat{\beta}/R$	χ^2_{12}/χ^2_{11}
Australia	0.39 *	0.78	1.11	0.76 *	0.93	1.22	0.60 *#	0.85	0.91
Austria	0.75 *	1.10	1.01	0.65 *	1.14	1.04	0.76 *	0.97	0.98
Belgium	0.60 *#	0.98	1.08	0.55 *	1.04	0.77	0.77 *	0.94	1.40
Canada	0.77 *	0.99	0.93	0.96 *	1.05	1.07	0.76 *	0.93	0.87
Denmark	0.62 *#	0.88	1.98	0.42 *#	0.81	0.89	0.87 *	1.09	2.22
Finland	0.25 #	0.89	0.70	0.55 *#	0.88	0.69	0.05 #	1.00	1.02
France	0.10 #	0.49	0.96	0.21 *#	0.47	0.66	0.66 *#	1.03	1.45
Germany (West)	0.77 *	0.95	1.67	0.74 *#	0.78	0.91	1.09 *	1.23	1.83
Greece	0.18 #	0.89	0.46	0.10 #	1.11	1.94	0.11 #	0.80	0.24
Italy	0.44 #	1.14	1.40	0.88 *	1.07	0.92	0.69 *	1.07	1.53
Japan	0.89 *	1.11	1.35	0.93 *	1.06	0.91	0.99 *	1.04	1.49
The Netherlands	0.73 *	1.00	1.17	0.85 *	0.97	0.99	0.71 *	1.03	1.18
New Zealand	0.19 #	0.89	1.31	0.41 *#	0.87	0.50	0.28 *	1.03	2.60
Norway	0.29 #	0.82	0.82	0.38 #	1.02	1.49	0.34 *	0.80	0.55
Portugal	0.12 #	0.93	0.92	0.42 #	1.02	1.43	0.15 #	0.91	0.64
Spain	0.18 #	0.79	0.92	0.07 #	1.16	1.29	0.53 *#	0.68	0.71
Sweden	0.45 *#	0.69	1.05	0.71 *	0.89	1.61	0.61 *#	0.78	0.65
United Kingdom	0.10 #	1.19	3.03	0.68 *#	1.08	1.85	0.60 *	1.10	1.64
United States	1.35 *	2.18	5.48	1.28 *#	1.39	2.08	1.08 *	1.57	2.63
Mean (unweighted)	*0.48*	*0.98*	*1.44*	*0.61*	*0.99*	*1.17*	*0.61*	*0.99*	*1.29*

Notes:
* denotes significantly different from zero at the 10% level. # denotes significantly different from unity at the 10% level (*t*-statistics calculated on the basis of White's heteroscedasticity consistent standard errors). For a description of the 19 sectors, see Table 5.4.

the export distribution of a given country and the total OECD divided by the OECD export distribution. The formula is:

$$\chi^2 = \sum_i [[(X_{ij}/\sum_i X_{ij}) - (\sum_j X_{ij}/\sum_i \sum_j X_{ij})]^2/(\sum_j X_{ij}/\sum_i \sum_j X_{ij})]. \tag{5.5}$$

If a country has an export structure exactly similar to all of the OECD, the value of the indicator will be zero. The size of χ^2 is an indication of how strongly each country is specialised. The more a country differs from the OECD average, the greater the value. Over time it indicates changes in the degree of specialisation for each country. Although different in construction, the aim of this measure is the same as $|\hat{\beta}/\hat{R}|$, i.e. to measure the changes in dispersion.

However, first we present the extent to which countries are specialised, as measured by the standard deviation of the specialisation pattern for each of the 19 OECD countries. The standard deviations are given in Table 5.1. From the table it can be seen that the level of specialisation is quite similar for export and patents for each country ($\rho=0.67$ and significant at the 1 per cent level). The table also confirms the findings of Balassa (1965) and Dosi, Pavitt and Soete (1990), for both exports and technology, showing that small countries are more specialised than large countries. Given the country size, countries less developed in 1972 (Greece, Spain, Portugal) were more specialised, compared to the other countries.

The results displayed in Table 5.2 confirm the findings of Chapter 4, showing that the OECD countries did in general tend to de-specialise in terms of export specialisation, over the period.[1] This conclusion stands, both when the χ^2 measure is used, and when the $|\hat{\beta}/\hat{R}|$ is applied. The evidence is less conclusive with regard to technological specialisation (Table 5.3), as the results are mixed in the sense that just about half of the countries tend to increase in terms of the level of specialisation (for the two sub-periods), while the other half tend to engage in de-specialisation. In each of the two sub-periods 11 out of 19 countries (1971-73 to 1980-82) and 10 out of 19 (1980-82 to 1989-91) countries, tend to increase the level of specialisation (measured as $|\hat{\beta}/\hat{R}|$). Over the full period only 6 out of 19 countries tend to increase in terms of specialisation. This finding is, however, not robust to the measure used, as 11 out of 19 countries tend to increase their level of specialisation over the full period, when using the χ^2 measure.

This finding appears to be in contrast to the results obtained by Cantwell (1991), and by Archibugi and Pianta (1992; 1994). Cantwell, using a classification encompassing 27 sectors, found that 11 out of 19 countries experienced an increase in technological specialisation, from 1963-69 to 1977-

83. Archibugi and Pianta (1992) found that 11 out of 16 countries (across 41 patent classes) tended to increase the level of specialisation over the period from 1975-81 to 1982-88.

There can be several explanations for the difference. Firstly, Cantwell did not adjust the *RTA* measure, in order to make it symmetric. As the use of the 'pure' *RTA* gives too much weight to values above one, not adjusting for symmetry can produce biased results. If, for instance, some *RTA* values above unity increase over time and some values below unity also increase, the conclusion by using the pure *RTA* might be that the level of specialisation has increased while in fact, it remained neutral.[2] Secondly, the chi square measure tends to produce more extreme values as the difference between the export structure of the country in question and the export structure of the OECD is squared. Hence, the measure is more erratic over time, as compared to the *RSTA*. Finally, the choice of time-periods might influence the results, as well as the level of aggregation applied. It should be pointed out, however, that our results appear not to be sensitive to the period applied in as far as the conclusion is that there seems to be no particular increase or decrease in terms of the level of technological specialisation, over the 1970s and the 1980s.[3]

As explained previously in this section, the size of $\hat{\beta}$ measures the degree of turbulence (or alternatively stability) of a specialisation pattern between two periods. However, as we are going to estimate a fuller model (in Sub-section 5.1.3, below), in a single estimation looking both at β-specialisation/de-specialisation (country-wise, across sectors), as well as β-divergence/convergence (sector-wise, across countries), we are only going to discuss the stability characteristics briefly, as measured by $\hat{\beta}$ in Tables 5.2 and 5.3. It should be pointed out, however, that while the model estimated in Sub-section 5.1.3 (Tables 5.4 and 5.5), below is based on data pooled over seven time periods, the results from Table 5.2 and 5.3 are based on comparing end-points. Hence, the results discussed in this section are of a more long term nature, as compared to the model estimated in the section below.

If Tables 5.2 and 5.3 are compared, it can be seen that trade specialisation patterns appear to be more stable than technological specialisation patterns. This is not surprising, as trade specialisation is to some extent bound to natural endowments; constraints which are not imposed on technological specialisation. In the shorter run (the two sub-periods 1971-73 to 1980-82 and 1980-82 to 1989-91) technological specialisation is cumulative (Table 5.3), as there is a significant and positive relationship between the specialisation pattern in the previous period, and the most recent period for 29 out of 38 pairs. Nevertheless, in the longer term (1971-73 to 1989-91) the relationship is only present in 9 out of 19 countries, showing that cumulativeness fades away over longer time periods. It can be also be seen that 5 (Finland, Greece, New Zealand, Portugal and Spain)[4] out of the 9 countries, for which no relationship could be detected in the longer run, are in fact OECD 'catching-up' countries. For 6 high-income countries (Austria, Canada, Germany, Japan, The Netherlands, and the United States) technological specialisation patterns are so stable, in the longer run, that the hypothesis of the specialisations patterns remaining unchanged, between the two periods, cannot be rejected.

For what concerns trade specialisation (Table 5.2), the picture is less clear-cut, as there appears to be no clear distinction between catch-up countries on the one hand (although Spain and Portugal do have the lowest $\hat{\beta}$'s), and high-income countries on the other. Especially striking is the low β for Germany. However, as argued in Chapter 4, the change in the German specialisation pattern has not been characterised by radical change. Rather, closer inspection of the specialisation pattern of Germany reveals that the country has been in a process of de-specialisation, meaning that Germany has become (slightly) weaker in nearly all areas where initially strong (but remains strong in these areas), while it has become stronger in areas of under-specialisation (but remains weak in these areas).

5.1.3. The Stability Characteristics of Specialisation Patterns Across Sectors and Countries

In order to investigate the degree to which both countries and sectors are stable in their specialisation patterns over time, in one single model, this chapter applies a regression model, used in a dynamic setting by Magnier and Toujas-Bernate (1994), but also applied by Amable and Verspagen (1995). The specification is as follows:

$$RSCA_{ij}^{t} = \alpha_{ij} + (\beta_\mu + \beta_i + \beta_j) RSCA_{ij}^{t-1} + \epsilon_{ij}, \ with \ \sum_i \beta_i = \sum_j \beta_j = 0. \qquad (5.6)$$

Each coefficient is the sum of an average coefficient (β_μ), a sector-specific coefficient (β_i), and a country-specific coefficient (β_j). One reason for applying this model is that it allows for direct comparison between the development of trade and trade specialisation patterns, as the size of the average coefficient, using export and patent data respectively, can be compared directly. However, if we wish to estimate a model with an average coefficient and variable slopes for each sector and country, such a model cannot be estimated, as it is not of full rank. However, the restrictions allow for estimating both sector- and country-specific coefficients in the same model. The basic procedure is to estimate the largest possible model of full rank, and then subsequently to estimate the remaining variables as a linear combination of the coefficients from the first step, while imposing the constraints (see Johnston, 1991, pp. 241-5). An alternative procedure (in order to make the model of full rank) would be to drop the average coefficient, and one other coefficient (e.g a sector slope) and make the interpretation in one dimension (e.g. in the sectoral dimension) relative to a benchmark (a sector). Nevertheless, in the model used in this chapter, the *levels* of the coefficients can be compared directly. The interpretation of the β's in Equation 5.5 is the same as in Equation 5.2. As mentioned in the previous section, the data has been pooled together over seven time periods[5] in this section, so that we get 2166 observations in total, for all sectors and countries.

The estimations, using Equation 5.5, can be found in Tables 5.4 and 5.5. It can be noted that the results have been found to be time invariant, for both trade and technology, using a Chow test for poolability over time. The *F*-statistics for the models in Table 5.4 and 5.5 are 0.012 and 0.091 for trade and technology, respectively. Hence, the hypothesis of no structural change cannot be rejected at any reasonable level (*p*-values of 1.000 in both cases). From Tables 5.4 and 5.5 it can be concluded that both trade specialisation and technological specialisation patterns are path-dependent in the sense that all country and sectoral patterns are correlated between seven three year intervals, within the period in question. In comparison however, trade specialisation patterns are more stable than are technological specialisation patterns, as the average coefficient for trade is 0.93, while the coefficient is 0.64 for technology. Of the sectors, most (textiles, footwear and leather; pharmaceuticals; petroleum refineries; rubber and plastics; ferrous metals; non-ferrous metals; non-electrical machinery; office machines and computers; electrical machinery; shipbuilding; other transport; motor vehicles; aerospace; and instruments) are turbulent to the extent that the hypothesis of an unchanged pattern of specialisation can be rejected at the 5 per cent level, for both trade and technological specialisation. Only for what concerns food, drink and tobacco; and industrial chemicals can the hypothesis of an unchanged pattern not be rejected for both types of specialisation. It can be seen from Tables 5.4 and 5.5 that textiles, footwear and leather is one of the sectors with the strongest difference between the development in trade and technological specialisation. The relatively low parameter for this sector in Table 5.5, indicates that technology is more fluid in this sector, while the production (exports) is found to be relatively more stable. In the case of office machines and computers the opposite pattern can be observed. In this case one interpretation could be that firms spread out their production (exports) facilities, while this is not the case to the same extent, when it comes to the production of technology. A similar (but stronger) conclusion can be made for what concerns fabricated metal products. The latter two cases are consistent with the models allowing for spatial separation of

Table 5.4 The development of trade specialisation patterns in terms of beta convergence (or divergence) over the period 1971-91

N = 2166 R² = 0.93	Estimate	*p*-value (H₀: β=1)	*p*-value (H₀: β=av. effect)	*p*-value (H₀: β=0)
Average coefficient	0.931	0.0000		0.0000
Coefficient per sector* Food, drink and tobacco	0.972	0.1219	0.0201	0.0000
Textiles, footwear and leather	0.950	0.0175	0.3659	0.0000
Industrial chemicals	0.936	0.0642	0.8767	0.0000
Pharmaceuticals	0.938	0.0064	0.7430	0.0000
Petroleum refineries (oil)	0.909	0.0320	0.6100	0.0000
Rubber and plastics	0.919	0.0030	0.6704	0.0000
Stone, clay and glass	0.986	0.5821	0.0232	0.0000
Ferrous metals	0.889	0.0006	0.1983	0.0000
Non-ferrous metals	0.941	0.0246	0.6922	0.0000
Fabricated metal products	0.904	0.0163	0.5007	0.0000
Non-electrical machinery	0.951	0.0285	0.3533	0.0000
Office machines and computers	0.932	0.0010	0.9531	0.0000
Electrical machinery	0.901	0.0078	0.4203	0.0000
Communication eq. and semiconductors	0.948	0.0242	0.4716	0.0000
Shipbuilding	0.909	0.0010	0.4247	0.0000
Other transport	0.879	0.0003	0.1182	0.0000
Motor vehicles	0.962	0.0418	0.0896	0.0000
Aerospace	0.916	0.0010	0.5630	0.0000
Instruments	0.941	0.0024	0.5775	0.0000
Coefficient per country** Australia	0.920	0.0040	0.6876	0.0000
Austria	0.954	0.1486	0.4565	0.0000
Belgium	0.963	0.2128	0.2760	0.0000
Canada	0.945	0.0186	0.5417	0.0000
Denmark	0.963	0.1281	0.1784	0.0000
Finland	0.924	0.0228	0.8458	0.0000
France	0.850	0.0050	0.1320	0.0000
Germany (West)	0.845	0.0022	0.0899	0.0000
Greece	0.947	0.0063	0.4196	0.0000
Italy	0.921	0.0031	0.7219	0.0000
Japan	1.014	0.3525	0.0000	0.0000
The Netherlands	0.893	0.0025	0.2880	0.0000
New Zealand	0.970	0.1504	0.0587	0.0000
Norway	0.962	0.0551	0.1060	0.0000
Portugal	0.858	0.0002	0.0561	0.0000
Spain	0.846	0.0000	0.0041	0.0000
Sweden	0.937	0.0206	0.8224	0.0000
United Kingdom	0.994	0.9039	0.1917	0.0000
United States	0.978	0.6133	0.2870	0.0000

Notes:
*/** Sum of the average coefficient and the sector specific coefficients; and the sum of the average coefficient and the country specific coefficients, respectively. Standard errors heteroscedasticity consistent, using White's method, corrected for d.f.

Table 5.5 The development of technological specialisation patterns in terms of beta convergence (or divergence) over the period 1971-91

N = 2166 R² = 0.44		Estimate	*p*-value (H₀: β=1)	*p*-value (H₀: β=av. effect)	*p*-value (H₀: β=0)
Average coefficient		0.643	0.0000		0.0000
Coefficient per sector*	Food, drink and tobacco	0.824	0.0609	0.0549	0.0000
	Textiles, footwear and leather	0.493	0.0000	0.1980	0.0000
	Industrial chemicals	1.173	0.0606	0.0000	0.0000
	Pharmaceuticals	0,635	0.0147	0.9575	0.0000
	Petroleum refineries (oil)	0.542	0.0000	0.2988	0.0000
	Rubber and plastics	0.504	0.0101	0.4705	0.0091
	Stone, clay and glass	0.595	0.0174	0.7777	0.0005
	Ferrous metals	0.574	0.0002	0.5544	0.0000
	Non-ferrous metals	0.546	0.0000	0.3394	0.0000
	Fabricated metal products	0.769	0.1194	0.3938	0.0000
	Non-electrical machinery	0.593	0.0247	0.7839	0.0011
	Office machines and computers	0.584	0.0016	0.6574	0.0000
	Electrical machinery	0.573	0.0200	0.7036	0.0018
	Communication eq. and semiconductors	0.830	0.0562	0.0360	0.0000
	Shipbuilding	0.599	0.0001	0.6581	0.0000
	Other transport	0.382	0.0000	0.0387	0.0025
	Motor vehicles	0.645	0.0007	0.9828	0.0000
	Aerospace	0.694	0.0029	0.6142	0.0000
	Instruments	0.658	0.0050	0.8991	0.0000
Coefficient per country**	Australia	0.600	0.0000	0.5252	0.0000
	Austria	0.767	0.0024	0.1053	0.0000
	Belgium	0.716	0.0003	0.3437	0.0000
	Canada	0.845	0.0420	0.0079	0.0000
	Denmark	0,598	0.0000	0.5498	0.0000
	Finland	0.653	0.0000	0.8898	0.0000
	France	0.473	0.0000	0.0209	0.0000
	Germany (West)	0.740	0.0000	0.1274	0.0000
	Greece	0.141	0.0000	0.0000	0.1431
	Italy	0.592	0.0000	0.5180	0.0000
	Japan	0.988	0.8766	0.0000	0.0000
	The Netherlands	0.870	0.0905	0.0032	0.0000
	New Zealand	0.128	0.0000	0.0000	0.2119
	Norway	0.531	0.0000	0.2125	0.0000
	Portugal	0.280	0.0000	0.0001	0.0019
	Spain	0.493	0.0000	0.0840	0.0000
	Sweden	0.722	0.0000	0.1307	0.0000
	United Kingdom	0.631	0.0001	0.9002	0.0000
	United States	1.445	0.0623	0.0008	0.0000

Notes:
*/** Sum of the average coefficient and the sector specific coefficients and the sum of the average coefficients and the country specific coefficients, respectively. Standard errors heteroscedasticity consistent, using White's method, corrected for d.f.

headquarter services (R&D and management) from production facilities, presented in Chapter 2.

Among the countries, Australia, Finland, France, West Germany, Greece, Italy, Portugal, Spain, Sweden and the United Kingdom display the highest degree of turbulence in the specialisation patterns, across sectors and time. Again the criterion is whether or not the hypothesis of an unchanged pattern can be rejected for both types of specialisation. In contrast, the specialisation patterns for Japan and for the US are path-dependent to the extent that the hypothesis of an unchanged specialisation pattern cannot be rejected, also for what concerns both technological and export specialisation. The case of Japan is worth noting, as it is confirmed that the specialisation of that country remained very stable over the 1970s and the 1980s, while the structural change took place in the 1960s (see Chapter 4, Table A4.2). It can be seen from Tables 5.4 and 5.5 that Denmark is one of the countries with the strongest difference between the development in trade and technological specialisation (there is also a striking difference for New Zealand). The trade specialisation pattern is very stable for Denmark, as the hypothesis of no change in the pattern of specialisation cannot be rejected. In contrast this hypothesis is strongly rejected for what concerns technology. In terms of technological specialisation Denmark has increased specialisation rather strongly in pharmaceuticals, but also to some extent in industrial chemicals. At the same time patenting activity has increased in almost all transport sectors, but starting from a very low level (Denmark remains under specialised in these sectors).

As stated in the introduction, we expect catching-up countries to experience the highest degree of turbulence in the specialisation patterns over time. For the OECD 'catch-up countries' in this sample (Finland, Greece, Italy, Spain, and Portugal) we do find that the specialisation patterns of these countries (Spain and Portugal in particular, given the low coefficients) belong to the group of countries experiencing the highest degree of turbulence, both in terms of trade and technology. It should be pointed out that Greece (the slowest growing of these countries) only display a very high degree of turbulence in the case of technological specialisation. In terms of trade specialisation, the hypothesis of no structural change for Greece can be rejected, but the parameter is around the size of the average coefficient. But as compared to high-income countries, Greece is (and remains) specialised in low-tech sectors, and has nearly no activity in other sectors.

5.2. CONCLUSIONS

The first aim of this chapter was to investigate whether the seemingly contradictory findings in the empirical literature on the development of technological specialisation and on export specialisation patterns, respectively, are due to a 'real world' phenomenon, or whether the explanation is purely technical, by comparing the development of export specialisation to specialisation in terms of US patents, using the same methodology, and level of aggregation. The second aim was to analyse the extent to which countries and sectors display stable specialisation patterns over time, also both in terms of exports and in terms of technology. The conclusions will be drawn by making reference to the propositions set up in Chapter 2.

The chapter confirmed that the OECD countries did in general *tend to* de-specialise in terms of export specialisation. The evidence was (even) less conclusive with regard to technological specialisation, as the results were mixed in the sense that just about half of the countries tended to increase in terms of the level of specialisation, while the other half tended to engage in de-specialisation. Based on the discussion of the weaknesses of the alternative analyses (in particular the bias due to the unadjusted *RCA* and the bias due to the heavy weight attributed to extreme values when using the chi-square measure), and based on the results found in this chapter, it can be concluded that the contradictory findings between the previous findings on exports and on patents are to a large extent due to differences in the applied methodology, rather than being due to 'real world' differences between the two measures.

In terms of country and sectoral stability of specialisation patterns [proposition (a)], it was concluded that both trade specialisation and technological specialisation patterns are path-dependent in the sense that all country and sectoral patterns were correlated between seven three-year intervals, within the period in question. In comparison however, trade specialisation patterns were more stable than were technological specialisation patterns [proposition (e)]. Among the countries, Australia, Finland, France, West Germany, Greece, Italy, Portugal, Spain, Sweden and the United Kingdom displayed the highest degree of turbulence in the specialisation patterns, across sectors and time. In contrast, the specialisation patterns for Japan and for the US were path-dependent to the extent that the hypothesis of an unchanged specialisation pattern could not be rejected, also for what concerns both technological and export specialisation. Concerning the hypothesis of OECD catching up countries experiencing the highest degree of turbulence [proposition (b)] in the specialisation patterns, the results were not as clear-cut as they were in Chapter 4, since only Finland, Greece, Italy, Spain and Portugal were consistently among the countries experiencing the highest degree of turbulence. The explanation has to do with the time periods considered, as Chapter 4 considered a period starting in 1965, while this chapter started in 1971. In this way it appeared that Japan encountered a high degree of structural change in the 1960s, while this process stopped from the 1970s onwards. Of the sectors, 14 sectors displayed structural change across countries and time, for both types of specialisation. Food, drink and tobacco; and industrial chemicals, on the other hand, were stable to the extent that the hypothesis of an unchanged specialisation pattern could not be rejected, in the case of both types of specialisation. Hence in general, the proposition (c) stating that 'low-tech' sectors are more footloose than 'high-tech' sectors could not be confirmed, either in the case of exports, or in the case of technology.

Concerning proposition (f), stating that trade and technological specialisation will in general tend to co-evolve in terms of divergence or convergence, some support can be said to be given for this proposition as the parameters for structural adjustment were in general high (or low) for the same countries and sectors for the two types of specialisation, as the 38 parameters for export and technology correlate, although the relation is not extremely strong ($\rho=0.29$). However, we have also seen in this chapter that there are a number of cases, when there is no co-evolution between the two types of specialisation.

A conclusion also coming out of this chapter is that, while European integration has been on-going throughout the period, there has been no tendency for European countries to specialise in terms of trade specialisation (similar to the findings of Chapter 4), or in terms of technological specialisation [in contrast to what was stated in proposition (g)]. Standard trade theory (Heckscher-Ohlin) would predict increasing specialisation - all other things being equal - if trade barriers are being reduced, given different factor endowments in various countries. However, as pointed out in Chapter 4, it is a 'stylised fact' that intra-industry trade grows in a period of economic integration. On the basis of these findings, one can speculate (as in the previous chapter) that instead countries increasingly specialise according to consumer preferences (within the same industries), rather than specialising in different industries. Hence, the findings are more in line with theoretical models allowing for increasing returns and (vertically or horizontally) differentiated products, presented in Chapter 2. Such a finding has important policy implications, in particular with respect to catching-up countries, since the growth opportunities of these countries appear not to lie in (static) gains from deepening the already existing pattern of specialisation. Instead, such opportunities can be realised in a process of structural change in the patterns of specialisation.

NOTES

1. This finding is consistent with e.g. Proudman and Redding (1997), who found that Germany and Great Britain showed no sign of increased export specialisation over a period from 1970 to 1993.

2. For further discussion of this topic, see Chapter 3.

3. The sensitivity to the time periods chosen, were not only tested using the two sub-periods, shown in Tables 5.2 and 5.3, but also on six sub-periods, not explicitly documented for reasons of space.

4. In fact all OECD 'catch-up' countries in our sample.

5. The observations are: 1971-73, 1974-76, 1977-79, 1980-82, 1983-85, 1986-88 and 1989-91.

PART III

The Determinants of International Trade
Specialisation

6. Horizontal Diversification as a Determinant of Specialisation: The Case of Denmark and Pharmaceuticals[1]

An important aim of the theory of national systems of innovation (Lundvall, 1992) is the attempt to assist in explaining the direction of technological development at the national level, by means of a combination of economic structure and national institutional set-up. Given that technology is an important - maybe the most important - determinant of comparative advantage in trade in more advanced sectors (Soete, 1981), theories of national systems of innovation have an important role to play in a trade specialisation context. This point has been elaborated from an empirical point of view by Fagerberg (1992; 1995).

A common denominator for this literature has been the focus on demand conditions as inducement mechanisms (cf. Hirschman, 1961) for technological innovation, thus to a large degree determining the pattern of comparative advantage among nations. In doing so, the authors have been influenced by the insights of Schmookler (1966) in his analysis of the effect of shifts in demand, influencing the allocation of resources to inventive activities, and from project SAPPHO (Rothwell *et al.*, 1974), showing that firms' attention to user needs is an important criterion for success in industrial innovation. However, this chapter is going to argue that, while demand-induced innovation has been of central importance in many sectors, there are sectors where this inducement mechanism is not so important. Rather, it will be shown that supply side factors play an important role in this regard. Specifically, the chapter aims at demonstrating that the cumulative mastery of core technologies has been a much more important inducement mechanism to innovation in the 'Danish insulin cluster' (cf. Porter, 1990). In other words this chapter aims at finding support for proposition (g) from Chapter 2, stating that internal technological activity is the most important factor in determining trade specialisation in science-based industries.

It can be said that technological accumulation along country-specific technological trajectories in developed countries, has led to the acquisition of personal, organisational and institutional competencies, which has enabled countries to adopt and develop product and process technologies of increasing sophistication. According to Bell and Pavitt (1993) such processes have evolved along with - and are increasingly a determinant of international competitiveness.

Accordingly - and as pointed out in Chapter 2 - Bell and Pavitt identify three types of mechanisms, which have been particularly important in influencing such trajectories in their rate and direction: (i) factor endowments; (ii) inter-sectoral linkages; and (iii) the cumulative mastery of core technologies.[2] The first mechanism has to do with the innovative response to alleviate for scarce factor endowments. The second mechanism has to do with inter-sectoral linkages, sometimes starting off with the exploitation of abundant raw materials, then later creating a base for competitiveness in downstream sectors. In turn (national) upstream sectors are reinforced through vertical linkages, making the sectors co-evolve. The third mechanism has to do with trajectories which are traced through horizontal technological diversification, and rooted in the R&D base.

The third mechanism is in the focus of this chapter. It has to do with the inherent characteristics of technology, namely that technology is firm-specific, cumulative and thus path-dependent. Given these characteristics, related diversification is feasible, as long as it is consistent with the underlying technological path dependency or/and imperatives of the individual firm (Teece, 1988). In other words, firms are not likely to survey all technological knowledge before making a technological choice, rather firms will conduct a local search which enables them to apply and enhance their existing technology-base (Dosi, 1982). In this context, and based on data concerning the 500 largest corporations in the US 1949-69, Rumelt (1974) has shown that in 1969 about 74 per cent of all firms were diversified into related markets or into technologically related areas, whereas only 19 per cent were diversified into technologically unrelated areas or markets, leaving about 6 per cent as single product firms. In addition, Rumelt showed that related diversity is associated with the financially best performance. Nevertheless, as stressed by Rumelt, one should be careful when determining the causation, since it makes no sense to diversify within the same product-family if the firm is situated within a dying industry.

In the context of the latter type of inducement mechanism it is useful to distinguish between technological diversification and product diversification. As pointed out by Granstrand and Sjölander (1990) the product-technology relationship is not one-to-one, since the development, production and use of a product usually involve more than one technology and each technology can be applied in more than one product. Given the complexity of products, firms are therefore often 'multi-technology' i.e. are able to orchestrate several technologies.

Thus, given a certain amount of complexity, technology with multiple applications has in itself become a central inducement mechanism in technologically advanced countries. Therefore, such trajectories are traced through horizontal technological diversification, rooted in an R&D base, often connected to a university environment. Thus, this type of inducement

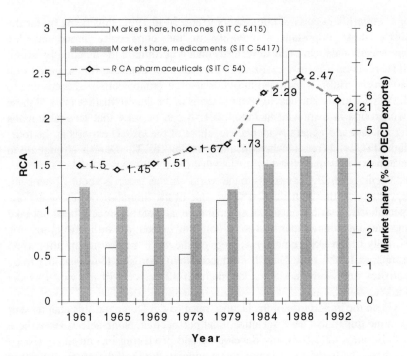

Source: Based on the IKE trade database.

Figure 6.1 Denmark's relative comparative advantage and market share of OECD exports to the world 1961-92.

mechanism might be relatively more important in science-based industries, as compared to production-intensive sectors.

Much attention has been paid to demand-led innovation in the Danish context, often focusing on production intensive sectors, while less attention has been given to the localised rate and direction of innovation in science-based sectors (e.g. Andersen, Dalum and Villumsen, 1981). Figure 6.1 shows that Denmark has become increasingly specialised in pharmaceuticals, as measured by the *RCA* index (see the definition in Chapter 3), over the more than 30 year period from 1961 to 1992. If compared to other OECD countries, only Ireland (3.13) and Switzerland display (5.01) higher degrees of export specialisation in this area in 1992. Hence, it seems that a pharmaceutical trajectory can be identified in Denmark. If one takes a closer look at Denmark's export of pharmaceuticals, using OECD export data, classified according to SITC revision 3, it can be shown that insulin export made up no less than 43 per cent of Denmark's exports of commodity group 54 in 1992, thus being by far the single most important commodity in the commodity group labelled pharmaceuticals. Unfortunately, trade data according to the detailed five-digit SITC revision 3 is only available in the IKE trade database for the year 1992. However, insulin is included in two four-digit groups classified according to SITC, revision 1. The development in terms of the Danish market share of these two groups is displayed in Figure 6.1. It can be seen that Denmark has a significant, and generally increasing, share of the OECD exports at the four-digit SITC level (rev. 1) where insulin is contained.[3] The Danish stronghold in insulin export is underlined by the fact that Denmark's export market share - as a percentage of OECD-exports to the world - in this group is about 72 per cent. Nevertheless, this statistic also shows one of the limitations of using export-specialisation, as a measure of comparative advantage, since it does not take into account commodities sold at the domestic market. According to observers, Eli Lilly of the US are nearly as large on the world market for insulin, when compared to the only Danish producer Novo Nordisk. However, the trade statistics only show a US market share of 12 per cent of the world *export* market.

Given the importance of the insulin trajectory in Denmark, this chapter will examine this trajectory from a historical perspective. Nonetheless, since there is only one single company developing and producing insulin today (Novo Nordisk), the focus will be upon this company. We shall therefore, in Section 6.1, begin by a chronological exposition of how technology was acquired by Novo. Sub-sections 6.1.1- 6.1.8 focus on specific product trajectories; on how they were created and influenced in their direction. It should be emphasised that in conducting the case-study, the focus will not be on why Novo has been particularly successful, compared to other firms (which would imply a focus on the innovation management aspect); rather the emphasis is on why the localisation in Denmark is so successful in pharmaceuticals.

In order to identify particularly important inducement mechanisms, it is useful to start by identifying the possible sources of innovation among business firms. Therefore, it can be useful to discuss briefly what innovation theory has to say about the sources of innovation. One starting point can be von Hippel's (1988) functional distinction between the contribution of manufacturers, suppliers, and users, to the process of innovation. The functional distinction fits in with Pavitt's sectoral taxonomy (1984), which identifies differences in the importance of different sources of innovation according to which broad sector the individual firm belongs. Four types of firms were identified accordingly; among these *science-based firms*. Science-based firms are found in the chemical and electronic sectors.

Given that Novo is a science-based firm, the literature on technological innovation suggests that one should look at sources of innovation among (i) *the manufacturer* (in this case Novo; its production engineering department and its R&D department), including technological links to former products or processes (ii) *suppliers*, (iii) *users* and (iv) *universities*. In addition, a source of technology can be (v) *cooperation between rivals* (see von Hippel, 1988, Chapter 6), based on complementary assets. Furthermore, as suggested by Rosenberg (1976), when looking directly for inducement mechanisms, one has to look for (vi) *the importance of different resource constraints* to the process of innovation, in addition to abundance of particular inputs. Using the aforementioned entities as the units of analysis, the general focus will be on how the company acquired its technologies, enabling the company to produce new products, or improve old ones. Sub-section 6.1.9 will focus on providing quantitative evidence (using patent data) for the 'technological relatedness' of products at Novo Nordisk. The relative importance of the sources of innovation, identified above, can then provide a framework for discussing the relative importance of inducement mechanisms, and their change over time. Section 6.2 will move back to the national level in focusing on the importance of a national science-base for the pharmaceutical industry. A final section contains concluding remarks, based on a 'match' between the conceptual framework, presented above, and the case-study which is to follow.

6.1. FROM CALF'S PANCREASES TO BIOTECHNOLOGY[4]

Novo Nordisk is today by far the largest Danish pharmaceutical company. This is illustrated by the fact that Novo's world-wide turnover in pharmaceuticals was as big as 78 per cent of total Danish production[5] (1992). Similarly, Novo Nordisk's world-wide turnover in other chemicals was 16 per cent of total Danish production[6]. Novo Nordisk's world-wide turnover in all chemicals was 36 per cent of total Danish production in chemicals in 1992. Hence, Novo Nordisk is completely dominating the Danish pharmaceutical sector, and prominent in the Danish chemical sector. The company had by the end of 1992 10,733 employees and two main product areas; insulin and industrial enzymes. Insulin made up around 50 per cent of total company turnover in 1992. The percentage for industrial enzymes was 29 per cent. Novo Nordisk is the world's largest producer in both areas. Other important products are human growth hormone, haemophiliac medicine, hormones for the treatment of women, central nervous system drugs, semi-manufactured penicillin and plant protection. In 1992, 96 per cent of total sales were sold outside Denmark. The company's R&D is located in four different countries and its production in six different countries.

6.1.1. The Start-up of Insulin Production in Denmark

In 1921, the two Canadians *Frederick G. Banting* and *Charles H. Best* managed to isolate insulin, a hormone situated in the pancreas, which was known to determine sugar-metabolism. This discovery made it possible to treat diabetes.

In the spring of 1922, a Danish biologist, August Krogh gave a series of lectures at the Yale University in the United States. August Krogh had in 1920 been awarded the Nobel prize for his work on the intake of oxygen in animal muscles. Krogh knew that insulin had been successfully used in the treatment of diabetes in both the USA and Canada. In order to set up possible Danish production, Krogh went on to Canada, when his lectures were finished at Yale. In Canada, Krogh visited professor *J.J.R. Macleod*, the head of the institute in Toronto where the first extraction of insulin from animal pancreases took place.

This personal contact was a very important reason why insulin production was set up in Denmark. Another important factor, was the abundant (at least in the beginning) availability of raw material in Denmark in the form of calf-, ox-, and pig-pancreases. These were all by-products from animal production in the predominantly agricultural country Denmark. In 1923 the first Danish production of insulin was set up. In this way Nordisk Insulin Laboratorium became the first Danish company producing insulin.

Nordisk Insulin Laboratorium was not, however, to become the leading insulin manufacturing company in Denmark. This role was to be played by *Novo*, a company set up in 1925 by the brothers *Harald* and *Thorvald Pedersen*, two brothers who had been working as an engineer and as a pharmacist at Nordisk Insulin Laboratorium from an early stage.

6.1.2. Diversifying into Industrial Enzymes

In early 1938, Novo had approximately 70 employees; the tasks within the company had become increasingly specialised, and a more formal research laboratory was set up. In the 1940s the laboratory came up with three major innovations; an improved insulin product; an improved production process and finally, based on knowledge accumulated in the laboratory about the raw-material for manufacturing insulin (the pancreas), Novo diversified into industrial *enzymes*.

World War II broke out in September 1939, and Denmark was occupied April 9, 1940. This was of course to have a drastic impact on a company exporting 90 per cent of its production. However, the main problem was not the lack of demand. Instead, the main problem was lack of pancreases, since the

Danish stock of pigs was halved, mainly as a consequence of a lack of imported feedstuffs, due to the war. This problem was exacerbated by the fact that (industrial) chemical companies used the same scarce raw material input. The *trypsin* enzyme was also extracted from pancreases. These enzymes were used in the tanneries mainly, for the purpose of softening leather.

According to conventional theory, insulin and enzymes could not be extracted from the *same* glands. Nonetheless, the scarcity induced Novo to do research on this topic; perhaps the theory was wrong? In 1940, research aiming to solve this problem was initiated. A systematic investigation of what happened to the enzyme when the insulin was extracted from the pancreas was conducted. The researchers at Novo discovered that the enzymes were not destroyed in the process, rather they were precipitated. This meant that it would be theoretically possible to extract enzymes from the waste of insulin-production.

Complex machinery, on an industrial scale, capable of extracting trypsin and another enzyme *chymotrypsin* from the 'waste' was accordingly developed by Novo. Initial problems were overcome, but more importantly, the experience with this first machinery could be used when a new trypsin-plant was set up in 1943/44. The new production became an instant success on the marketplace; the demand and hence production of insulin, determined the amount of enzymes produced.

6.1.3. Diversifying into Fermentation and Penicillin in the 1950s

The Scottish bacteriologist *Alexander Fleming*, discovered penicillin in 1928, but he did not make any clinical products, and the discovery was more or less forgotten until shortly before World War II, when the two English scientists *Florey* and *Chain*, took an interest in Fleming's work, and developed clinical products. Florey took the discoveries to America in 1941, and production on a large scale was initiated.

At Novo, the Pedersen brothers and the head of research *Hallas-Møller* thought that fermentation (penicillin) production would fit into Novo's structure. Novo already had some experience in fermentation, manufacturing citric acid. This fermentation process had been possible due to the hiring of an Italian fermentation chemist, *B. Steinhardt*, in 1939. However, the citric acid was a commercial failure, and was given up when the war broke out. Nevertheless, without any knowledge of the technological advances that had been achieved in the States, the first experiments with penicillin fermentation were set up at Novo in 1943. The experiments did produce penicillin, but in too small amounts to form the basis of industrial production. After the war Hallas-Møller went to the States, to visit leading public institutions heavily involved in the development and production of penicillin. During his stay Hallas-Møller visited *Cornell University* in New York, and became acquainted with crystalline penicillin. This product had the advantage of being non-perishable and could hence be stored for years, without losing any effect, while the standard penicillin could be stored for half a year only. Furthermore, the new drug did not need any (expensive) freeze-drying.

Hallas-Møller went back to Copenhagen and set up a research team searching for a method for producing crystalline penicillin. Included in this team was Steinhardt who had fermentation production experience. Comprehensive fermentation experiments including trial and error tests were conducted. However, penicillin production is not only about fermentation, but also about purification. In this area the research team came up with new methods, capable of making a very clean product. The intermediate product could now be manufactured (ammonium penicillin). But the final step crystallising the penicillin was extremely troublesome, and required months of trial and error. But in the summer of 1947 these problems were overcome.

The new penicillin-trajectory was to become a very important part of the company, in the following years, both directly in terms of products, but also as a means of further diversification. In this latter context the fermentation capability became of utmost importance.

6.1.4. Microbiological Enzymes

Novo's enzyme products were until the early fifties, based on pancreas-extracts only. However, as already noted, the access to the raw-material was the limiting factor. Furthermore, the demand for enzymes became more diverse. As a response to this situation, in the late forties Novo's fermentation expert Bruno Steinhardt suggested that enzymes could be produced by means of fermentation, utilising capabilities acquired in penicillin fermentation. By means of processing a culture of bacteria, he succeeded in making bacteria capable of producing the enzyme *amylase*. Subsequently, methods for concentration and purification were developed. These methods shared many similar characteristics with methods used in penicillin production. Consequently, experimental production was set up, and the new product was introduced to the market in 1952. However, even though the product (with further improvements) became a relative success, its impact on total company turnover remained, for nearly a decade, very limited.

Nevertheless, markets for enzymes grew significantly, when Novo, in 1960, managed to manufacture an enzyme (*alcalase*), which had an efficient impact in clothes washing. In 1965, the success was so evident, that the multinational manufacturers could not leave this area unattended. Negotiations with multinationals such as Procter & Gamble, Unilever, Colgate-Palmolive and Henkel were initiated in 1965.

6.1.5. Other Diversification in the 1960s

Until the 1960s, Novo's products had been almost solely biology-based. But in the early sixties, Novo diversified into purely synthetic drugs. Products introduced in the early sixties included psycho-pharmaceuticals, sleeping medicine, gynaecological and contraceptive products. Even though diversification into these areas did not have as obvious links as in previous cases, a number of reasons for moving into synthetic drugs can be listed. First of all the company had accumulated a general skill in biochemistry (from insulin and penicillin R&D and production). In this context a closer inspection of Novo's patenting activity in the US shows that the 'synthetic' based drugs (central nervous system drugs and hormones for women) involve one of the same patent classes (organic compounds series, class 532-570), as do the 'biology' based drugs such as insulin, enzymes and blood products. Secondly, general skills in testing effects of drugs had been acquired from an early stage. This skill could also be utilised in the new areas.

6.1.6. Human Insulin

Until 1982, all insulins manufactured had been bovine or porcine products. However, rapid scientific advances in the areas of molecular biology and peptide chemistry made it possible to make an insulin identical to the one produced by the human pancreas. The animal insulins are only slightly different from the human one, but these insulins are still alien proteins to the human body, so therapeutic advantages from such products could be expected.

Based on the advances in science, human insulin could (theoretically) be produced in two ways. It could be manufactured by means of fermentation, using genetic engineering, or by means of converting porcine insulin into human insulin, by means of (synthetic) biochemistry. Novo went both ways. But the first human insulin Novo put on the market was based on porcine insulin. It had been known since the sixties, that both porcine and human insulin are made up of 51 amino acids. Only one of these acids differs between the two types of insulin. However small this difference might seem, it is an extremely complex biochemical process to get rid of the 'wrong' amino acid and replace it with the 'right' one, without damaging the complete molecule. It was well-known that the enzyme trypsin could decompose the 'wrong' amino acid. So the problem was to fasten the 'right' amino acid to the molecule. In 1978, American researchers showed that enzymes could be used both in order to decompose and to link the amino acids. Progress was also made on this front in Japan.

As we have seen, knowledge concerning both enzymes and insulin had been accumulated at Novo. Based on this knowledge and the latest scientific advances abroad, researchers at the company managed to come up with a very elegant method, which could separate and link the amino acids in one single industrial process. The product was put on the market in 1982, and became the world's first human insulin. Clinical tests showed subsequently, that the amount of antibodies produced were very low. In some instances allergic responses could be avoided as well.

In the US Eli Lilly had high expectations of breaking into the European market, while defending its strong position in the US, based on its genetically engineered human insulin. Lilly's product was put on the market three months after Novo's. While Novo's human insulin was 'old fashioned', in terms of its biochemical production processes, the *product*s were similar (Hall, 1988).

However, Novo did not ignore the progress within molecular genetics. The company had already gained experience in the field of biotechnology, since the mid-seventies, due to the development of enzymes. Two benefits from producing enzymes can be identified in a biotechnological context. Firstly, enzymes are essential in recombinant DNA (rDNA) techniques, since they are used to cut and splice genes. Hence, knowledge about the *artefact* 'the enzyme' is very useful. Secondly, knowledge about how to *manufacture* enzymes is important, as fermentation technology is very important in this context, and fermentation is an essential part of biotechnological manufacturing.

Bacteria producing enzymes are found in nature (e.g. in soil) and can hence be changed incrementally, using biotechnological techniques, to produce enzymes with the desired characteristics. But there are no natural bacteria producing insulin; the bacteria have to be created (reprogrammed) synthetically. Hence, producing insulin by means of biotechnology is a more complex technology than producing enzymes using biotechnological techniques.

But even though Novo had biotechnological capabilities, they were not enough *per se*, in order to make a genetically engineered insulin. External capabilities were bought in. In 1981, a contract was formed with *Biogen* in the US. Biogen is closely connected to Harvard University. Due to the very upstream nature (i.e. close to basic research) of the race to synthesize the human insulin, in which Genentech and Biogen took part (Hall, 1988), it was natural that Novo wanted to acquire very upstream capabilities concerning the insulin gene. A more long-term relationship was developed with a smaller *dedicated biotechnology firm* (DBF), namely *ZymoGenetics* in Seattle. ZymoGenetics had, and still has, strong links with the University of Washington. A minority share was bought in this company in 1982. This company had know-how in the area of genetic engineering in yeast. In 1988 (when the collaboration had worked successfully), Novo bought the rest of the shares in the American company.

Based on a combination of these bought-in capabilities and in-house experience, Novo came up with new methods of making insulin by means of fermentation, in 1987. Experimentation targeted at optimising the yield of human insulin was conducted, and different yeast cells, producing different pre-stages to insulin, were made. Subsequently, new enzymatic methods of converting these pre-stages into human insulin were developed. In some cases this process of conversion could be conducted with methods very similar to the ones used when converting porcine insulin into human insulin.

6.1.7. A Variety of Enzymes

Whereas the 'enzyme boom', in the late 1960s had been virtually based on enzymes for detergents, the new expansion in the 1970s, in the area of industrial enzymes, was based on a broader variety of enzymes. Nevertheless, these areas were not technologically new to Novo, since a part of the development of these enzymes was conducted in the early 1960s. But the large scale commercial exploitation of these products was not conducted before the mid-seventies. Other areas where sales and product development were expanded were enzymes for the textile industry; the brewing and alcohol industry; the paper industry; the dairy industry; and the food & beverage industry, among others.   In the mid 1980s Novo had approximately 60 per cent of the world market in enzymes. The success can partly be explained by the company's ability to tailor-make enzymes according to user needs. This responsiveness is indicated by the fact that Novo Nordisk's Bioindustrial Group in 1992, had 40 basic fermentation products, but more than 500 different end-products. In contrast to innovations in insulin, innovations in enzymes have been induced, to a great extent, by means of interaction with the user. An example of such interaction is the recent co-development of the enzyme *Carezyme*, with Procter & Gamble. In this case researchers from the two companies collaborated; Novo Nordisk's researchers primarily utilising the company's knowledge of the properties of enzymes, while Procter & Gamble's researchers could make contributions based on more general knowledge of detergents.

6.1.8. The Increasing Importance of Biotechnology

Novo Nordisk has strengthened research and sales in the areas of blood products, and central nervous system drugs (*CNS*; psycho pharmaceuticals). Furthermore the company has diversified into growth hormones, diagnostic kits and biological pesticides. In the context of technology-based product diversification, biotechnology has become a very important basis for

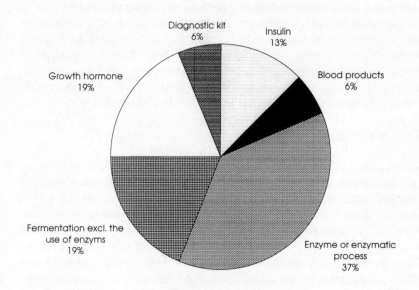

Diagnostic kit
6%

Insulin
13%

Growth hormone
19%

Blood products
6%

Fermentation excl. the
use of enzyms
19%

Enzyme or enzymatic
process
37%

Source: Based on data supplied to SPRU by the U.S. Department of Commerce, Patent and Trademark Office.

Figure 6.2 Distribution of patents involving a biotechnological technique on product groups (N=16)

diversification at Novo, since biotechnological techniques are important to all the products mentioned above, except CNS.

Patent data show that biotechnological techniques are very important in the technological activity of Novo Nordisk A/S today, since 25 per cent of all patents taken out by Novo in the period 1986-90 have a biotechnological component.[7] Only 4.7 per cent of the patents in the previous period (1980-85), involved genetic engineering. The first 'biotechnological' patent was taken out in Denmark in 1981 (an enzyme). Figure 6.2 shows in which 'old' product groups biotechnological activity was detected, and how much of total biotechnological patenting was done in the different areas. Thus, Figure 6.2

demonstrates that biotechnology is a *generic process* technology, since it is present in many (and quite different) product areas. In this way the movement into biotechnology can be seen as technological diversification which provides a basis for product diversification (Diagnostic kits, enzymes, growth hormones) or product/process improvements (insulin, enzymes, blood products).

6.1.9. Shared Structural Characteristics Between Products and Processes

Table 6.1 is an attempt to classify Novo Nordisk's patents according to product groups. Given that the technology-product relationship is not one-to-one, it is not an easy task, since the US classification scheme relates to technological fields, rather than product fields. Nevertheless, the classification was attempted, drawing upon a knowledge of Novo's product portfolio and an interview with a PhD student in molecular biology in addition to assistance from Novo Nordisk's own patent department. Table 6.1 shows a high degree of overlaps in terms of the same patent classes (as a proxy of structural characteristics) being present in different product/process groups. The two products that Novo Nordisk no longer does significant research on (penicillin and hormones for women), all belong to patent classes 532-570 ('organic compounds series'). However these patent classes are present in six of today's product groups.

Such observed 'overlaps', in terms of several patent classes being present in a given product group, add to the understanding of why product diversification is possible, when technology is cumulative and has a strong tacit dimension; some competencies (knowledge of structural characteristics of chemicals/ materials) can be utilised in many different product groups. Hence, such cross-product capabilities provide a basis for product diversification.

Table 6.1 shows that technological diversification[8] does take place across product groups at Novo Nordisk A/S, since five out of six product groups (the six groups where data are available for both periods) display more patent classes involved (i.e. the product groups are more dispersed in terms of patent classes involved) in the period 1969-79, than in the period 1980-90. The table is inspired by similar calculations conducted by Granstrand *et al.*(1990).

Concerning Table 6.1 it should be noted that the indexes in two of these groups are very fragile, since they rely on only one observation in the first period (1969-79). Another distinctive feature of Table 6.1 is, that three of the 'new' product groups (growth hormones, diagnostic kits and pesticides) involve many technologies. Thus, the index is very low (< 0.40) in these areas. Since group 935 (Genetic engineering) is a new one, it was excluded in order to test for sensitivity. However, even under these, (for the hypothesis of technology diversification) unfavourable circumstances the *pattern* remains the same.

Table 6.1 The depth and width of the technology base at Novo Nordisk, 1969-90

No. of patents = 153, no. of patent classifications = 262 Product Group	Patent Classes[A]									Technology diversification index[C]	
	424	426	435	436	514	530	532-570	935	Other (71/13/252)[B]	unmod	mod[D]
Insulin (5.9%) 1969-1979			1		1	1				0.33	0.33
1980-1990			4		3	2	1	1		0.26	0.30
Blood products 1969-1979	1		1			3				0.44	0.44
(6.5%) 1980-1990	1		2		1	7	1	1		0.34	0.39
Other peptides/ 1969-1979											
polypeptides (3.5%) 1980-1990	1				5	4				0.42	0.42
Enzyme or enzymatic 1969-1979		2	16			1				0.72	0.72
process (34.3%) 1980-1990		12	38				1	5	9	0.40	0.46
Ferment. excl the use 1969-1979		1								1.00	1.00
of enzymes (6.5%) 1980-1990		7	8		1		1	2		0.33	0.40
Saccharides 1969-1979		1	5						1	0.55	0.55
(6.5%) 1980-1990		1	6							0.76	0.76
CNS 1969-1979							1			1.00	1.00
(13.6%) 1980-1990					20	22				0.50	0.50
Growth hormone 1969-1979											
(4.1%) 1980-1990			5		4	3	1	3		0.23	0.30
Diagnostic kits 1969-1979											
(1.8%) 1980-1990			3	3				1		0.39	0.39
Pesticides 1969-1979											
(3.6%) 1980-1990	1		1		1				1	0.25	0.25
Antibiotics 1969-1979							19			1.00	1.00
(3.0%) 1980-1990											
Hormones 1969-1979							12			1.00	1.00
(for women) (5.3%) 1980-1990											
Number of patent - class references	4	24	90	3	35	22	59	13	11	261	241

Notes:

A) No. of patent classes is the number of *different* patent classifications at each individual patent times the total number of patents examined. B) The fact that 'other' includes more than one patent class, does not affect the results, since they are only different across product groups (i.e. only one 'other' patent class is found in each product group). C) = H, where H is Herfindahls index, and p is number of patent classes, n_i is the number of references in category i and N is total number of patent classifications. D) Modified by excluding patent class no. 935.

Source:　Calculations based on data supplied to SPRU by the US Department of Commerce, Patent and Trademark Office.

6.1.10. Product and Technological Trajectories at Novo (Nordisk) 1925-92

The case study has identified strong *internal* horizontal linkages between old and new products and core technologies, which were crucially important in the process of innovation. Figure 6.3 below, summarises the product trajectories present at Novo Nordisk today, in which years they emerged and how these trajectories have been linked to one another. The first major product diversification (from insulin manufacturing) took place (*A* in Figure 6.3) during and after the second world war. The movement into the area of industrial enzymes was based on knowledge of the raw material (animal pancreases), used for manufacturing the two quite different products; insulin and enzymes. Knowledge concerning the pancreases had been accumulated, while researching, developing and producing insulin, since 1925. Furthermore, knowledge concerning the extraction of insulin (mainly mechanical engineering) could be utilised in the new area.

The second main product diversification was the movement into penicillin production (*B*). Even though the technology used for manufacturing penicillin (fermentation) was quite different from what the firm had been doing previously, the company could still build on its general skills in the areas of biology, biochemistry, testing and mechanical engineering. In addition to being product diversification, it was also a technological diversification; future products could be based on the new capabilities acquired.

Further diversification into blood products (*C*) was based on the specific knowledge of the enzyme *trypsin*, an enzyme centrally important in extracting the blood product (*heparin*), from ox lungs. Heparin is capable of impeding blood coagulation, and is therefore useful in the treatment of patients with heart/vessel diseases. Also, Novo had more general capabilities in the purification and extraction from biological material (acquired in insulin and enzyme research and production).

As indicated above, the acquisition of fermentation skills was to become much more important for the company, than the penicillin product itself. Based on the acquired fermentation capability in penicillin, Novo managed to diversify technologically into enzymes manufactured by means of fermentation (*D*), in the 1950s. The ability to make enzymes by means of fermentation, made it possible to produce enzymes on a much bigger scale; but also more diverse enzymes. Fermentation capabilities were also of utmost importance when Novo assimilated biotechnology (along with knowledge of enzymes) in the 1970s and 1980s.

Diversification into central nervous system drugs (*E*) was primarily based on a skill in the area of synthetic biochemistry, acquired through research and development in many different areas of pharmaceuticals. Nevertheless, the

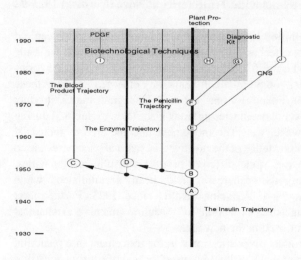

Figure 6.3 Technological links between product trajectories at Novo 1925-91

takeover of a Danish company (Ferrosan A/S) (*J*) has led to a significant enhancement of this technology within the company.

Furthermore, the Novo Nordisk A/S has moved into new areas, such as growth hormones (PDGF) (*I*), plant protection (*H*) and diagnostic kits (*G*), primarily based on biotechnological competences. However, the diagnostic kit products also had backward horizontal linkages (*F*), based on in-house testing abilities. Besides the product diversification, innovation in existing products and processes has taken place; based on advances in science, the products have been improved. Most important were improvements in the main business area, insulin. Most recently significant improvements have been made in the manufacture of a human insulin, first based on advances in peptide chemistry, later based on biotechnological techniques. In both these cases knowledge accumulated in connection with another product trajectory (enzymes) was crucial in developing new products and methods in insulin. This is remarkable since enzymes originally spun off the insulin trajectory.

Nevertheless, one should be cautious taking Figure 6.3 as evidence of smooth technical change at Novo Nordisk, since the figure only involves the 'successes' in the sense of the product groups still being present at Novo. However, branches of Novo's 'product tree' have withered away as well. The descaling of activities in the area of penicillin and hormones for women has already been mentioned, but many more areas have 'been opened' and then later closed or sold off, when the company decided that resources were better spent elsewhere. Novo did, for instance, produce surgical threads, based on sheep's intestines between 1938 and 1967 when the production was closed down. In 1990, Novo Nordisk sold their veterinary department off to a competitor. Very large research projects have also failed. One prominent 'failure' was the heavy investment in research on a drug containing an enzyme, in the early 1960s, which could theoretically dissolve thromboses. The expectations turned out to be too high, and the research did not produce any commercially useful products. The 'new' product groups at Novo Nordisk should be viewed in this light; because of fundamental technological uncertainty, new areas are opened up, of which some will 'survive' and grow, and others will be 'closed' again. New technology or product areas are invested in order to increase option values (Mitchell and Hamilton, 1988). So even though R&D spending does not secure specific success in a product or technology area, high levels of R&D spending remain crucially important, since it increases option values in a complex, and uncertain world. If technological capabilities are present, *some* of the projects will be successful.

In spite of substantial technological uncertainty, some of the product diversifications have brought about technological diversification (i.e. new core technologies have been created), which in turn has provided a basis for further product diversification in the future.

6.2.   BACK TO THE NATIONAL LEVEL

So far, the case study has primarily dealt with technical change at the firm level. In this section the focus will shift to Denmark's specialisation in a science-based sector, and the quality and impact of the local science-base will be analysed. Even though basic research has a strong public good element to it, this is not the full agenda. Recent research by Hicks *et al.*(1994) has shown that publications produced by Japanese companies (basic research) tend to over-cite the national science system by approximately 30 per cent, which in turn suggests that the economic benefits are geographically and linguistically localised, since they are embodied in persons and institutions, and mainly transmitted through personal contacts. Similar findings have been made by Narin and Olivastro (1992) showing that national patents cite national science and vice versa. A strong position in basic research at the national level is economically important, because it provides research training, state-of-the-art development and use of research techniques and instrumentation, and access to high-quality international networks (Gibbons and Johnston, 1974; Pavitt, 1993).

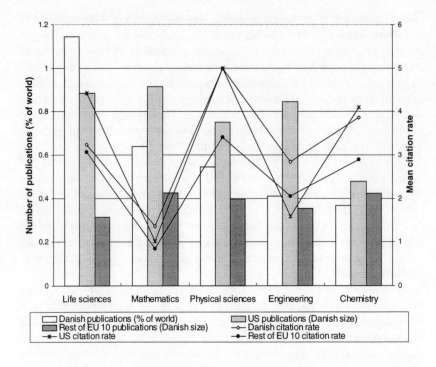

Source: Schubert, Gläzel and Braun (1989)

Figure 6.4 Number of publications and citations per paper in major scientific fields, 1981-85. Denmark versus rest of EU 10 and the USA

In addition basic research provides an important country-specific incentive to science-based firms, providing recent results from national as well as international state-of-the-art-research as an input to commercial research.

The main source used in this analysis is Schubert, Gläzel and Braun (1989), which provides a comprehensive data set based on 2649 journals, in the period 1981-85. The journal set was fixed in the sense that all journals were cited in all years. In all science-fields Denmark ranks fifth in terms of mean citation per paper, which can be applied as an imperfect proxy for the quality of the general science-base. Additionally, Denmark ranks third in terms of numbers of papers published as a percentage of world publications, adjusted for population size. It can be seen from Figure 6.4, that Danish scientists publish more papers in relation to population size (except from the field of chemistry) and has a higher mean citation ratio, than the 'rest of EU' in all science fields. The number of

Table 6.2 Relationships between country specialisation in pharmaceuticals and bibliometric variables (n=23)

RSCA54	=	-88.5	+	24.7 ASF	R^2=0.31
		(26.7)*		(8.8)*	
RSCA54	=	-80.6	+	23.5 LS	R^2=0.24
		(25.6)*		(9.1)**	
RSCA54	=	-42.5	+	0.0022 RGDP92	R^2=0.02
		(46.1)		(0.0034)	

Notes:
Standard error in brackets. */** denotes significant at the 1% and at the 5% level, respectively. Variables: *RSCA54* is the 'revealed symmetric comparative advantage' for pharmaceuticals, 1992, defined as $(RCA-1)/(RCA+1)$.

Source: The dependent variable: IKE trade database. *ASF* is the citation rate for 'all science fields' and *LS* is the citation rate for 'life sciences', 1981-85. Source: Schubert, Gläzel and Braun (1989). *RGDP92* is the real GDP per capita 1992, expressed in international prices, with base 1985. Source: Penn World Tables mark. 5.6.

Danish papers published in life-sciences is significantly above the number of papers published by the rest of EU. Bibliometric data of this kind may be misleading, however. Martin (1994) argues that since these measures take into account all scientific output, they might be biased, due to many relatively small and trivial contributions. Furthermore, scientific progress might to some extent rely on major breakthroughs (Kuhnian 'scientific revolutions'). In this context Martin suggests that a possible measure of such breakthroughs can be the number of Nobel Prizes a country has won. In the period 1957-92 Danish scientists were awarded three Nobel Prizes in the areas of Physics, Chemistry and Medicine or Physiology, which makes Denmark rank third in the world, when looking at Nobel Prizes won per citizen. Even though these figures should be taken with a pinch of salt, given the small number of observations, the numbers do indicate that Danish science has the ability to produce some major breakthroughs. Another measure of contributions to scientific breakthroughs is papers among the 1000 most cited papers in the world. Based on ISI data, Nørretranders and Haaland (1990) has shown that Denmark ranks sixth in the world, when such a measure is applied and adjusted for population size.

The importance of a strong science-base as an incentive to innovation in science-based sectors can also be examined in more quantitative terms. The relationship between the trade specialisation in pharmaceuticals and the quality of the science-base can be examined by means of cross-country regression analysis. Based on numbers of references on patents to scientific papers Narin and Olivastro (1992) showed that the linkage between science and technology is by far the strongest in pharmaceuticals, when compared to other product groups. Table 6.2 supports these results in showing that there is a significant and positive relationship between national trade specialisation in pharmaceuticals and the quality of the national science base, measured as mean citation per academic paper. There is also a positive and significant relationship between the quality of national life-sciences - which are supposed to be the sciences most closely linked to pharmaceuticals - and trade specialisation, however significant only at the 5 per cent level. Nevertheless, Patel & Pavitt (1993) show that national citation rates are correlated with GDP per head. Therefore, one would suspect that specialisation in pharmaceuticals is a simple function of GDP per capita. Nevertheless, this is not the case, as displayed in Table 6.2. Overall, the regressions in Table 6.2 point to a high quality science-base as being a necessary condition for being specialised in pharmaceuticals.

6.3. CONCLUSION AND IMPLICATIONS

As pointed out in the introduction to this chapter, three types of localised inducement mechanisms seem to have been particularly important in determining the direction of technological trajectories at the national level strongly influencing the trade specialisation pattern of advanced countries. They were (i) factor endowments; (ii) inter-sectoral linkages; and (iii) the cumulative mastery of core technologies. However, in order to identify the relative importance of these mechanisms, a number of sources of innovation were identified according to the literature on technological innovation. They were *suppliers*, *users*, *the manufacturer* and *universities*. I shall deal with these in turn.

This chapter has stressed the crucial importance of technology and product diversification, based on mastery of in-house core technologies, as inducers of technological innovation at Novo Nordisk A/S. However, interaction with upstream capital good *suppliers* does take place. Novo Nordisk does not build their highly complex fermentation factories on its own. The highly advanced electronic control equipment is for example developed together with suppliers. Nevertheless, there is no 'semi-turnkey' fermentation factory available on the market; different parts are developed together with different suppliers, since it is Novo Nordisk which have the overall fermentation competence (the overall design of the plants is conducted by Novo Nordisk). In this context the company has a big engineering department, with the single function of setting up new production capacity world-wide. But this is somehow beside the point, since the opening question of this chapter asked about important 'inducement mechanisms' to innovation. So even though suppliers play a part in the process of innovation, they can not be said to have played an important part in *inducing* innovation at Novo Nordisk. This is so, because the breakthroughs in product and process innovations have always been pioneered in the research laboratories and internal production engineering departments; suppliers have only been brought in at much later stages. These findings are in line with the results of Klevorick *et al.* (1995) who, based on attitudinal data, show that suppliers are not creating important technological opportunities in pharmaceuticals, whereas university research does.

When it comes to downstream *users*, they cannot be said to have played any significant part in inducing innovation in pharmaceuticals. In the area of biochemicals, the situation is different, since the enzymes are intermediate (capital) goods, which have a variety of uses, across sectors. Hence, the enzymes are incrementally adapted according to specific user needs. The products are often developed jointly with the user. Nonetheless, it should be stressed that the major breakthroughs in the field of biochemicals did not have any users involved.

The central source of innovation has been a combination of *the manufacturer* and related university activities. This finding is consistent with proposition (g) from Chapter 2, stating that internal technological activity is most important for specialisation in science-based sectors. In Section 6.1, the path dependent nature of technological development was demonstrated, since technology-based diversification - based on competencies developed in the context of previous products - were shown to be present and very important in the movement into enzymes, penicillin, blood products and a number of new biotechnology based products. In this context an interaction between the movement into new product areas and the adoption of new core technologies can be observed. In other words the (few) movements into new core technologies were often motivated by a wish to strengthen existing products, or by a wish to move into new product areas, which required an additional technology. The new technology could then be the basis for future product diversification. Such product diversification can take place because firms are often 'multi-technology'. Furthermore, external horizontal linkages to other firms, or to science, was strongest while assimilating new core technologies.

As mentioned in Section 6.2, the economic benefits from basic research (conducted at universities) include research training, state-of-the-art development and use of research techniques and instrumentation, and access to international professional networks. These economic benefits accrue, not only because of the research conducted by the scientists of a given country, but (mainly; at least in a small country case) because of the ability to assimilate the results of basic research conducted by other countries, an ability which in turn partly depends on the home country's ability to perform high quality basic research itself. In the Novo case, major breakthroughs were nearly always conducted at foreign universities. In this context, the *research skills* developed at Danish universities have been of utmost importance in assimilating and commercialising inventions made abroad. Another potential impact of basic research was found in many cases, through the entire history of Novo, namely the *ready access to high-quality international scientific networks*, a story which began with Krogh himself, ending up with contacts to 'centres of excellence' in biotechnology, situated in California. These more indirect impacts from national science to national technology might also assist in explaining why the correlation is stronger between the general quality of the science base (all science fields) and the degree of trade specialisation in pharmaceuticals, when compared to the more specific quality of the science bases (life sciences) and its correlation with specialisation in pharmaceuticals.

Based on the relative importance of the *manufacturer* and *universities* as the sources of innovation, compared to the importance of *users* and *suppliers*, it has to be concluded that the relatively most important inducement mechanism identified in the Novo case was the *cumulative mastery of core technologies* with multiple applications, together with related assimilation of new core technologies. In addition, the study has presented two instances where *factor endowments* constituted an inducement of innovation. The start-up of insulin production was based on the abundant availability of the raw material (animal pancreases). In addition, the initial acquisition of enzyme technology was spurred by a scarce supply of pancreases during the second world war. However, as indicated above, the case study has also demonstrated, that the importance of inducement mechanisms may change over time. Initially, factor endowments, in terms of availability of raw materials, were necessary for insulin production in Denmark, while today's more sophisticated production has lost its direct connection to the factor endowment.

But why does the importance of users and producers differ among industries? More specifically, why is user-producer interaction not so important in pharmaceuticals? One explanation is of course that technological opportunity emerges from science in the pharmaceutical industry, mainly. The research and development of e.g. capital goods can be viewed as a by-product of opportunities created by up-to-date science. In this context a distinction between directly providing technological opportunity, and science which creates technological opportunity by adding to a pool of (not necessarily new) knowledge (Klevorick *et al.*, 1995) is to be kept in mind. Whereas both the pharmaceutical industry and e.g. the industry for electronic components can be said to be science-based, since they are both heavily dependent on science in the latter sense, only *new* scientific advances are highly relevant for the pharmaceutical industry (ibid). In addition, technological leads in making capital goods for the production of pharmaceuticals were - at least in the Novo-case - important for appropriating returns from innovation, thus not being in the interest of the company to out-source the production of crucial parts of capital equipment.

An innovation system can be defined in terms of a common knowledge-base, and it is therefore more than just the sum of its parts. Previous studies (Andersen, Dalum and Villumsen, 1981; Lundvall, Olesen and Aaen, 1984) of the Danish innovation system have shown that this knowledge-base often consists of a national user-producer interaction. Nevertheless, this study has found that the most important knowledge-base can in some cases reside inside large firms and in related university activities.

The story of Novo's initial acquisition of insulin technology is to some extent the story of the importance of small events in determining the direction of technological change (Arthur, 1989). However, as contrasted to Krugman (1987) this chapter maintains that nations matter in a technological context, by showing that two country-specific factors were necessary conditions for the insulin production in Denmark, namely the availability of the raw material and the presence of high quality science. The explanation of trade-specialisation is richer than just chance and scale-economies. Hence we shall explore the explanation further in the next chapter in a more general setting.

NOTES

1. This chapter draws on Laursen (1996).

2. See Carlsson and Stankiewicz (1991) for a discussion on how technological accumulation can be related to 'technological systems'.

3. In 1992 - the only year where insulin can be detected exactly in the database - insulin made up 49 per cent of the Danish export of commodity group 'medicaments' (SITC 5415, rev. 1), while insulin made up 99 per cent of the export of the group 'hormones' (SITC 5417, rev. 1).

4. The case study draws on Richter-Friis (1991), as it provides very detailed descriptions on how the technologies were appropriated and developed at the company. The book is consistent with other sources, such as annual reports and newspaper articles.

5. Defined as SITC (rev. 3) three digit numbers 541 and 542.

6. SITC commodity group 5** (three digit), excl. pharmaceuticals (541 and 542).

7. Defined specifically as patent classes 435/70.1-75 and the complete patent class 935.

8. The Herfindahl index expresses the concentration of certain technologies (measured as patent class) involved in a given product. Thus, an index value of one implies that there is one technology (patent class) only, involved in making the product.

7. Do Inter-sectoral Linkages Matter for International Export Specialisation?[1]

Whereas the previous chapter focused on a single inducement mechanism to trade specialisation in a rather detailed manner, this chapter is broader in scope, in being an econometric analysis of several inducement mechanisms determining the direction of specialisation amongst advanced countries. Bearing in mind the lacking explanation power of the traditional factor endowment theory (see Chapter 2), but without totally discarding it, this chapter adopts a 'technology gap' approach for explaining international trade (export) specialisation, by testing the effect of two different sources of technology ('own' sector effort versus the role of national inter-sectoral linkages) on export specialisation.

Using the Pavitt taxonomy as a starting point for the reconciliation of two different inducement mechanisms, this chapter statistically investigates the importance of variables reflecting different inducement mechanisms for trade specialisation, in 19 manufacturing sectors (see Table A7.1 for a description of the sectors), across 9 OECD countries. From the discussion of the Pavitt taxonomy found in Chapter 2, the following propositions can be recapitulated: (g) *internal technological activity* is most important for specialisation in science-based sectors, but is also expected to be of some importance for scale intensive sectors; (h) *upstream and downstream linkages* are more important in the case of specialised suppliers, but should also be of importance in the case of scale intensive sectors. Downstream linkages should be of importance for supplier dominated sectors; (i) it is anticipated that investment will be important in the case of scale intensive sectors; while (j) low *labour costs* are predicted to be an important determinant of specialisation in the case of supplier dominated types of sectors.

A criticism of the taxonomy, which should be mentioned, is that industries undergo evolutions. For instance, Pavitt and colleagues (Tidd, Bessant and Pavitt, 1997), have added a fifth sector, labelled *information intensive firms*. These firms are highly innovative firms within retailing, finance and other services; a type of firm that almost did not exist in 1984. However, since our sample is confined to manufacturing sectors, we do not consider the emergence of these firms to be a relevant issue for the analysis in this chapter. It should be stressed however, that while the Pavitt taxonomy has held up reasonably well in subsequent tests (Cesaratto and Mangano, 1993; Arundel, van den Paal and Soete, 1995), it inevitably simplifies.

The chapter is organised as follows. Sub-section 7.1 starts off by briefly outlining previous empirical findings related to the topic of the current chapter, while the section ends up by taking up the discussion of what an input-output based measure of vertical linkages is really measuring, by relating to the literature on the effect of spillovers on productivity growth. Section 7.2 describes the data to be applied, as well as the empirical set-up and findings of the chapter. Finally, Section 7.3 sums up and concludes.

7.1. THE RELATION TO OTHER RESEARCH

7.1.1. Previous Empirical Work

From an empirical point of view, the technology gap theory has gained support from Soete (1981) and Dosi, Pavitt and Soete (1990). Based on cross-country regression analysis, for a single year, these two studies showed that among 40 sectors about half of these were found to be influenced in their direction by technological specialisation (measured as US patents) in the same sector. From a panel data perspective - in an aggregate country perspective - Amendola, Dosi and Papagni (1993) found convincing support for the hypothesis as well. Also applying panel data - and from a sectoral as well as a country-wise perspective - Amable and Verspagen (1995) showed that competitiveness in trade was significantly influenced by technological capabilities (US patenting) in eleven out of the eighteen sectors in question. Furthermore - while looking at bilateral trade between advanced countries - Verspagen and Wakelin (1997) found support for the hypothesis of technology being an important factor in explaining trade performance. Carlsson (1991) found that trade performance was not only determined by innovative activities in relation to products, but also by the application of advanced production technology.

Empirically, the home market hypothesis has gained some support at the descriptive level by Andersen, Dalum and Villumsen (1981) and econometrically by Fagerberg (1992; 1995). However the tests conducted by Fagerberg only applies one variable reflecting a 'backward spillover', and is not based on data on economic transactions. Instead the independent variable is the trade specialisation (Balassa figure) of a country in an 'upstream sector' with respect to the dependent variable (also measured as Balassa). This chapter will apply data on actual economic transactions (I-O data) used as weights (see Sub-section 7.2.1, below) on the technological output from upstream or downstream sectors with respect to the sector to be explained.

7.1.2. Input-output Tables as Measures of User-producer Relationships

As a starting point for this discussion, it should be stressed that linkages can be interpreted as localised 'spillovers'. However, before discussing the differences and similarities between the 'home market hypothesis' and the spillover literature, it can be useful to distinguish between rent-spillovers, as opposed to pure knowledge spillovers as done in a seminal paper by Griliches (1979). *Rent-spillovers* consist of the R&D embodied in purchased inputs. One example of this type of spillover is the contribution to aggregate productivity from the computer industry. Because of competitive pressure within the industry, the full effect could not be appropriated by the industry itself, but instead improved the productivity of purchasing firms in other industries.[2] In contrast to rent-spillovers, Griliches argues that real *knowledge spillovers* are the ideas borrowed by the research teams of industry *i* from the research results of industry *j*, and that it is not clear that this kind of borrowing is particularly related to input purchase flows.

The aim of a large part of the now large (mainly empirical) spillover literature (for important recent contributions, see Coe and Helpman, 1995; Verspagen, 1997), is to estimate the effect of technological spillovers on productivity, while the aim of the 'home market hypothesis' is to give an explanation for international trade specialisation. It should also be pointed out that spillovers can be both national or international in scope, whereas home market linkages are localised (national) per definition.

In this chapter we are going to apply an input-output measure of linkages. In the spillover literature, the input-output measure would be equivalent to rent-spillovers. The argument concerning rent-spillovers is that when commodities flow freely across sectors, the firms of a sector in question have access to the R&D stock of all sectors (in an extreme case - where all sectors' outputs are equally 'relevant' to each other), because independently of in which sector an input has been developed or improved, the firms of any sector can purchase the input and employ it in manufacturing (cf. Coe and Helpman, 1995). Hence, in comparison with the idea of rent-spillovers, the 'home market hypothesis' is a more dynamic argument, in the sense that the focus is on how *new* technologies and products are created, in terms of exchange of information between suppliers and users of a product, rather than on diffusion issues, as is dealt with in the case of rent-spillovers. Nevertheless, as real knowledge spillovers are the ideas borrowed by the research teams of industry *i* from the research results of industry *j*, one can argue that home market linkages are a particular kind of knowledge spillover, related to input purchase flows (Los, 1996).

It is also worth noting that the qualitative mechanisms, discussed by both Linder and Lundvall are hard to measure *per se*. In fact the interaction as described by both authors need not necessarily be large, as reflected in exchange of commodities between firms situated in different sectors. However, we assume in this chapter, that the quantity of useful information will on average be related to the quantity of commodities exchanged.

7.2. EMPIRICAL ANALYSIS

7.2.1. The Data

Patent data are taken from the US patent office, and concern patents, dated by the year of grant. All other data applied are taken from the OECD STAN database (1995 edition). The main limiting factor is the use of the STAN input-output tables, which are only available for nine OECD countries (Australia, Canada, Denmark, France, Germany, Great Britain, Japan, the Netherlands, and the United States). Also the input-output data are only available for five points in time (early 1970s, mid 1970s, early 1980s, mid 1980s and 1990). It should be noted that the I-O tables are not exactly from the same year. For instance, the 'mid 1970s' observation is 1974 for Australia, while this observation for Canada was obtained in 1976. Even though the inclusion of I-O data severely reduces the amount of observations, the inclusion allows for the calculation of up- and down-stream 'technology flows', based on 'real' economic transactions. Often, in this kind of study, the intensity of economic transactions between sectors is calculated on the basis of one country. Accordingly, the *intensity* of transactions between sectors of that country is then assumed to be the same in other countries in the analysis, while e.g. the structure of production differs. So this advantage has to be judged against the smaller number of observations, and a number of missing values. Concerning the selection of years, the other variables were picked so that they match the I-O data more or less (i.e 1973, 1977, 1981, 1985 and 1990).

The dependent variable is the Revealed Comparative Advantage (Balassa, 1965):

$$RCA_{ij} = \frac{X_{ij} / \sum_{i} X_{ij}}{\sum_{j} X_{ij} / \sum_{i} \sum_{j} X_{ij}}. \tag{7.1}$$

The numerator represents the percentage share of a given sector in national exports - X_{ij} are exports of sector i from country j. The denominator represents the percentage share of a given sector in OECD exports. For further details of the measure, see Chapter 3. As in the previous chapters, the index is made symmetric (the *'RSCA'*), obtained as *(RCA-1)/(RCA+1)*.

The downstream linkage-variable can be defined as:

$$DL = (y_{ab}/Y_a)P, \quad \text{for } a \neq b, \tag{7.2}$$

where y_{ab} is a matrix of the deliveries of intermediates from the sector in question and Y_a is a vector of total output. P is a vector of US patents taken out by the sectors trading with sector a (normalised for country-size), as a proxy of the technological competence of these sectors. In other words the variable measures sector b's importance as a user of sector a's output. Likewise for the upstream linkage variable:

$$UL = (y_{ab}/Y_b)P, \quad \text{for } a \neq b, \tag{7.3}$$

where Y_b is a vector of total input. Thus, the variable measures sector a's importance as a supplier to sector b.

7.2.2. Applying the Pavitt-taxonomy in an International Trade Context

Each of the 19 sectors have been assigned to the four Pavitt sectors. The classification is shown in Table A7.1. However, since any such assignment is somewhat arbitrary on the boundaries, the chosen classification deserves some comments. First of all, the classification, according to the Pavitt taxonomy, used in this chapter follows to a large extent OECD (1992), and differs only from this in the case of 'industrial chemicals'; 'instruments'; and 'fabricated metal products'. In the first two cases, the sectors are on the boundaries of the 'Pavitt sectors'. Firms in the 'industrial chemicals' sector possess both science based characteristics, but also some scale intensive characteristics, and firms in the instruments sector both carry specialised supplier characteristics, but also some science based characteristics. In both cases we opted for the original Pavitt classification, as science based and specialised suppliers respectively. If one looks at the ISIC nomenclature, under 'fabricated metal products', it can be seen that this sector produces mainly standard products (nails, screws, steelwire etc.). In contrast to the OECD, we argue that this type of production is not mainly carried out by specialised supplier firms.

The *a priori* reasons for including 'food, drink and tobacco' and 'petroleum refineries' as supplier dominated sectors, even though the firms in these sectors are probably to some extent scale-intensive, is that we are dealing with national specialisation. Thus the specialisation in these sectors is to some extent determined by what goes on in the (related) primary sectors, which in turn are supplier dominated, in addition to being influenced by natural resource availability. Other sectors on the boundary that should be mentioned are non-ferrous metals (classified as supplier dominated, but could be classified as scale intensive) and electrical machinery (classified as supplier dominated, but have some science based properties). Because of the arbitrary assignments of some of the sectors, we have made some test for sensibility to the aggregation chosen. The results of these experiments will be briefly presented at the end of this section.

For now, the empirical model can be set up as follows:

$$RSCA_{ij} = \alpha_{ij} + \beta_1 \, INV_{ij} + \beta_2 \, LC_{ij} + \beta_3 \, RSTA_{ij} + \beta_4 \, UL_{ij} + \beta_5 \, DL_{ij} + \epsilon_{ij}, \qquad (7.4)$$

where *RSCA* is the 'revealed symmetric comparative advantage'; *INV* is the equivalent measure for investment. The representation of the variable is chosen, in order to reflect the size of the capital stock in each sector, as we are dealing with levels in this chapter. A variable like the ratio of investment to production would for instance reflect the growth of the capital stock, rather than the level. In addition, we wish to treat investment and technology in an analogous way. *LC* is labour cost, measured as labour compensation per employee, in the sector in question (relative to the average). *RSTA* is 'revealed symmetric technological advantage' (see Chapter 5 for a description of this measure). *UL* is a proxy for upstream linkages with producers, measured as technological output (US patents) performed in upstream sectors (normalised for country-size), weighted by the input-output-coefficients. *DL* is finally a proxy of downstream linkages with users (technological activity, performed in downstream sectors, normalised for country-size, weighted by the output-coefficients).

Our expectations on behalf of the specific 'Pavitt-sectors' were described in the introduction in terms of the set of propositions (g)-(j). However, we do also have more general expectations, which will be described subsequently. The investment variable is expected to turn out with a positive sign, as we would expect physical capital to be a necessary condition for being specialised in a given sector. We have no specific expectation for the wage variable as it might reflect low labour costs (negative sign), as well as a high skill requirement (positive sign). The technology variable is expected to have a positive impact, as are the both of the 'linkage' variables.

Table 7.1 Regression results for explaining international trade specialisation (n=662)

Sector Type	Variable	Model (i) R² =0.40		Model (ii) R² =0.40		Model (iii) R² =0.40	
		Estimate	*p*-value	Estimate	*p*-value	Estimate	*p*-value
Supplier	*INV*	0.616	0.0000	0.612	0.0000	0.617	0.0000
dominated	*LC*	-0.107	0.1831	-0.107	0.1826	-0.108	0.1757
	RSTA	0.306	0.0023	0.336	0.0007	0.321	0.0014
	DL	0.480	0.3582				
	UL			-0.194	7395		
	PI					0.008	0.7444
Science	*INV*	0.395	0.0000	0.429	0.0000	0.411	0.0000
based	*LC*	0.059	0.1017	0.067	0.0591	0.064	0.0758
	RSTA	0.480	0.0000	0.465	0.0000	0.472	0.0000
	DL	0.339	0.2473				
	UL			-0.131	0.7109		
	PI					0.006	0.7017
Scale	*INV*	0.460	0.0000	0.453	0.0000	0.458	0.0000
intensive	*LC*	0.075	0.0000	0.071	0..0000	0.073	0.0000
	RSTA	0.077	0.4659	0.056	0.5943	0.069	0.5112
	DL	0.734	0.0085				
	UL			0.672	0.0352		
	PI					0.036	0.0092
Specialised	*INV*	0.388	0.0000	0.446	0.0000	0.416	0.0000
suppliers	*LC*	-0.036	0.0001	-0.042	0.0000	-0.039	0.0000
	RSTA	0.047	0.8143	0.227	0.2300	0.137	0.4774
	DL	1.242	0.0000				
	UL			1.244	0.0000		
	PI					0.058	0.0000

Note: Country and (Pavitt) sector specific constants documented in Table A7.2.

INV = Investment specialisation.
LC = Level of labour costs; relative to the average.
RSTA = Revealed symmetric technological advantage
DL = Downstream linkages. Technological activity, performed in downstream sectors (normalised for country-size), weighted by the output-coefficients.
UL = Upstream linkages. Technological output (patents) performed in upstream sectors (normalised for country-size), weighted by the input-output-coefficients.
PI = Principal component, based on *BL* and *FL*.

We pool all countries, all sectors, and all years, and estimate a model for the whole sample, using ordinary least squares. We shall allow for the slopes of the different variables to vary according to which Pavitt-sector each individual sector belongs. The results are reported in Table 7.1. The estimations are heteroscedasticity consistent. As country specific mechanisms are likely to be present, we included country-specific dummies in addition to the Pavitt-sector constants present in the model. The estimations of the country and (Pavitt) sector specific constants are shown in Table A7.2.

Given the presence of multicollinearity[3] between *DL* and *UL*, three separate models have been estimated. In other words, if sectors have many linkages downstream, they have many linkages upstream as well. Hence, first we estimated two separate models (models (i) and (ii)), each including *UL* and *DL*, respectively. In addition to that, principal component regression has been applied, which is one way of tackling multicollinearity. Principal component analysis is a type of factor analysis, and the analysis computes linear combinations of the original variables. Given a data set with p numerical variables, p principal components can be computed. The first principal component has the largest variance of any linear combination of the observed variables, and the last principal component has the smallest variance of any linear combination of the observed variables. In other words, each principal component maximises 'the explained residual variance' in p rounds. As the synthetic variables (i.e. the principal components) are jointly uncorrelated, by definition, the methodology can sometimes be useful in addressing multicollinearity. Thus, in Table 7.1 synthetic variables have been computed for *UL* and *DL* (model iii). Only the first principal component is used in the regressions, as the explained variance exceeds 0.86. In other words, we only leave out 14 per cent of the variance of the two variables. The parameters of the so-called factor loadings (i.e. the parameters relating the original variables to the principal components) display identical signs (positive); i.e. the contribution of each of the two original variables to the first of the principal components goes in the same direction.

Specification tests are reported in Table 7.2. Using the Chow test, the null hypothesis of no structural change (across the five time periods included) cannot be rejected at any reasonable level (F-values of around 0.03). For what concerns normality of the error terms, the null hypothesis of normality cannot be rejected at a very high level, using the Jarque-Bera test.

The results of the estimations for the *supplier dominated sectors* are found in the top of Table 7.1. It can be seen that the first principal component (i.e. the synthetic combination of *UL* and *DL*) is not significant[4], indicating that national linkages do not appear to be of importance for specialisation in these sectors. However, from proposition (h) we would have expected upstream linkages to be of importance for specialisation in this type of sector. One possible explanation for this might be that strongholds of countries in these sectors are to some extent determined by the ability to absorb technology developed elsewhere. If that is the case, upstream linkages need not be national. *LC* and

Table 7.2 Specification tests for the regressions

	Model (i)	Model (ii)	Model (iii)
	p-value	*p*-value	*p*-value
Chow test (poolability over time)	1.0000	1.0000	1.0000
Jarque-Bera test	0.4155	0.5130	0.4475

INV come up with the expected signs, although *LC* is insignificant [proposition (j)]. Surprisingly enough technological specialisation appears to be positively related to export specialisation. While this finding is not untenable, it should be pointed out that these sectors might be particularly influenced by natural resource availability, such as arable land, forest, oil and so on. Since such factors are not included in the present chapter, the regressions, presented in Table 7.1, might be exposed to mis-specification in relation to the supplier dominated types of sectors.

As expected [proposition (g)], with regard to the *science-based sectors*, the coefficients for technological specialisation are found to be highly significant. The coefficient is relatively high, both when compared to the other variables in the regression, but even more so, when compared to the other types of sectors. In contrast, the insignificant linkages confirm the findings of Klevorick *et al.* (1995) and Chapter 6, concluding that inter-sectoral linkages do not seem to be of critical importance for science-based sectors more generally, and for pharmaceuticals in particular.

For what concerns *scale intensive sectors* a number of points should be made. First of all, the (direct) technology variable does not seem to be of importance for these sectors, in contrast to what was expected from proposition (g). Secondly, investment is (also) highly significant in this case [in line with proposition (i)]. Thirdly, it is worth noting that the wage variable is significant, but that it has a positive sign, thus probably implying the importance of high-skill requirements for human capital in these sectors. Finally, the linkage variables are significant in this case, as we would expect for one of the two 'production intensive' types of sectors [consistent with proposition (h)].

The results with regard to the *specialised supplier* type of sectors, display a negative correlation between trade specialisation and relative labour costs of the sectors. In other words, those countries which are specialised in these sectors, also appear to have the relatively lowest labour costs, although the parameter is rather small. Both of the linkage variables are significant, and have a high parameter. This finding corresponds neatly to the idea, stated in proposition (h), that specialised suppliers have the most technological linkages to the surrounding system (cf. Figure 7.1).

Finally, we reclassified 'food, drink and tobacco'; 'petroleum refineries'; and 'non-ferrous metals' to scale intensive sectors from supplier dominated sectors, and 'electrical machinery' to science based from specialised supplier sectors, in order to test for the sensitivity to the chosen 'sectoral affiliation'. The results of this experiment display (not explicitly documented for reasons of space), that for supplier dominated sectors only investment is significant. In this context it should be pointed out that only 'textiles, footwear and leather' is left in this Pavitt sector. For science based sectors, investment and US patent specialisation are robust to the change made. For scale intensive sectors investment, labour costs and the linkage variables are all robust to the changes made, while the parameter for the technology variable becomes positive and significant, given the changes made. For specialised suppliers, investment and the linkage variables retain their sign and significance.

7.3.   CONCLUSIONS

This chapter has distinguished two approaches, within the broad label 'technology gap' theory. One of them has emphasised the importance of own technological activity of the sectors or firms in question, while another approach has emphasised the importance of up- and downstream technological linkages.

Thus we estimated a model including all time periods, all countries and all sectors, but allowing for different slopes, according to which Pavitt-sector each individual sector belongs (as well as allowing for sector and country specific constants). The results displayed that investment in physical capital appears to be important for all types of sectors. Labour costs had a negative impact in the case of specialised supplier types of sectors, whereas the positive relationship for scale intensive sectors might well imply the importance of high skilled labour in these sectors. Revealed technological advantage had the expected positive impact for science-based sectors, but surprisingly also a positive impact for supplier dominated sectors. The linkage variables appeared to be important for scale intensive sectors, but even more so for specialised supplier sectors. This is much in accordance with what was expected. In *general* it can be concluded that the findings of this chapter are in line with the set of propositions found in the introduction, although a couple of exceptions were found.

Hence, it seems fair to conclude that the two types of technological activities, discussed in Chapter 2, namely technological activities in the 'own' sector, and inter-sectoral linkages are both important in the determination of national export specialisation patterns. However, the importance differs according to the mode of innovation in each type of sector.

NOTES

1. This chapter draws on Laursen and Drejer (1999).

2. In should be pointed out that rent spillovers are mainly related to the market structure in the technology producing industry, rather than being true externalities in the strict sense of the word (Griliches, 1979; Verspagen, 1997).

3. The variance inflation factor (VIF) displays high values for *UL* & *DL*, which indicates that these variables might be involved in multicollinarity. For the ith independent variable, the variance inflation factor is determined as $1/(1-R^2_i)$, where R^2_i is the coefficient of determination for the regression of the ith independent variable on all other independent variables. The VIF statistic show how multicollinarity has increased the instability of the coefficient estimates.

4. More generally, the results based on the application of principal components did not differ in any dramatic way from the results of the estimation based on separate estimations of *UL* and *DL*.

Table A7.1 Sectors used in the analysis; classified according to Pavitt sector; and compared to other studies applying the Pavitt taxonomy

		Pavitt (1984)	Amable/Verspagen (1995)	OECD (1992)	This chapter
1	Food, drink and tobacco	SCAI	SDOM	SDOM	SDOM
2	Textiles, footwear and leather	SDOM	SDOM	SDOM	SDOM
3	Wood, cork and furniture	-	-	SDOM	-
4	Paper and printing	-	-	SCAI	-
5	Industrial chemicals	SCIB	SCIB	SCAI	SCIB
6	Pharmaceuticals	SCIB	SCIB	SCIB	SCIB
7	Petroleum refineries (oil)	-	-	SDOM	SDOM
8	Rubber and plastics	-	PROD	SCAI	SCAI
9	Stone, clay and glass	SCAI	PROD	SCAI	SCAI
10	Ferrous metals	SCAI	PROD	SCAI	SCAI
11	Non-ferrous metals	SCAI	PROD	SDOM	SDOM
12	Fabricated metal products	SCAI?	PROD	SDOM	SCAI
13	Non-electrical machinery	SPEC	PROD	SPEC	SPEC
14	Office machines and computers	SCIB	SCIB	SCIB	SCIB
15	Electrical machinery	SPEC	SCIB	SPEC	SPEC
16	Communic. eq. and semiconduct.	SCIB	SCIB	SCIB	SCIB
17	Shipbuilding	SCAI	PROD	SCAI	SCAI
18	Other transport	-	PROD	SCAI	SCAI
19	Motor vehicles	SCAI	PROD	SCAI	SCAI
20	Aerospace	-	SCIB	-	SCAI
21	Instruments	SPEC	PROD	SCIB	SPEC

Notes:

SDOM = Supplier dominated
SCAI = Scale intensive
SPEC = Specialised suppliers
SCIB = Science-based
PROD = Production intensive (SPEC+SCAI)
–   = Not included in the analysis

Table A7.2 Country specific effects for the regression (n=662)

Sector Type	Effect	Model (i) Estimate	p-value	Model (ii) Estimate	p-value	Model (iii) Estimate	p-value
Supplier	Australia	-0.080	0.5440	0.000	0.9981	-0.021	0.8393
dominated	Canada	-0.017	0.8915	0.062	0.6091	0.042	0.6543
	Denmark	0.156	0.1928	0.237	0.0336	0.220	0.0103
	France	0.100	0.4351	0.192	0.1163	0.162	0.0810
	Germany	0.099	0.4131	0.190	0.0938	0.166	0.0564
	Great Britain	0.131	0.2770	0.223	0.0524	0.196	0.0221
	Japan	-0.008	0.9519	0.091	0.4549	0.061	0.5172
	The Netherlands	0.084	0.4907	0.149	0.2039	0.138	0.1214
	United States	-0.009	0.9457	0.089	0.4760	0.056	0.5687
Science	Australia	-0.296	0.0000	-0.251	0.0003	-0.262	0.0001
based	Canada	-0.234	0.0000	-0.190	0.0012	-0.199	0.0002
	Denmark	-0.060	0.2265	-0.014	0.7931	-0.022	0.6617
	France	-0.117	0.0223	-0.059	0.3056	-0.080	0.1075
	Germany	-0.118	0.0175	-0.062	0.2695	-0.075	0.1097
	Great Britain	-0.086	0.0613	-0.029	0.5819	-0.046	0.3182
	Japan	-0.224	0.0000	-0.161	0.0038	-0.181	0.0009
	The Netherlands	-0.133	0.0120	-0.102	0.0770	-0.103	0.0528
	United States	-0.225	0.0001	-0.162	0.0074	-0.185	0.0002
Scale	Australia	-0.406	0.0000	-0.402	0.0000	-0.316	0.0000
intensive	Canada	-0.343	0.0000	-0.341	0.0000	-0.253	0.0000
	Denmark	-0.170	0.0000	-0.165	0.0001	-0.075	0.0324
	France	-0.226	0.0000	-0.210	0.0000	-0.133	0.0000
	Germany	-0.227	0.0000	-0.213	0.0000	-0.129	0.0001
	Great Britain	-0.195	0.0000	-0.180	0.0002	-0.099	0.0028
	Japan	-0.333	0.0000	-0.312	0.0000	-0.234	0.0000
	The Netherlands	-0.242	0.0000	-0.253	0.0000	-0.157	0.0000
	United States	-0.335	0.0000	-0.313	0.0000	-0.239	0.0000
Specialised	Australia	-0.310	0.0000	-0.310	0.0000	-0.155	0.0063
suppliers	Canada	-0.247	0.0000	-0.248	0.0000	-0.092	0.0116
	Denmark	-0.074	0.1178	-0.072	0.0990	0.085	0.0115
	France	-0.130	0.0056	-0.117	0.0069	0.027	0.3889
	Germany	-0.131	0.0040	-0.120	0.0037	0.031	0.2795
	Great Britain	-0.099	0.0145	-0.087	0.0166	0.061	0.0252
	Japan	-0.238	0.0000	-0.219	0.0000	-0.074	0.0350
	The Netherlands	-0.146	0.0013	-0.160	0.0003	0.004	0.9230
	United States	-0.239	0.0000	-0.220	0.0000	-0.079	0.0092

PART IV

The Effects of International Specialisation

8. The Impact of Technological Opportunity on the Dynamics of Trade Performance[1]

The traditional explanation for trade flows assumed that technology was equally available to all countries and had its focus on factor endowments, and hence concentrated on factor prices. However, empirical studies show that price effects are rather weak, if at all significant (see e.g. Bairam, 1988). However, alternative theoretical explanations can been found in different strands of literature. Within the neoclassical New Trade Theories, authors like Paul Krugman (1985) have stressed the importance of technology as an explanation, in terms of product differentiation and increasing returns to scale on the supply side, as well as in terms of differences in consumer preferences on the demand side. Within the framework of evolutionary economics, e.g. Dosi *et al.*(1994) has underlined the importance of sector and country specific learning processes resulting in (stochastic or 'uncertain') technological innovations, in determining trade flows. Because it is assumed in evolutionary approaches, that agents have limited computational capabilities, the so-called mechanism of transmission secures a certain degree of stability in trade specialisation patterns.

Common to all of the approaches mentioned so far in this chapter, is that they have considered various *resources* only, as determinants of trade flows. However, as pointed out in Chapter 2 various theoretical contributions predict [stated in proposition (k)] that the growth rate of an economy (including the rate of growth in exports) depends, at least partly, on what the country is specialised in and how the specialisation pattern changes over time. This proposition can be termed the Ricardian or the specialisation-based growth proposition.

This chapter shares common characteristics with the papers of Fagerberg (1988) and Amendola, Dosi and Papagni (1993) in exploring the determinants of market share dynamics ('or competitiveness') at the aggregate level of the country. Still, those papers aim at examining the effect of general technological activity on trade performance. The question which this chapter aims at answering concerns whether countries' specialisation in, or movement into sectors offering high levels of technological opportunity (proxied by growth in US patents) has any effect on the growth of export market shares of countries.

The remainder of the chapter is organised as follows. Section 8.1, starts off with a presentation of the data to be used (Sub-section 8.1.1), as well as with a presentation of growth rates, related to the average, in both trade and technology (Sub-section 8.1.2). Subsequently, the 'structural decomposition analysis'

133

methodology to be applied is presented and the results of the analysis will be discussed, both for what concerns technological development and for the development of trade performance (Sub-section 8.1.3). Sub-section 8.1.4 contains regression analysis, applying the decomposed effects (as well as other variables) from Sub-section 8.1.3 in an attempt to assess the impact on aggregate export performance of countries' ability to get access to sectors with low versus high degrees of technological opportunity. Section 8.2 concludes.

8.1. EMPIRICAL ANALYSIS

8.1.1. Technological Opportunity and Trade Growth

Hence, following the 'technology gap' approach presented above (i.e. assuming that technology is an important determinant of trade growth and that technology is not perfectly 'fluid' across countries), one would expect countries' ability to expand markets shares to be affected by whether the countries manage to get into the sectors offering high (low) levels of technological opportunity. It should be stressed that the focus of this chapter is not on what creates differences in technological opportunities, but on how differences in getting access to sectors containing high levels of technological opportunities might affect trade performance at the country level.

8.1.2. The Data

In order to avoid too much influence of cyclical variations in export market shares (expressed in current prices), four 'peak' years were selected from the IKE trade database; namely 1965, 1973, 1979 and 1988 (for a description of the database, see Appendix A4.1). These years broadly correspond to peaks in business and trade cycles. Concerning the country patenting in the US, these data were chosen to correspond to the trade data. However, because of problems of small numbers the patents[2] were aggregated three years back, so that, for example, the first observation in terms of patents consists of the years 1963-64-65; and the last observation consists of the years 1986-87-88. Another reason for such a procedure is that technological development is expected to influence trade performance with some lag. The patent data used is taken from the US patent office, and concerns patent grants, dated by the year of grant.

Before exploring the relationship between technological opportunity and development in export market shares, we take a closer look at how fast the 17 sectors have grown from 1965 to 1988, both in terms of trade and technology.

Table 8.1 Annual growth rates expressed in percent of total world patenting in the US and of total OECD exports to the world 1965-88. Relative to the average

	1965-88	
	Patents	Exports
Food, drink and tobacco	-30.69	-12.21
Textiles, footwear and leather	23.28	-15.51
Industrial chemicals	-22.32	6.60
Pharmaceuticals	246.90	6.10
Rubber and plastics	39.78	12.84
Stone, clay and glass	16.18	-3.91
Basic metals	2.20	-20.41
Fabricated metal products	-50.52	-9.48
Non-electrical machinery	-80.51	-6.76
Office machines and computers	128.23	47.49
Electrical machinery	-16.44	11.01
Communication eq. and semiconductors	89.11	29.32
Shipbuilding	-106.28	-29.68
Other transport	-77.44	-17.32
Motor vehicles	12.84	16.83
Aircraft	-55.99	-1.43
Instruments	91.62	11.44
Standard deviation	88.34	19.36

Source: IKE trade database & patent data delivered to MERIT by the US Department of Commerce, Patent and Trademark Office.

Table 8.1 shows that annual growth rates in terms of trade and technology, related to the averages, are related to each other.[3] When sectors grow faster than average of the world total in technology, sectors also seem to grow faster in terms of exports. There are exceptions however; the sectors textiles, footwear and leather; stone, clay and glass; basic metals; and electrical machinery all have different signs.

The table also shows that the growth rates in relation to the mean are much more dispersed (measured by the standard deviation) across sectors in technological activity, than are the growth rates in export growth across sectors.

8.1.3. Structural Decomposition Analysis

One way of looking at the dynamics of technological activity can be by way of applying a 'structural decomposition analysis' (SD) methodology, often used in an empirical trade context (cf. Fagerberg and Sollie, 1987), here known as constant market share (CMS) analysis. This chapter is going to apply SD analysis to technology, as well as to exports.

In the case of technology, the starting point is whether or not a country manages to get more US patents granted as a percentage of total world US patenting over time, between two periods. As an example, Canada's share of the world's US patenting activity made up 1.28 per cent in 1965, rising to 1.76 per cent in 1988, this being equivalent to a growth rate of 37.9 per cent. The basic idea of the method is then to decompose the growth rate, in such a way that structural change gets isolated. It is then possible to say something about whether a rise (or fall) of a country's share of world US patenting is due to (i) the 'right' ('or wrong') specialisation pattern; (ii) a movement into sectors with fast-growing (or stagnating) technological activity; (iii) a movement out of sectors with generally stagnating technological activity (or fast-growing); and finally (iv) whether the rise (or fall) is due to the fact that the country has gained shares of patenting, assuming that the structure is the same in the two periods in question.

Below is a presentation of the methodology to be applied. Superscript t-1 denotes the starting year, while t denotes the end year. Δ denotes a change from year t-1 to year t.

$$p_j = \sum_i P_{ij} / \sum_i \sum_j P_{ij} \qquad \text{(a country's aggregate share of total world patents);}$$

$$p_{ij} = P_{ij} / \sum_j P_{ij} \qquad \text{(a country's share of a given sector in terms of patents);}$$

$$o_i = \sum_j P_{ij} / \sum_i \sum_j P_t \qquad \text{(a sector's share of total world patents),}$$

where P_{ij} denotes patents granted to firms in country j in sector i. The rate of change of a given country's aggregate share of total world patents (Δp_j) can be decomposed into:

$$\Delta p_j = \sum_i (\Delta p_{ij} o_i^{t-1}) + \sum_i (p_{ij}^{t-1} \Delta o_i) + \sum_i (\Delta p_{ij} \Delta o_i). \qquad (8.1)$$

Technology	Structural	Technology
share effect	technology effect	adaptation effect

Thus, the technology share effect measures whether a country is gaining or losing shares of world patents, assuming a fixed structure in the two periods.

The structural technology effect measures whether a country is gaining or losing patent shares because of a 'right' or a 'wrong' specialisation pattern. Finally, the technology adaptation effect measures whether a country is gaining or losing shares because of an active movement into (or out of) the 'right' sectors or a movement out of (or into) the 'wrong' sectors. However, since for instance, a positive value of the latter effect can be caused by either a movement into 'right', or a movement out of the 'wrong' sectors, it can be useful to further decompose the 'technology adaptation effect' and distinguish between a 'technology growth adaptation effect' (positive, if a country moves into the fast-growing sectors) and a 'technology stagnation adaptation effect' (positive, if a country moves out of the stagnating sectors):

$$\sum_i (\Delta p_{ij} \Delta o_i) = \sum_i (\Delta p_{ij} (\Delta o_i + |\Delta o_i|)/2) + \sum_i (\Delta p_{ij} (\Delta o_i - |\Delta o_i|)/2). \qquad (8.2)$$

| Technology | Technology growth | Technology stagnation |
| adaptation effect | adaptation effect | adaptation effect |

Thus, in other words, if (8.2) is inserted into (8.1), the four components, namely 'the technology share effect', 'the structural technology effect', 'the technology growth adaptation effect', and the 'technology stagnation adaptation effect' add up to the total rate of change (Δp_j) of a given country's share of the world's total patents granted in the US.

The relative growth of a sector in terms of patents arguably reflects, whether growth in technological opportunity is relatively high or low in that sector. In this way e.g. Cantwell and Andersen (1996) and Meliciani and Simonetti (1998) have applied growth rates of patents as measures of technological opportunities. Applying the results of the Yale Survey as a more direct indicator of technological opportunity Nelson and Wolff (1997) showed that technological opportunity and R&D intensity are indeed closely related.[4] If growth rates in patents are used as a proxy for technological opportunities, a possible interpretation of the three latter effects is that these effects measure a given country's access to sectors with relatively high levels of technological opportunity.

If the structural effect for a country is positive and high, this means that the country has been 'fortunately' specialised in the initial year; being specialised in sectors which have generally experienced high levels of technological opportunity (indicated by high levels of patenting growth). Following the same logic, if the two latter effects are high and positive, it indicates that a country has *actively* moved into sectors with higher levels of technological opportunity (the growth adaptation effect), or actively moved out of a sector with lower technological opportunity (the stagnation adaptation effect).

A drawback using the SD methodology on patents is that it is well known that the propensity to patent differs across sectors (Levin *et al.*, 1987; Pavitt, 1988). As the methodology applies first differences, large sectors will tend to grow faster than small sectors. However, this problem is common to all studies looking at aggregate patenting (e.g. Fagerberg, 1988; Amendola, Dosi and Papagni, 1993).[5] An alternative procedure could, in the present setting, be to use a specialisation figure for the fastest growing sectors (say the top 20 per cent) as e.g. done by Cantwell and Andersen (1996) and by Meliciani and Simonetti (1998). However, such a procedure suffers from the exclusion of a large part of the variation in the data material. The SD analysis looks at all the data. A more general problem in applying SD analysis is the fact that it is looking at the development of shares. When looking at shares, a country might appear to be doing badly because other countries (e.g. newly industrialised countries) are doing very well, when in fact the domestic performance of that country is rather good. While this chapter argues that the SD methodology is well suited for the analysis of the effects of specialisation and structural change on performance, the drawbacks of the methodology should be kept in mind.

The decomposition can also be conducted for growth in export market shares:

$$\Delta x_j = \sum_i (\Delta x_{ij} y_i^{t-1}) + \sum_i (x_{ij}^{t-1} \Delta y_i) + \sum_i (\Delta x_{ij} \frac{\Delta y_i + |\Delta y_i|}{2}) + \sum_i (\Delta x_{ij} \frac{\Delta y_i - |\Delta y_i|}{2}), \quad (8.3)$$

| Market share effect | Structural market effect | Market growth adaptation effect | Market stagnation adaptation effect |

where:

$x_j = \sum_i X_{ij} / \sum_i \sum_j X_i$ (a country's aggregate share of OECD exports to the world);

$x_{ij} = X_{ij} / \sum_j X_{ij}$ (a country's share of a given sector in terms of exports);

$y_i = \sum_j X_{ij} / \sum_i \sum_j X_i$ (a sector's share of total OECD exports to the world),

where X_{ij} denotes exports by firms situated in country j in sector i.

Table 8.2 displays the results of the 'constant market share' calculations. Generally speaking, 'catching up' countries (such as Japan, Austria, Finland, Greece, Ireland, Italy, Portugal, Spain and Turkey)[6] have had high levels of growth rates in terms of aggregate exports. The initial (1965) sectoral specialisation of these countries has, however, had a significant negative impact on the overall export performance, since the structural market effect is negative for all these 'catch up' countries. Likewise most of these countries (all, except Japan) have further moved into sectors offering low levels of market opportunity, as displayed by the negative impact of the 'market stagnation effect' on overall performance. The reason for these countries moving increasingly into sectors offering low levels of market opportunity might be path-dependence (David, 1985; Arthur, 1989) in trade specialisation, as countries might deepen their specialisation in sectors where already strong (Krugman, 1987), disregarding the fact that these sectors might be offering low market opportunities. The table also shows that only a small group of countries has been initially specialised in sectors offering high levels of market opportunity, namely initially rich countries such as the US, Germany, Switzerland and the UK. Thus, these countries appear to have benefited from the observed strong stability in export specialisation (Dalum, Laursen and

Table 8.2 Changes in market shares of total OECD exports to the world 1965-88

Country	Share 1965	Share 1988	Total Change (%)	MS-effect	Structural market effect	Market growth adap.ef.	Market stagnation adap.ef.
Canada	3.90	4.25	8.84	1.10	-8.34	10.57	5.51
USA	21.20	14.64	-30.92	-37.49	8.43	-6.90	5.03
Japan	8.24	16.21	96.76	70.19	-13.40	39.81	0.16
Austria	1.22	1.60	31.20	47.00	-15.51	8.04	-8.35
Belgium	5.66	4.51	-20.32	-11.79	-13.46	-0.15	5.08
Denmark	2.01	1.38	-31.32	-17.88	-16.15	-1.34	4.05
Finland	0.42	0.72	72.66	116.27	-23.19	12.56	-32.97
France	8.72	8.77	0.50	4.77	-1.64	-2.35	-0.29
Germany	16.89	18.19	7.68	7.40	7.40	-3.93	-3.20
Greece	0.15	0.25	70.18	140.92	-23.62	1.18	-48.30
Ireland	0.37	1.05	187.28	165.66	-23.88	65.07	-19.57
Italy	6.31	7.05	11.65	26.79	-0.94	-5.60	-8.60
Netherlands	5.21	5.05	-3.07	4.57	-2.52	-3.97	-1.16
Norway	1.17	0.78	-33.68	-10.61	-24.45	-0.23	1.62
Portugal	0.43	0.56	29.14	62.71	-20.90	5.72	-18.40
Spain	0.65	2.05	214.69	239.51	-17.04	39.50	-47.28
Sweden	2.63	2.27	-13.57	-13.86	-0.38	-5.44	6.11
Switzerland	2.78	2.73	-1.54	1.85	5.62	-5.89	-3.11
Turkey	0.13	0.58	359.38	535.21	-29.60	15.95	-162.18
United Kingdom	11.93	7.37	-38.23	-36.85	5.01	-9.64	3.25

Source: Calculations based on the IKE trade database

Villumsen, 1998).

Table 8.3 shows the results of the 'constant technology share' analysis. It can be seen that most 'catching up' countries (Japan, Finland, Ireland, Spain, Austria, Italy and Turkey) have experienced very high levels of growth in terms of technology, measured as shares of US patents. At the same time these countries generally appear to have been specialised in the 'wrong' (i.e. sectors offering lows levels of technological opportunity) sectors in 1965, since the structural technology effect is negative for most of these countries. An interesting feature is that in 1965 Japan already tended to be specialised in sectors offering higher levels of technological opportunity than the average in the period 1965-88. This is to be compared with the Japanese export specialisation in 1965, which offered relatively low levels of market opportunities in the period 1965-88. Thus, early on Japan were already specialised in the technologies, which grew above the average in the period 1965-88. Both with regard to adjustment into sectors offering high levels of technological opportunity and especially with regard to the active movement

Table 8.3 Change in shares of world patenting in the US by country 1965-88

Country	Share 1965	Share 1988	Total Change (%)	TS-effect	Structural technology effect	Technology growth adap.ef.	Technology stagnation adap.ef.
Canada	1.28	1.76	37.95	46.65	-5.75	4.85	-7.80
USA	79.87	51.32	-35.74	-35.70	0.06	-4.83	4.72
Japan	1.28	20.78	1523.27	1412.04	8.00	252.01	-148.77
Austria	0.20	0.44	114.17	138.11	0.89	2.66	-27.49
Belgium	0.27	0.37	34.72	37.37	6.32	-1.18	-7.80
Denmark	0.14	0.24	70.24	80.38	-2.11	6.10	-14.12
Finland	0.03	0.30	857.71	983.23	-10.76	69.21	-183.97
France	2.18	3.47	59.41	61.23	-0.84	7.15	-8.12
Germany	5.52	9.96	80.42	92.91	1.07	3.35	-16.90
Greece	0.01	0.01	66.45	64.03	8.19	3.04	-8.81
Ireland	0.00	0.05	1221.44	1204.65	-16.44	171.77	-138.54
Italy	0.71	1.41	96.83	108.49	-2.26	10.17	-19.58
Netherlands	0.82	1.11	36.03	31.04	7.72	2.39	-5.12
Norway	0.08	0.14	75.29	92.20	-12.51	11.16	-15.57
Portugal	0.01	0.01	-8.91	7.50	-6.73	-10.41	0.74
Spain	0.06	0.15	158.26	188.36	-5.30	12.30	-37.11
Sweden	0.86	1.11	29.04	42.05	-5.42	0.74	-8.33
Switzerland	1.51	1.70	12.52	19.63	-2.53	0.37	-4.95
Turkey	0.00	0.01	361.74	263.99	-10.36	106.72	1.38
United Kingdom	4.24	3.45	-18.64	-19.16	-1.04	-1.41	2.97

Source: Calculations based on data from the US Patent and Trademark Office

into sectors offering high levels of market opportunity, Japan has done extraordinarily well, since e.g. the 'market growth adaptation effect' made up 40 per cent of the increase in export market shares of 97 per cent (from a relatively high level). Thus, it would seem that the Japan has had a strong ability to adjust to changes in opportunities in both trade and technology. This finding is in line with the observations of Freeman (1988), who furthermore argues that social and institutional changes played a major role in this context.

8.1.4. The role of Technological Opportunity in Competitiveness

This section is going to apply some of the SD effects from the previous section as explanatory variables (as well as other variables) in regression analysis, in attempting to explain market share dynamics. In order to reach conclusions, an empirical model of the determinants of growth of aggregate market shares will be tested. The model to be tested is:

$$\hat{x}_j = \alpha_j + \beta_1 U\hat{L}C_j + \beta_2 INV_j + \beta_3 TL_j + \beta_4 DUS_j + \beta_5 S\hat{M}E_j + \beta_6 S\hat{T}E_j + \beta_7 T\hat{G}AE_j + \epsilon_j. \qquad (8.4)$$

The dependent variable is the growth of aggregate market shares across countries. The independent variables are growth in unit labour costs (*ULC*); the investment-output ratio (*INV*, a proxy for the growth of the capital stock); a proxy of the technological level of a country, relative to the world leader (*TL*); a dummy for the US (*DUS*); a proxy for the effect of structural change in world demand (*SME*, i.e. the structural market effect from Table 8.2); a proxy for the effect of change in technological opportunity (*STE*, i.e. the structural technology effect from Table 8.3); and finally a proxy for the ability of countries to actively move into sectors with above average growth in technological opportunities (*TGAE*, i.e. the technology growth adaptation effect from Table 8.3). The observations from the three sub-periods (1965-73, 1973-79 and 1979-88) are pooled. Since some of the additional variables are not available for Turkey and Portugal these countries are excluded in the present part of the analysis. Since data (export data) are only missing for Australia in 1965, Australia was included.

The unit labour costs, investment, GDP and population data have been taken from OECD Economic Outlook and Reference Supplement (No. 59). The growth in unit labour costs is expressed as annual growth rates. Both the growth of unit labour cost variable and the investment variable are expressed in relation to the average values of the 19 countries for each period. This procedure has been followed, since the export variable is expressed in relation to the total (as shares).

The investment variable is used as a proxy of the growth of 'physical production equipment, transport equipment and infrastructure', in the same manner as done by Fagerberg (1988). The *TL* variable is constructed in order to pick up effects, related to catching-up (see Verspagen, 1993, for a discussion of theories of catch-up). The variable is analogous to a variable used by Fagerberg (1988). Following Fagerberg, the variable is calculated as per capita patenting activity in the US, divided by the highest value found in the sample in each period, adjusted for the degree of openness of the economy.[7] Thus, the variable varies between 1 (the country at the world's technological frontier in the initial year) and 0 (a hypothetical country with no technological activity in the initial year). However, Fagerberg used a synthetic mix of the R&D measure and US patent data. But since the weight of the measures is somewhat arbitrary, the patent measure was chosen on its own.

Also included in the model is the measure of the impact of change in world demand on the market share of the individual country (*SME*). The measures of technological opportunity are the structural technology effects (*STE*) and the technology adaptation effects (*TGAE*). Because it is expected that US firms have relatively many patents due to a 'home-market' effect, a dummy for the US is included in the regressions (*DUS*).

Concerning the signs of the variables, the sign of the dummy for the US; the sign of the catch-up variable; as well as the sign of the unit labour cost measure are expected to be negative. Nevertheless, the labour cost measure deserves a brief discussion. From a production cost perspective, one would expect high wage costs to lead to low competitiveness. Regardless, high growth in wage costs might also reflect highly growing skill levels (as argued in Chapter 7), so that low growth of wages implies low growth in levels of skills. Thus, in some sectors with high-skill requirements, the sign might be positive. However, as the estimated model is a macro model, a negative sign is expected. The other variables are expected to have positive signs.

The results of the regressions are displayed in Table 8.4. Specification tests are reported at the bottom of the table. Using the Chow test, the null hypothesis of no structural change (across the three time periods included) cannot be rejected at the 1 per cent level. For what concerns normality of the error terms, the null hypothesis of normality cannot be rejected at any reasonable level, using the Jarque-Bera test. The estimations are heteroscedasticity consistent (using the White estimator).

The estimate of the growth of unit labour costs has the expected sign, but is not significant. This observation might be due to the fact that the model estimated in this chapter is of a long-term nature, while price factors such as *ULC*, might be more important in the shorter run. The catching-up variable has

Table 8.4 Regression results for the impact technological opportunity on aggregate trade performance (n=57)

Variable	Model (i) $R^2 = 0.38 \ (0.29)$		Model (ii) $R^2 = 0.38 \ (0.29)$	
	Estimate	*p*-value	Estimate	*p*-value
k	-1.49	0.8724	-20.9	0.8192
ULC	-0.12	0.2390	-0.01	0.2876
INV	0.24	0.0031	0.06	0.0018
TL	-39.63	0.3852	-36.96	0.4423
DUS	21.17	0.6007	62.36	0.6759
SME	1.56	0.0239	1.62	0.0187
STE	1.44	0.1085	0.01	0.0778
TGAE	1.30	0.0000		
TTG			0.08	0.0000
Chow test		0.0299		0.0276
Jarque-Bera test		0.3210		0.8089

Note: Adjusted R^2 in brackets.

ULC = Growth in unit labour costs; relative to the average
INV = Investment-output ratio; relative to the average
TL = Technological level of a country, relative to the world leader
DUS = Dummy for the US
SME = Structural market effect
STE = Structural technology effect
TGAE = Technology growth adaptation effect
TTG = Total technology growth

the expected sign, but is also insignificant as is the dummy for the US. The non-price factors all have the expected positive signs. The demand variable, i.e. the measure of being specialised (initially) in the fastest growing sectors in terms of exports is significant. Also significant, at the 1 per cent level, is the proxy for the growth of 'physical production equipment, transport equipment and infrastructure' (*INV*).

Of the 'technological opportunity variables' only the technology adaptation growth effect is significant at the 1 per cent level, whereas the variable reflecting the effect of being initially specialised in sectors offering above average technological opportunity (*STE*) is insignificant. Thus, it can be concluded that it appears to be more important for countries to actively move into sectors offering above average technological opportunity, rather than being 'fortunately' specialised initially.

It would have been desirable to have included a proxy for the total growth of technological activity in a country in the model, as well as the variables capturing technological opportunity. However, due to problems of multicollinearity, the total growth of technological activity (*TTG*) could not be included in the same model as the technology growth adaptation effect (*TGAE*). Hence, an additional model have been estimated (model (ii)), including the *TTG* variable instead of the *TGAE* variable. However, the two models fare equally well, and the *TGAE* and the *TTG* variables are both significant at the 1 per cent level.

8.2. SOME CONCLUSIONS

The aim of the chapter was firstly to assess the impact of differences in technological opportunity among sectors, upon trade growth at the country level.

Concerning the dynamics of trade performance *per se*, 'catching up' countries (Japan, Austria, Finland, Greece, Ireland, Italy, Portugal, Spain and Turkey) have experienced high levels of growth rates in terms of aggregate exports. The initial (1965) sectoral specialisation of these countries has however, had a significant negative impact on the overall export performance, since the structural market effect is negative for all these 'catch up' countries in the period 1965-88. Likewise most of these countries (all, except Japan) have further moved into sectors offering low levels of market opportunity. In addition it was shown that only a small group of countries have been initially specialised in sectors offering high levels of market opportunity, namely initially rich countries such as the US, Germany, Switzerland and Great Britain.

With regard to the dynamics of 'technological capabilities' *per se* it can likewise be seen that most 'catching up' countries (Japan, Finland, Ireland, Spain, Austria, Italy and Turkey) have experienced very high levels of growth in terms of technology, measured as shares of US patents. At the same time these countries generally appear to have been specialised in the 'wrong' sectors (i.e. sectors offering low levels of technological opportunity) in 1965.

Based on a regression analysis of the determinants of growth of country export market shares, some support was found for the specialisation-based growth proposition (k), as there is a significant relationship between growth rates in trade performance and the individual country's ability to move into (faster than average) technological sectors, offering above average technological opportunity. However, the results did not support a hypothesis stating the importance for trade growth, of being specialised in the fastest growing technological sectors initially.

Finally, it should be pointed out that the present chapter (as most other papers in this field) probably underestimates the effects of technology as a determinant of market share dynamics, as technological spillovers from other sectors are not included in the model. The task of including such spillovers in the analysis of market share dynamics is an important one for future research.

NOTES

1. This chapter draws on Laursen (1999).
2. The use of patents as a proxy for technological capabilities, will not be discussed at length here. For a good survey of the pros and cons of the use of patent data in this context, see Pavitt (1988).
3. $\rho = 0.58$, significant at the 1 per cent level.
4. Using industry-specific constants, Geroski (1990) has shown that technological opportunity is an important factor in explaining innovativeness across industrial sectors.
5. If a country is specialised in sectors with a high propensity to patent, aggregate patent growth will be higher compared to a situation in which the country is specialised in a sector with an average propensity to patent.
6. $\Delta x_j > 10$ per cent.
7. Whether one adjusts for the degree of openness of the economies or not, did not make any significant difference in the estimations.

9. Does Specialisation Matter for Growth?[1]

As was argued in Chapter 2, in the survey on the literature on growth in open economies, an important issue in this literature is whether or not the specialisation pattern of a country has an impact on growth. Thus, the question is whether countries which are specialised in a particular activity have a higher growth potential than other countries. The literature identifies two sources for such a relationship: demand side sources (e.g. income and price elasticities of demand) and supply side factors (e.g. technological opportunities).

The aim of this chapter is to test the hypothesis that specialisation matters for growth at the sectoral level [proposition (k)] from Chapter 2 and to confront it with the two other perspectives on growth indicated above (purely resource based growth and purely technology based growth). To this end, a new data set will be presented and used in a regression model in which the different sources of growth are modelled. This model will be developed in Section 9.1, and subsequently estimated in Section 9.2 of the chapter. Section 9.3 summarises the argument and draws some conclusions on the policy implications of the findings.

9.1. THE EMPIRICAL MODEL

The hypothesis we derive from the discussion in Chapter 2 is that there are some 'activities' which are more conducive for growth than others. What we mean by 'activities' will be specified below. An alternative hypothesis is that economic growth is solely determined by resources (labour and investment, as in the Solow model) or technological change (as in new growth models of endogenous R&D).

In order to test these hypotheses, we set up a model that we derive from the general set-up that is often used in cross-country growth regressions (e.g. Barro and Sala-i-Martin, 1995, Ch. 12). This specifies the growth rate of output as follows:

$$q = f(y_0, \beta x). \tag{9.1}$$

Here, q is the growth rate of output, y_0 is initial productivity, β is a parameter vector, and x is a set of (exogenous) variables determining the steady state (or long-run) growth rate.[2] βx is thus the expression for the long-run growth rate, while y_0 measures the initial deviation from the long run path. In other words, we assume that growth is influenced on the one hand by a set of variables with a long-run impact, and on the other hand by 'transitory dynamics'. Note that these transitory dynamics can be interpreted in many different ways. For example, it may indicate 'catching-up' based growth (see Fagerberg, 1994), as well as convergence in a Solow-based model.

The variables associated to our hypotheses are assumed to be included in the vector x, and (apart from the specialization variable) can be said to be standard variables in cross-country growth regression models (Levine and Renelt, 1992; Fagerberg, 1994).[3] The model is then made operational in the following way:

$$\hat{Q}_{ijt} = \alpha_{it}\hat{L}_{ijt} + \beta_{it}\hat{K}_{ijt} + \gamma_{it}T_{ijt} + \delta_{it}U_{ijt} + s_{it}S_{ijt}. \tag{9.2}$$

In this equation, Q is value added (in fixed prices), L is labour input, K is capital input, T is a proxy for technology investment, U is a variable related to international technology diffusion, S is a vector of specialization variables to be defined more precisely below, α, β, γ and s are parameters, and the subscripts i, j and t indicate a sector, country and time period, respectively. Hats indicate proportionate growth rates. L and K capture the effect of purely resource driven growth. T captures the effect of active technology investment as it is found in new growth theory (e.g. Romer, 1990). U is a variable related to technological catch-up or convergence, i.e., it captures the effect of a country's growth path deviating from its long-run path (steady state). Our preferred interpretation of this variable is that countries with an initially backward position may be expected to grow relatively fast due to international diffusion of technology (see, e.g., Fagerberg, 1994, for an overview of theories on catch-up), but as argued above, it may also be interpreted as 'Solowian' convergence.

S is the variable of main interest for our chief hypothesis. In order to explain this variable, we need to specify what we mean by 'activities'. The national accounts framework usually divides economic activities into sectors. At the usual level of aggregation (say, 20 sectors within manufacturing), these sectors are still made up of rather heterogeneous activities. For example, in a sector 'transport equipment', one would find both the manufacturing of bicycles and aeroplanes, while in 'office machines', one would find photocopiers and computers. In order to capture this heterogeneity, we use a database on export values for 75 products, each of which can be assigned to one of 11 manufacturing sectors. These trade data are taken from the IKE trade database.

We interpret the 75 product classes as homogeneous 'activities'. Thus, when we speak about a country being specialised in a certain activity, we mean that it scores a high value on the specialisation index (to be defined below) for that particular product class. Because of the assignment of the 75 product classes to the 11 industrial sectors, we are able to say something on specialisation within those sectors.

In setting up the 75 product groups, our aim was to establish relatively homogeneous groups. Thus, in some cases (where the sector itself is already relatively homogeneous) we get a relatively small number of products (e.g., wood and wooden products). In case of a more heterogeneous sector we define a larger number of products, like in the case of 'transport equipment', where we have 11 products within one sector. The breakdown of the 11 sectors into activities (product classes) is documented in the appendix tables.

The variable S is measured using the trade data for the 75 product classes. The first step in this measurement procedure is to define a sectoral specialisation index, for which we use the *RCA* index, for measuring *intra-sectoral specialisation*. In raw form, this index is written as:

$$RCA_{pj}^{i} = \frac{X_{pj} / \sum_{p} X_{pj}}{\sum_{j} X_{pj} / \sum_{p} \sum_{j} X_{pj}},$$

(9.3)

where X is the value of exports, the superscript i indicates within-sector *RCA*, and the subscript p is a product group belonging to sector i (j, as before, indicates a country). Thus, the *RCA* index for product p in country j and sector i is defined as p's share in total exports of i by country j divided by p's share in total exports of sector i, from all countries. Because the *RCA*-index is not symmetric, we apply the usual transformation $RSCA = (RCA-1)/(RCA+1)$. In summary, a positive (negative) value for product p indicates that the corresponding sector i in the country is specialised (de-specialised) in that particular product.[4]

In principle, one could define S simply as the vector of product-wise specialisation indices, in which case S would have as many elements as there are product classes in a sector. This procedure has the major disadvantage, however, that in many cases, there are many product classes as compared to the number of countries in our data set. In other words, using such a procedure, the number of degrees of freedom would become quite low.

We therefore implement a second step in our procedure of measuring S by applying principal components analysis (as applied in Chapter 7) to the data for $RSCA^{i}$ for four key years: 1965, 1973, 1979 and 1988. These years all (roughly) correspond to peaks in the business and trade cycles, so that our data are not too much influenced by cyclical variations in export market shares or exchange rates. Recall, that principal components analysis, a form of factor analysis, is a technique aimed at data reduction, which estimates linear combinations of the underlying variables, in this case the specialisation indices, which 'explain' the highest possible fraction of the remaining variance in the data set. Thus, the first principal component is estimated to explain the highest possible fraction of the total variance, the second principal component the highest possible fraction of the variance not explained by the first principal component, etc. By maximising the 'explained residual variance' in each round, the first m principal components will explain a relatively large proportion of the total variance, which is why the technique is used for data-reduction.

The result of this procedure is a number of variables (usually two or three) for each sector, which give a 'synthetic' impression of differences in specialisation patterns per country. The value of each variable itself does not have a direct interpretation, because they are a linear combination of the underlying *RSCA* values. The coefficients of this linear combination (the so-called factor loadings) are documented in the appendix tables. The next section will make use of the signs of these factor loadings in combination with the estimated regression coefficients. In this section, it is only the question of whether or not the estimated regression coefficients are significant which interests us, not the numeric value or sign of the estimated coefficients.

9.2. GROWTH AND SPECIALISATION: REGRESSION ANALYSIS

The regression analysis makes use of data for the period 1965-88, and 20 OECD countries (Austria, Belgium, Canada, The Netherlands, Portugal, Spain, France, Germany (West), Switzerland, Denmark, Sweden, Norway, Finland, Japan, United Kingdom, United States, Greece, Turkey, Ireland, Italy). We estimate separate equations for three periods: 1965-73, 1973-79 and 1979-88. The breakpoints between these periods correspond to the peaks of the international business cycle. All our variables, except the ones related to specialisation and catch-up, are simple means over the complete period, with growth rates defined as annual compound rates. Besides the specialisation variables, we include four other variables, as in Equation 9.2: the growth rate of employment (*GL*, measured in persons, rather than hours), the investment-output ratio (*I*, as a proxy for the growth rate of capital), the number of patents granted in the US per employee (*P*) as an indicator of investment in technical change, and the ratio of value added per employee in the country/sector relative to the maximum value for the sector in the 20 countries sample (CU). The latter variable is measured for the initial year of the period for which growth rates are measured. Given the interpretation of this variable as a catch-up variable, we would expect a negative sign for it in the regressions. The signs for the other non-specialisation variables are all expected to be positive.

The patent data we use are taken from the US patent office, and concern patent grants, dated by the year of grant. Because we would expect US firms to have relatively more patents due to a 'home-market' effect, we include a dummy for the US in the regressions ($DUSA$). The data for the growth rates of value added, CU, GL, I and the employees data used in P is taken from the UNIDO Industrial Statistics Database.

As Equation 9.2 specifies, we expect the value of parameters to be estimated to differ between sectors. Given the limited number of observations within each sector, however, we choose to pool our data in the cross-section dimension, allowing for two broad classes of sectors; so-called *high-tech* sectors (defined as chemicals, machines, electrical goods, transport equipment, and instruments), and *low-tech* sectors (all other sectors). This broad classification has proven to be useful in estimating production structures and the impact of R&D on productivity (Verspagen, 1995).

The resulting data set is one in which we have 11 sectors (no patent data is available for two other sectors, i.e. wood and other manufacturing), and 20 countries, leading, in principle, to 220 data points for each period. Due to missing values in some of the data, however, we have a smaller number of observations in each case. For the first period, this problem is worse, with only 98 data points available. We estimate the impact of the variables I, GL, CU and P separately for the two groups of sectors, and denote this by the variable symbol together with '-high' or '-low'.

The specialisation indices are defined meaningfully only at the sectoral level, so we estimate their impact for each sector separately. We included up to three of the principal components in the final estimates presented below, although we experimented with more in some sectors. The resulting setup is one in which the principal components included in the regression pick up at least 60 per cent of the total variance of the specialisation data (see Table A9.2). Including the fourth, sometimes fifth principal component, did not change the results in a major way. We denote the principal components by $Fi\text{-}sA$, where A is the number of the sector, and i is the i-th principal component

Because we would expect that the impact of specialisation on the growth performance of large countries may be smaller than in the case of small countries, an additional variable is included for all of the three principal components included in the regressions, defined as $Fi\text{-}sA*DL$, where DL is a dummy variable set to one for large countries.[5] Note that this variable, because it is entered in the equation in an additive manner, is only meaningful if the sectoral specialisation variables all enter the regression equation with the same sign. However, because of the way the specialisation variables are constructed, we do not have *a priori* expectations on this sign. In order to assure the meaningfulness of the large countries' specialisation variable, we started with an initial regression including all specialisation variables with their original sign. In a next step, we multiplied all specialisation variables with a negative sign in the regression by -1, thus expecting that they would turn up with a positive sign.[6] This yields a regression in which we would expect the large country specialisation variable to turn up with a negative sign. However, in order to allow for a direct comparison between Table 9.1 and Table A9.1 (see the next section), Table 9.1 presents those factors which were multiplied by -1 with a negative sign.

Table 9.1 documents the regression outcomes for the three periods. We discuss the outcomes for the non-specialisation variables first. The growth rate of labour input is highly significant and positive in all cases. The values of the coefficients for this variable differ between periods and sectors, with the highest value found in low-tech sectors during the period 1965-73. In the period 1973-79, the values for these coefficients are relatively low.

The coefficients for the investment-output ratio are significant in all but one case. The one exception is low-tech industries during the period 1973-79. For all three periods, the value of this coefficient is higher for the high-tech sectors, while the value of the coefficients tends to fall over time. The patents variable is significant and positive, as expected, in only two cases; high tech industries during 1965-73 and 1973-79. For low-tech industries, this variable is always negative, during the last period even significantly so, a result which is hard to explain. The US dummy is negative during the first period, in line with our expectations about the 'home market' effect for US firms in the patents variable, but it is perfectly conceivable that this variable also picks up other influences specific to the US.[7] For the other two periods, the US dummy is positive and significant.

Overall, the regressions tend to explain a decreasing fraction of the total variance as time increases. The adjusted R^2 falls from roughly two-thirds in the first period to slightly less than one half in the second, to barely one fifth of the total variance in the last period.

With regard to the specialisation variables, which are the crucial part of our argument, we do indeed find many significant variables. Only in textiles (2) and basic metals (7), none of the specialisation variables are significant. For the other nine sectors, there is at least one, but often more, principal component for one time period that is significant. In the first period, roughly half of all of the specialisation variables are significant (14 out of 29), for the second period this

The Effects of International Specialisation

Table 9.1 Regression results for the Specialisation-Growth relationship*

	1965-73		1973-79		1979-88	
R²-adj	0.67		0.47		0.22	
N	98		158		164	
Variable	estimate	*t*-value	estimate	*t*-value	estimate	*t*-value
GL-low	**1.269**	6.73	**0.587**	7.14	**0.764**	5.85
GL-high	**0.532**	5.95	**0.583**	3.29	**0.817**	3.51
I-low	**0.215**	2.73	-0.012	-0.32	**0.072**	1.63
I-high	**0.388**	6.29	**0.248**	3.52	**0.223**	2.92
DUSA	**-0.025**	-1.83	**0.022**	2.58	**0.018**	1.91
Pat-low	-5.179	-0.83	-4.704	-1.10	**-13.157**	-1.84
Pat-high	**6.482**	3.83	**2.446**	1.80	4.643	1.23
CU-low	**-1.990**	-5.00	**-0.632**	-3.40	-0.092	-0.41
CU-high	**-2.780**	-8.18	**-1.596**	-4.47	-0.566	-1.53
F1-s1	**-0.011**	1.89	-0.002	0.30	0.006	0.68
F1-s2	0.004	0.53	0.001	0.22	0.004	0.96
F1-s4	**0.029**	1.91	**-0.023**	2.16	-0.007	1.07
F1-s5	-0.008	1:19	0.000	0.09	-0.007	1.58
F1-s6	**0.008**	2.74	0.000	0.19	-0.003	0.90
F1-s7	-0.006	0.67	0.007	1.17	-0.004	0.53
F1-s8	**-0.017**	2.51	**0.008**	3.25	-0.001	0.08
F1-s9	-0.007	1.05	**0.024**	3.53	-0.009	0.95
F1-s10	-0.007	0.79	-0.006	1.46	**-0.013**	1.62
F1-s11	**-0.014**	3.16	-0.001	0.08	-0.005	0.61
F1-s12	**0.011**	1.74	0.013	1.55	0.012	1.12
F1-large	-0.007	-1.28	**-0.016**	-3.41	-0.009	-1.21
F2-s1	**-0.015**	1.98	-0.001	0.16	**0.013**	1.81
F2-s2	-0.003	0.57	-0.005	1.31	-0.002	0.45
F2-s4	**-0.022**	4.68	**-0.027**	4.40	-0.008	1.21
F2-s5	-0.002	0.14	**-0.010**	1.60	**-0.010**	1.85
F2-s6	**-0.010**	3.17	**-0.010**	2.63	**-0.013**	2.63
F2-s7	-0.005	0.53	-0.008	1.38	-0.006	1.14
F2-s8	-0.001	0.21	-0.002	0.49	**-0.010**	2.02
F2-s9	0.016	1.54	-0.007	0.58	-0.017	1.34
F2-s10	-0.001	0.18	0.003	0.44	-0.006	0.74
F2-s11	**0.010**	2.60	-0.014	1.28	**0.012**	1.62
F2-s12	**0.026**	5.03	**-0.023**	1.83	**-0.024**	2.52
F2-large	-0.003	-0.46	0.002	0.34	0.009	1.22
F3-s1	-0.006	1.10	0.002	0.31	**0.012**	2.34
F3-s4	**-0.022**	3.51	**0.028**	3.88	0.002	0.69
F3-s7	0.005	0.78	-0.001	0.07	-0.005	0.71
F3-s8	0.011	1.31	**0.009**	1.60	-0.002	0.22
F3-s9	-0.001	0.27	**-0.028**	2.67	0.005	0.74
F3-s10	**-0.018**	1.84	-0.006	1.02	0.000	0.04
F3-s11	**-0.015**	4.23	**0.022**	2.37	-0.006	0.56
F3-large	0.005	1.02	0.004	0.76	-0.004	-0.93
C	**0.066**	7.47	**0.030**	4.44	**0.025**	2.37

Note: *Cells with coefficients significant at a level >10% in a 2-tailed *t*-test are printed in bold.

is slightly less (11 out of 29), and for the last period, it is even less (8 out of 29). We thus conclude that there is indeed some evidence that sectoral growth rates of production are related to within-sector specialisation patterns of international trade, although the impact seems to become weaker over time.

We can only speculate as to why the specialisation variables are becoming less important over time as a factor explaining growth. It might be related to the fact that our sample is not a balanced one (some observations in the sample for the last period are not present in the early period), thus reducing the phenomenon at least partly to an artificial one. It might also be the case that a 'real' phenomenon, such as trade liberalisation, the increased importance of FDI, or technological developments underlying the production structure, have a role in this. For the time being, we will not discuss this part of our findings from a statistical point of view, but instead focus on a more 'qualitative' interpretation of our regression results in the next section.

9.3. INTERPRETATIONS AND CONCLUSIONS

The regression results presented in the previous section seem to indicate that specialisation does indeed matter for economic growth, as asserted by proposition (k) in Chapter 2. Compared to a model in which a combination of resource based and technology based explanations of growth are offered, the specialisation factor adds explanatory power. The theoretical frameworks that were discussed in Chapter 2, suggest that there are various factors that may account for these results. On the supply-side, there are factors such as the learning opportunities offered by various activities or products, while from the demand side, income elasticities are important.

The result that the variables such as technology (as measured by patents), specialisation and catching-up potential all show a weaker impact on growth during the 1980s, suggests that there might be an interaction between them. For example, while catching-up in the 1960s and 1970s was mainly due to a non-activity-specific rapid learning of relatively backward economies, in the 1980s, it became an activity specific phenomenon. Some activities provided 'windows of opportunity', while others, e.g. due to their relatively cumulative technological nature, provide more opportunities for relatively advanced countries. It has to be stressed, however, that such an interpretation is rather speculative, and more research would be necessary to substantiate these ideas.

In order to obtain a more precise notion of which activities have had a 'positive' impact on growth, the methodology can be taken one step further. If the factor loadings from Table A9.1 (numerically above 0.5, admittedly an arbitrary value) are combined with the regression results in Table 9.1, it is possible to analyse the impact of intra-sectoral specialisation patterns on sectoral growth, i.e. to obtain a positive or negative impact on growth. It should, however, be kept in mind that the data reduction, itself a central aim of the principal components methodology, by definition leaves out some of the underlying information. Therefore such specific conclusions at the product level should be interpreted with caution. It should also be stressed that the specialisation patterns referred to are calculated at the intra-sectoral level - the weighted average of the specialisation indicator sums to up zero for each of the sectors.

Applying this procedure yields a number of products which have a 'significant' impact on sectoral growth in each of the three periods. Such a procedure shows that the interpretation of our regression results is indeed one which involves a rather complex set of interacting supply and demand side factors. In e.g. the electrical goods sector, specialisation in semiconductors in 1979 turns out to have had a negative impact on real growth in value added (of the electrical goods sector) 1979-88, in spite of high growth of the value of international trade in semiconductors over that period. Inspection of underlying data shows that only a few countries are specialised in semiconductors, including 'established' technology leaders such as Japan, the US and the Netherlands (Philips), as well as less advanced countries such as Austria (where Philips has many of its production facilities) and Portugal (which has a relatively low export volume in electrical goods). Although these countries (perhaps with the exception of Portugal) have seen the volume of their semiconductors exports increase significantly over the period, they have also experienced increasing competition by catching-up nations, which has been growing rapidly, but only in selected product-segments, like telecommunication equipment. Thus, our interpretation of the negative impact of semiconductors specialisation on growth in electrical goods production, is that in the semiconductors segment, the 'technology leaders' are in the best position, due to for example the short product life cycle and high investments in this sector. The appropriability conditions in semiconductors seem to foster considerable barriers to entry. Other segments of the electrical goods industry, however, seem to provide a 'window of opportunity' for catching-up for relatively backward nations, which implies that catching-up related rapid growth is correlated with negative specialisation in semiconductors. Or, in other words, the capability to use (imported) semiconductors in a wide array of products may be of far more importance for economic growth than the capability to produce and export the semiconductors.[8]

This example (others could be mentioned) indeed brings out the complicated nature of the causal relationship between specialisation and growth. Demand related mechanisms (e.g. the high income elasticities of semiconductors) may not always work in the same direction as supply side effects (e.g. the small opportunity for catching-up in semiconductors), and the net result is rather unpredictable from the theories that we have discussed in Section 9.2.

Perhaps more interesting is the mixed pattern that emerges when we compare the impact of one product group across periods. In 29 cases, a single product group appears with a similar impact (negative or positive) for different periods. However, in 35 cases, the same product group appears with different impacts for different periods.[9] This seems to indicate that the stickiness with regard to the sign of the impact of specialisation on growth is not very large. This finding has some interesting policy implications, which we shall return to in the conclusion (Chapter 11).

NOTES

1. This chapter draws on Dalum, Laursen and Verspagen (1999).
2. Note that it is more common to use GDP per capita at the lhs of the equation. However, we will include the growth rate inputs, including labour, in x, so that our specification encompasses the common one.
3. It should be pointed out that the specification of the model is not strictly consistent with the post-Keynesian theories, discussed in Chapter 2, as factors of production are seen as being endogenous within this approach.
4. Note that within each sector, a country is always specialised in some products. Thus, even if a country is de-specialised in the sector taken as a whole, it will be specialised in some of the product classes.
5. France, Germany, Japan, United Kingdom, United States, Italy are defined as large countries.
6. In no cases did this procedure change conclusions about the significance levels of any of the variables in the regressions.
7. We have also experimented with dummy variables for other countries, but in no cases did these prove to influence the results in the table in an important way, even if some of the country dummies were statistically significant for some periods.
8. One might thus call the negative correlation a 'statistical artifact'.
9. These numbers are 'double-counted', i.e. if a product group appears twice with the same impact, we counted it twice.

Table A9.1 Factor loadings, principal components analysis of within-sector specialisation patterns of export-values, 1965-79*

	Principal Component 1			Principal Component 2			Principal Component 3		
	1979	1973	1965	1979	1973	1965	1979	1973	1965
1. Food, beverages and tobacco									
1 Meat	**0.85**	**0.78**	**0.55**	0.21	0.04	0.21	0.22	0.45	**0.71**
2 Fish	**-0.54**	**-0.51**	**-0.52**	0.37	0.16	-0.10	**-0.50**	-0.19	-0.31
3 Cereals	0.00	**0.50**	**0.52**	**-0.86**	-0.06	0.17	-0.23	**-0.63**	**-0.61**
4 Vegetables	**-0.58**	-0.48	-0.17	**-0.63**	-0.34	-0.38	0.19	-0.42	**-0.59**
5 Animal-food	0.39	0.06	-0.21	0.02	**0.82**	**0.70**	**-0.66**	0.04	-0.12
6 Oils	**-0.51**	-0.47	-0.42	-0.18	**0.54**	**0.65**	**-0.69**	**-0.55**	**-0.55**
7 Non-alco	**0.51**	**0.67**	**0.80**	**-0.71**	-0.44	-0.23	-0.04	-0.48	-0.25
8 Alco	-0.19	-0.12	0.33	-0.15	**-0.78**	**-0.77**	**0.68**	0.11	-0.28
9 Tobacco	**0.74**	**0.77**	**0.74**	0.02	0.28	0.43	-0.21	0.02	-0.21
10 Other	**0.78**	**0.84**	**0.84**	-0.17	0.12	0.27	-0.18	-0.33	-0.16
2. Textiles, clothes and leather									
11 Raw	**0.69**	**0.64**	0.26	0.06	0.41	**0.87**	**0.72**	**0.65**	0.41
12 Yarn	**0.92**	**0.91**	**-0.92**	0.03	-0.21	0.27	-0.27	-0.24	-0.16
13 Leather	**-0.81**	**-0.65**	**0.92**	-0.46	**0.72**	-0.27	0.25	-0.12	-0.14
14 Clothing	**-0.55**	**-0.69**	-0.31	**0.82**	**-0.58**	**-0.86**	0.10	0.40	0.41
3.Wood and wooden products									
15 Products	0.35	**0.67**	**0.74**	**0.93**	**0.72**	**0.66**	0.09	0.14	0.12
16 Raw	**-0.97**	**-0.97**	**-0.97**	-0.02	0.03	0.06	0.22	0.26	0.25
17 Furniture**	**0.90**	**0.79**	**0.84**	-0.39	**-0.58**	**-0.51**	0.21	0.19	0.18
4. Chemicals									
20 Plastic**	0.32	0.13	0.35	0.02	**0.90**	**0.83**	**0.82**	0.14	0.10
21 Organic	**-0.54**	**-0.52**	-0.05	0.48	0.30	0.44	**0.54**	0.41	**0.86**
22 Inorganic	**0.80**	**0.91**	**0.80**	-0.42	-0.09	-0.25	-0.19	0.04	0.23
23 Other	-0.14	-0.24	-0.21	**0.80**	0.23	0.45	-0.36	**-0.88**	-0.72
24 Dyeing	**-0.80**	**-0.69**	**-0.54**	0.25	0.20	**0.61**	-0.19	-0.24	0.08
25 Fertilisers	**0.64**	**0.70**	0.25	0.41	-0.29	0.22	-0.45	-0.23	0.08
26 Drugs	**-0.82**	**-0.87**	**-0.94**	-0.32	-0.32	0.02	-0.21	0.02	0.15
27 Oils	**-0.57**	-0.40	**-0.57**	**-0.64**	**-0.61**	**-0.57**	-0.16	0.09	0.27
5. Rubber and plastic products									
28 Other	0.19	0.09	**0.69**	**0.98**	**0.99**	**0.73**	0.02	0.04	0.03
29 Rubber	**-0.96**	**0.97**	**0.90**	0.13	0.04	-0.31	-0.24	-0.23	0.29
30 Plastic	**0.97**	**-0.96**	**-0.92**	-0.07	0.14	0.24	-0.24	-0.23	0.31

Notes:
*   Factor loadings with absolute values above 0.5 printed in bold.
** We have two more product groups for the sector 'printing and publishing', however, for two product groups it does not make sense to calculate principal components, so the numbering in the table is non-consecutive.

[Table continues on next page]

	Principal Component 1			Principal Component 2			Principal Component 3		
	1979	1973	1965	1979	1973	1965	1979	1973	1965
6. Glass, clay, etc.									
31 Pottery	0.30	0.38	0.05	**0.85**	**0.81**	**0.77**	0.03	0.36	**0.54**
32 Sanitary	0.48	**0.60**	**-0.57**	**-0.71**	-0.16	**0.68**	0.23	**0.53**	0.04
33 Glass	**0.78**	**0.70**	**-0.93**	-0.12	**-0.57**	-0.23	**-0.57**	0.06	0.03
34 Building	**-0.95**	**-0.95**	**0.87**	-0.08	-0.05	0.19	0.10	0.08	-0.02
35 Other	**0.74**	**0.60**	-0.06	0.14	0.24	**0.53**	**0.57**	**-0.69**	**-0.82**
7. Basic metals									
36 Steel	**0.90**	**0.88**	**0.91**	0.23	0.16	0.09	0.01	0.15	0.29
37 Wires	0.23	0.34	0.58	**0.69**	**-0.73**	-0.02	0.16	0.14	-0.31
38 Aluminium	**-0.55**	**-0.54**	-0.49	**-0.66**	**0.68**	**0.67**	0.37	-0.21	0.27
39 Uranium	-0.08	-0.19	0.46	0.47	0.36	0.07	**0.83**	**0.78**	**-0.57**
40 Silver	**-0.73**	-0.48	-0.04	0.29	-0.17	**0.64**	0.07	**0.62**	**-0.53**
41 Copper	-0.48	**-0.70**	-0.49	**0.74**	**-0.57**	**-0.56**	-0.34	-0.06	**-0.60**
42 Other	**-0.72**	**-0.86**	-0.03	0.17	-0.08	**0.76**	-0.16	-0.12	-0.22
8. Simple metal products									
43 Structural	0.07	0.31	0.31	0.38	0.49	**0.61**	0.48	0.05	0.57
44 Wires, screws	0.44	**-0.88**	0.44	**-0.54**	-0.06	**0.74**	**-0.53**	-0.15	-0.14
45 Hand tools	0.06	-0.45	**0.64**	**0.76**	**-0.76**	**-0.51**	**-0.52**	-0.14	-0.28
46 Stoves	**-0.85**	**0.92**	**0.66**	-0.37	-0.17	-0.41	0.21	-0.08	0.31
47 Furniture	**-0.57**	0.07	**0.66**	**0.56**	-0.42	0.44	-0.19	**0.89**	-0.48
48 Scrap	**0.70**	**-0.55**	**-0.88**	0.25	**0.65**	0.24	0.43	0.34	-0.20
9. Machines									
49 Agriculture	**0.55**	0.11	**0.58**	0.02	**0.77**	0.48	0.40	0.46	0.24
50 Turbines	**0.70**	-0.38	**0.65**	0.35	**0.59**	0.23	0.32	0.17	-0.43
51 Computers	**0.51**	**-0.62**	**0.71**	**0.65**	**0.63**	0.48	-0.44	-0.17	-0.15
52 Office	-0.04	**-0.69**	**0.69**	**0.76**	0.19	-0.28	0.04	-0.38	-0.12
53 Metal working	-0.39	**-0.72**	**0.79**	0.43	-0.05	-0.48	**0.73**	0.42	-0.02
54 Textile	**-0.62**	**-0.52**	0.47	0.44	**-0.71**	**-0.74**	**0.55**	-0.04	-0.05
55 Specialised	**0.52**	**0.69**	0.12	-0.46	0.18	0.38	**0.61**	0.37	-0.76
56 Other	-0.13	**0.85**	**-0.82**	**-0.67**	0.08	0.09	0.21	-0.30	-0.22
57 Firearms	**-0.68**	-0.11	0.42	-0.04	**-0.55**	0.42	-0.18	**0.60**	**0.68**
10. Electrical goods, excl. computers									
58 TV etc	**0.72**	**0.63**	0.49	0.18	0.04	0.06	0.29	0.08	**0.80**
59 Generating	0.29	0.03	0.33	-0.23	**0.71**	-0.45	**-0.87**	**0.50**	-0.04
60 Telecom	**-0.59**	0.18	0.24	-0.38	**-0.89**	**0.73**	0.24	0.16	**-0.52**
61 White goods	**-0.74**	**-0.88**	**0.78**	0.09	0.05	-0.34	0.26	0.23	-0.23
62 Medical	0.07	0.34	**0.86**	**-0.85**	-0.21	0.17	0.31	**0.85**	-0.16
63 Other	0.40	0.42	**-0.88**	**-0.70**	0.30	0.19	0.00	-0.01	0.05
64 Semiconductors	**0.71**	**0.67**	0.33	0.16	0.16	**0.71**	0.49	-0.27	0.35

[Table continues on next page]

		Principal Component 1			Principal Component 2			Principal Component 3		
		1979	1973	1965	1979	1973	1965	1979	1973	1965
	11. Transport equipment									
65	Aero engines	**0.53**	**0.69**	**0.55**	**0.56**	0.39	**0.73**	0.38	0.36	0.12
66	Auto engines	0.44	**0.50**	**0.71**	**0.51**	0.04	-0.25	-0.27	0.41	**0.51**
67	Non-motor	0.06	-0.10	0.27	**0.75**	-0.38	**-0.67**	0.01	**0.80**	**0.56**
68	Locomotives	**0.74**	0.39	**0.54**	-0.37	**-0.66**	-0.24	-0.05	-0.18	-0.21
69	Oth. railway	**0.61**	0.36	**0.58**	-0.27	**-0.75**	**-0.74**	-0.42	0.23	0.03
70	Cars	**0.52**	**0.54**	**0.53**	-0.45	0.03	-0.02	0.28	**-0.64**	-0.47
71	Trucks	-0.28	0.22	0.76	**-0.58**	-0.12	-0.19	-0.34	-0.03	-0.36
72	Auto parts	**0.83**	**0.87**	**0.84**	0.01	0.04	0.31	0.06	-0.31	-0.10
73	Motorcycles	0.03	-0.03	0.32	0.11	**-0.82**	**-0.79**	**-0.89**	-0.20	-0.25
74	Aircraft	**0.77**	**0.78**	**0.69**	0.27	0.21	**0.53**	-0.22	0.29	0.23
75	Ships	**-0.50**	**-0.87**	**-0.86**	**0.56**	0.03	-0.35	-0.23	0.02	-0.05
	12. Instruments									
76	Measuring	**0.89**	**0.86**	**0.77**	0.27	0.25	0.43	0.11	0.06	0.27
77	Medical	0.04	**0.66**	**-0.73**	**-0.84**	-0.45	0.28	-0.33	-0.16	-0.11
78	Optical	**-0.62**	-0.23	0.39	**0.51**	**-0.53**	-0.17	0.28	**0.81**	**-0.89**
79	Photo	**-0.57**	-0.11	**0.79**	-0.46	**0.82**	-0.11	**0.57**	0.39	0.08
80	Clocks	**-0.59**	**-0.89**	-0.02	0.27	-0.06	**-0.93**	**-0.69**	-0.32	0.24
	13. Other manufacturing									
81	Pearls	**0.87**	**0.93**	**0.92**	0.34	0.24	0.28	0.05	0.03	0.16
82	Music	-0.31	-0.29	-0.53	**0.87**	**0.95**	**0.71**	-0.37	-0.12	-0.46
83	Toys, sports	**-0.74**	**-0.84**	**-0.63**	0.48	-0.14	0.40	0.46	-0.48	**0.66**
84	Other	**-0.84**	**-0.79**	**-0.87**	-0.39	0.07	-0.43	-0.22	**0.59**	-0.03

Table A9.2 Cumulative R^2 values for subsequent principal components

	Sector	1979			1973			1965		
		F1	F2	F3	F1	F2	F3	F1	F2	F3
1	Food etc.	0.32	0.51	0.70	0.33	0.53	0.68	0.31	0.52	0.70
2	Textiles, etc.	0.57	0.79	0.96	0.53	0.80	0.96	0.46	0.87	0.96
3	Wood, etc.	0.63	0.97	1.00	0.67	0.96	1.00	0.73	0.96	1.00
4	Chemicals	0.39	0.61	0.79	0.38	0.58	0.71	0.30	0.53	0.71
5	Rubber and plastic	0.63	0.96	1.00	0.63	0.96	1.00	0.71	0.94	1.00
6	Glass, etc.	0.48	0.73	0.87	0.45	0.67	0.85	0.39	0.67	0.87
7	Basic metal	0.35	0.61	0.75	0.38	0.60	0.75	0.27	0.52	0.70
8	Simple metal	0.29	0.55	0.72	0.37	0.61	0.77	0.39	0.65	0.79
9	Machines	0.26	0.50	0.69	0.34	0.58	0.71	0.38	0.57	0.72
10	Electrical	0.31	0.52	0.71	0.28	0.48	0.65	0.38	0.58	0.74
11	Transport	0.30	0.51	0.64	0.32	0.50	0.65	0.40	0.65	0.75
12	Instruments	0.37	0.63	0.83	0.41	0.65	0.84	0.38	0.62	0.81
13	Other	0.53	0.84	0.94	0.57	0.82	0.96	0.57	0.81	0.97

10. How Structural Change Differs, and Why it Matters (for Economic Growth)

As pointed out in the previous chapter, the proposition that economic structure matters for economic growth is not an uncontroversial one in the mainstream of economic theory and analyses. The underlying notion of 'competitiveness' has been attacked recently by Krugman (1994) for being theoretically meaningless. The main point of the argument in this context is that the standard of living of a country is related to growth in productivity in the domestic country, and is not related to growth of productivity with respect to other countries. However, this thesis argues that if comparative advantage (stemming from economies of scale or from endowments) forces countries to specialise in certain sectors, and sectors differ in terms of learning opportunities and/or asymmetric demand structures, 'competitiveness' (as a relativistic concept) makes a difference for economic growth of countries.

The previous chapter examined the 'Ricardian' proposition (k) asserting that the growth rate of an economy depends, at least partly, on what the country is specialised in and how the specialisation pattern changes over time. The general issue was dealt with in the preceding chapter as well. However, more specifically the previous chapter examined the role of (Ricardian) *intra*-sectoral specialisation in explaining growth at the level of the sector, across countries. The aim of this chapter is to investigate empirically, whether or not *inter*-sectoral trade specialisation matters for economic growth at the level of the country (18 OECD countries); that is, whether or not initial specialisation in, or a movement into fast-growing sectors, matters for economic growth.

The chapter is structured as follows. In Section 10.1, we briefly outline some earlier empirical findings on the topic (for a theoretical treatment see Chapter 2). Section 10.2 accommodates the empirical analysis. The first part of the section is devoted to regression analysis (using fixed- and random effects models), including effects stemming from constant market share analysis. One advantage of this procedure is that while we would like the variables to be time invariant, from a technical point of view, the CMS methodology allows for (possibly) time invariant effects, while the underlying sectoral composition can change quite dramatically over time (like in the case of 'computers', where this sector grew much faster in the 1980s, as compared to the growth in the 70s).

Of the CMS effects, the parameter for the variable expressing the movement into fast-growing sectors turns out to be positive and significant. Following up on that result, the last part of the section (Sub-section 10.2.2) deals with the question of whether fast-growing sectors are (in general) high-tech. Finally, Section 10.3 contains the conclusions of the chapter.

10.1. PREVIOUS EMPIRICAL WORK

This section will briefly outline some of the previous empirical work in relation to the empirical analysis to be carried out in Section 10.2.

From an empirical point of view, the hypothesis of Ricardian specialisation being of importance for economic growth has gained support from e.g. Amable (1997). Amable looked at the effect of inter-industry specialisation on economic growth in a sample of 39 countries over the period 1965-90, using the Michaely-index as the indicator of specialisation. Amable included (among other variables) one 'Smithian' specialisation variable (measuring the level of specialisation); and two variables measuring aspects of 'Ricardian' specialisation (one measuring the degree to which a country's specialisation profile matches international demand; the other measuring whether or not a country is seen to be specialised in electronics). The conclusions are that the level of specialisation does matter for growth, as does specialisation in electronics, although the effect of the latter seemed to be rather small. However, the results also suggest (against intuition) that being specialised in fields where international demand is rather low, has a significant and positive impact on growth, over the period. However, it should be pointed out that this result could be the outcome of the (arbitrary) size of the commodity classification applied. Meliciani and Simonetti (1998) made a similar set-up to that of Amable, but used technological specialisation (measured as the 'revealed technological advantage') in fast-growing fields (specialisation in top 8, out of 91 US patent classes), as well as specialisation in information and communication technologies, as the specialisation variables applied. The authors found a positive impact of both types of specialisation, but the relationship appears to hold only for the 1980s, and not for the 1970s.

10.2. THE IMPORTANCE OF STRUCTURAL CHANGE FOR ECONOMIC GROWTH

10.2.1. Regression Analysis

The investment, GDP (volume) and population data have been taken from OECD Economic Outlook and Reference Supplement (No. 59). The patent data used are taken from the US patent office, and concern patent grants, dated by the year of grant. The export data are taken from the STAN data base, as these data are available from 1970 and onwards on an annual basis.

The starting point for the type of structural decomposition analysis, conducted on trade data, namely constant market share (CMS) analysis, is whether or not a country expands its exports as a percentage of total OECD exports over time, between two points in time (for a more detailed elaboration on the subject, see Chapter 8). The basic idea of the method is then to decompose the growth rate, in such a way that structural change gets isolated. It is then possible to say something about whether a rise (or fall) of a country's share of OECD exports is due to (i) *the structural market effect* (SME); i.e. having the 'right' ('or wrong') specialisation pattern in the initial year; (ii) *the market growth adaptation effect* (GAE); i.e. a movement into sectors with fast-growing (or stagnating) exports; (iii) *the market stagnation adaptation effect* (SAE); i.e. a movement out of sectors with generally stagnating market activity (or fast-growing), and finally; (iv) *the market share effect* (MSE); i.e. whether the rise (or fall) is due to the fact that the country has gained shares of markets, assuming that the structure is the same in the two periods in question. The decomposition can be conducted for growth in export market shares as follows:

$$\Delta x_j = \sum_i (\Delta x_{ij} y_{ij}^{t-1}) + \sum_i (x_{ij}^{t-1} \Delta y_{ij}) + \sum_i (\Delta x_{ij} \frac{\Delta y_{ij} + |\Delta y_{ij}|}{2}) + \sum_i (\Delta x_{ij} \frac{\Delta y_{ij} - |\Delta y_{ij}|}{2}), \quad (10.1)$$

| Market share effect | Structural market effect | Market growth adaptation effect | Market stagnation adaptation effect |

where:

$x_j = \sum_i X_{ij} / \sum_i \sum_j X_{ij}$ (a country's aggregate share of OECD exports to the world);

$x_{ij} = X_{ij} / \sum_j X_{ij}$ (a country's share of a given sector in terms of exports);

$y_{ij} = \sum_j X_{ij} / \sum_i \sum_j X_{ij}$ (a sector's share of total OECD exports to the world),

where X_{ij} denotes exports by firms situated in country j in sector i.

The CMS effects are calculated as a kind of three year moving average. An example of this procedure is that for the first period we decompose the change in market shares, that is the change of market shares between 1970 and 1973; the second period is 1971 and 1974, and so on. The (aggregate country level) technology variable has been calculated as follows:

$$T_{jn}^{stock} = \sum_{t=1}^{n} t/n \; T_{jt},$$ (10.2)

where T_{jn}^{stock} is the stock of technology in period n in country j, measured as numbers of US patents granted to firms in country j. T_{jn}^{stock} is in other words the sum of US patents in n (in our case $n=9$) periods held by the firms of country j, allowing for linear depreciation over the (nine) years. The reason for choosing a nine year period was the data availability, as data on US patenting was made available electronically from 1963 onwards, and in combination with the fact that we want to use the variable together with growth rates in GDP from 1972 onwards.[1]

As pointed out in the previous chapter, the variables associated with our hypotheses can be said to be standard variables in cross-country growth regression models (see e.g. Levine and Renelt, 1992; Fagerberg, 1994), apart from the specialisation variables. Hence, the basic empirical model explaining economic growth among 18 OECD countries, can be set up as follows:

$$\hat{y}_j = \alpha_j + \beta_1 Y0_j + \beta_2 \hat{K}_j + \beta_3 \hat{T}_j + \beta_4 M\hat{S}E_j + \beta_5 S\hat{M}E_j + \beta_6 G\hat{A}E_j + \beta_7 S\hat{A}E_j + \epsilon_j,$$ (10.3)

where $\hat{y}_j$ is the annual growth rate of GDP. $Y0_j$ is the level of income per capita in country j, relative to the US, in the initial year (a catch-up variable, or 'expressing transitional dynamics'); $\hat{K}_j$ is the annual growth rate of the stock of physical capital (investment with nine years depreciation) for each country (capital accumulation, as in the Solow model); while $\hat{T}_j$ is the growth rate of the stock of technology (nine years depreciation), measured as US patents, and held by the firms of country j (technological change, as in new growth models of endogenous R&D). Both the variable expressing the growth of the stock of technology and the variable expressing the growth of capital are expressed in relation to the average values of the 18 OECD countries[2] for each period. As mentioned above, we apply a three year 'moving average' for the CMS variables in order to avoid too much short term fluctuation in the figures. When we subsequently compare the annual growth rates of GDP to the CMS variables, we apply the end year as the connecting point. Hence, e.g. growth in GDP 1972-73 is to be measured against CMS variables, calculated on the basis of growth rates between 1970 and 1973. For what concerns expectations of the direction of the parameters, one would expect all variables to have a positive sign, apart from the catching up variable.

It should be pointed out that the CMS variables, as well as the patent variable are based on manufacturing only, while the rest of the data includes all of the economy. This is of course a limitation of the analysis, as it would have been preferable to have included specialisation in the service sector as well. However, with the present data set such a procedure is not possible.

The results of the regressions are given in Table 10.1. As we are dealing with a panel data set, the model has been estimated as both a random effects model, as well as a fixed effects model. However, OLS estimates are also shown in Table 10.1, as a kind of benchmark in relation to the more appropriate panel data techniques. In the fixed effects model, the intercept is taken to be a group specific constant in the regression model. In the random effects model, the intercept is a group specific disturbance, and for each group, there is but a single draw that enters the regression identically in each period. As the cross sectional dimension is countries in the model, it might be expected *a priori*, that there are country-specific fixed effects present, especially if the literature on national systems of innovation (see Lundvall, 1992; Nelson, 1993) is correct in asserting national differences in terms of the institutional set-up (e.g. differences in firm organisation; technological support systems; education systems; financial systems; and university systems). In this context, two specification tests were conducted. Since it is assumed in the random effects model that the individual effects are uncorrelated with the other regressors, the random effects model may suffer from the inconsistency, due to omitted variables. Hence, a Hausman test was carried out. The Hausman (1978) test is devised to test for orthogonality of the random effects and the regressors. The test (see Table 10.1) rejects the hypothesis that the individual effects are uncorrelated with the other regressors in the model, at the two per cent level. Thus, the test strongly indicates that the assumption behind the random effects model does not hold. In addition, the outcome of the *F*-test for the hypothesis stating that the country effects are the same can be rejected at any plausible level. Given the outcome of the specification tests, with regard to the technique applied, it can be concluded that the fixed effects model appears to be the most appropriate one. This finding is in accordance with the *a priori* expectations, based on the literature on national systems of innovation, emphasising differences among countries.

The fixed effects model estimated in Table 10.1 is significant overall, at any reasonable level (as are the two other models). The capital stock variable has a positive sign and is significant at a six per cent level, while the catching up variable has the expected negative sign, and has a significant (and large) parameter at any reasonable level. It can be seen from Table 10.1 that the catching up variable is only significant, when fixed country effects are controlled for. Hence country-specific developments appear to be 'crowding out' the catch-up variable, when the fixed effects are not included. The

Table 10.1 The effect of different variables on economic growth in a panel of 18 OECD countries and across the years 1972-90 (n=324)

	OLS $R^2 = 0.09$		Random effects model $R^2 = 0.09$		Fixed effects model $R^2 = 0.16$	
	Estimate	p-value	Estimate	p-value	Estimate	p-value
$Y0$	0.627	0.2213	0.539	0.3541	-11.890	0.0018
K	0.210	0.0448	0.204	0.0548	0.223	0.0534
T	0.031	0.3673	0.035	0.3290	0.045	0.2547
MSE	-0.009	0.6671	-0.009	0.6649	-0.014	0.5018
SME	-0.035	0.3461	-0.029	0.4366	-0.018	0.6451
GAE	0.504	0.0045	0.492	0.0057	0.464	0.0107
SAE	-0.254	0.0954	-0.246	0.1068	-0.229	0.1386
Hausman test			0.0187			
F Test for No Fixed Effects						0.2009

aggregate technology (stock) growth variable has the expected sign, but is not significant. However, it should be pointed out that the link between technology and growth is very (too) simple in this set-up. First, it has been shown that not all sectors are technology intensive in the sense that the firms in those sectors base their competitiveness on R&D (Soete, 1981; Pavitt, 1984; Amable and Verspagen, 1995). Second, the patenting activity is mainly related to manufacturing, while the dependent variable includes all of the economy. However, an analysis allowing for the variables to interact, reveals that the technology (patent) variable does play a role in the present setting, but in an indirect way. Hence, it can be seen from Table 10.2, that the effect of technology in this setting travels through the channel of growth in physical capital. High growth in terms of technological competence exerts a positive impact on growth in an interaction with high growth of physical capital, as the interaction variable $(K*T)$ between the capital variable and the technology variable always turns out to be significant.

Of the effects from the constant market share analysis, only the 'growth adaptation effect' is significant (at the two per cent level), in Table 10.1. In this context it is interesting to note that the variable measuring whether a country has been 'fortunately' specialised in the initial year, with respect to trade growth in the period in question (i.e. the 'structural effect') is far from being significant. Hence, it can be concluded that, whether a country has a 'dynamic' specialisation pattern initially does not appear to be important for economic growth. However, a certain dynamism in terms of structural *change* (i.e. countries actively moving into fast-growing sectors) is required by countries in

Table 10.2 The effect of different variables on economic growth in a panel of 18 OECD countries and across the years 1972-90. Various fixed effects specifications (n=324)

	(1) $R^2=0.15$		(2) $R^2=0.13$		(3) $R^2=0.15$		(4) $R^2=0.16$		(5) $R^2=0.17$	
	Estimate	*p*-value	Estimate	*p*-value	Estimate	*p*-value	Estimate	*p*-value	Estimate	*p*-value
Y0	-12.149	0.0014	-13.310	0.0005	-12.318	0.0011	-12.817	0.0000	-12.515	0.0010
K	0.214	0,0608	0.267	0.0194	0.211	0.0616	0.271	0.0164	0.239	0.0381
T	-0.018	0.7073	0.001	0.9785	-0.006	0.9008	-0.014	0.7619	-0.013	0.7804
*K*T*	0.057	0.0178	0.056	0.0205	0.051	0.0312	0.059	0.0138	0.053	0.0254
MSE	0.032	0.0083							-0.012	0.5577
SME			-0.008	0.8421					-0.019	0.6229
GAE					0.415	0.0008			0.430	0.0178
SAE							-0.287	0.0146	-0.241	0.1160

order to achieve high levels of economic growth at the macro level, given the positive and significant impact of the 'growth adaptation effect'.

Table 10.2 tests for the stability of the 'specialisation' (CMS) variables. In this context it can be noted that the growth adaptation effect is not sensitive to the removal of any of the CMS variables. In addition, interactions between the 'standard' variables (*Y0*, *K* and *T*) was also tested for. The interaction between the technology variable and the physical capital variable, mentioned above, was the only significant of these three interaction variables.

10.2.2. Are Fast-growing Sectors High-tech?

As mentioned previously, one can interpret the elasticities with respect to demand in the post-Keynesian growth literature as being related to the sectoral composition of countries' exports. Building on this literature, Verspagen provided an evolutionary model, which incorporates this feature in an explicit manner, highlighting that one of the reasons for some countries growing faster than others is higher learning opportunities on the supply side, and non-symmetric consumption structures on the demand side. In both of these types of literature, what matters for economic growth (in the context of trade) is whether or not a country is specialised in fast-growing sectors in terms of trade. The empirical set-up of this chapter basically corresponds to that. However, in the neoclassical literature, only supply side factors matter (i.e. higher learning opportunities in some sectors, as compared to others). Hence, in order to be in accordance with the neoclassical predictions, the fast-growing sectors need to be high-tech, as these models focus exclusively on learning opportunities,

Table 10.3 Trade growth and R&D intensity in the 1970s and in the 1980s

No.	Sector	Sum of CMS trade growth vectors (TG)*		Annual trade growth (relative to the average)		R&D intensity (R&D as % of value added)	
		1973-81	1982-90	1973-81	1982-90	1977	1986
1	Food, drink and tobacco	-9.82	-31.86	0.87	0.88	0.75	1.11
2	Textiles, footwear and leather	-64.64	-9.48	0.69	1.13	0.34	0.59
3	Wood, cork and furniture	0.60	-4.06	0.77	1.16	0.33	0.40
4	Paper and printing	-16.64	13.78	0.96	1.22	0.58	0.57
5	Industrial chemicals	84.97	-0.56	1.21	1.09	6.54	8.47
6	Pharmaceuticals	-1.38	6.01	1.01	1.09	14.66	17.17
7	Petroleum refineries (oil)	53.87	-60.95	1.54	0.11	3.99	5.50
8	Rubber and plastics	5.13	2.26	1.07	1.19	2.73	2.67
9	Stone, clay and glass	1.46	-4.64	0.99	1.03	1.33	2.75
10	Ferrous metals	-36.14	-56.30	0.77	0.54	1.50	2.62
11	Non-ferrous metals	-9.08	-15.05	0.86	1.01	2.30	3.70
12	Fabricated metal products	23.54	-27.01	1.22	0.78	0.82	1.47
13	Non-electrical machinery	-46.45	-24.45	0.95	1.00	2.97	4.68
14	Office machines and computers	0.61	65.09	1.13	1.77	24.04	27.42
15	Electrical machinery	24.72	12.68	1.24	1.19	9.63	8.58
16	Communic. eq. and semiconductors	2.52	59.48	1.05	1.44	14.77	20.74
17	Shipbuilding	-41.08	-18.35	0.33	0.10	0.78	1.33
18	Other transport	-6.08	-8.65	0.88	0.52	3.76	10.32
19	Motor vehicles	11.32	69.85	1.05	1.24	6.57	11.35
20	Aerospace	3.50	22.79	1.26	1.31	44.78	42.30
21	Instruments	11.04	15.39	1.18	1.18	6.08	9.86
22	Other manufacturing	8.03	-6.00	0.98	1.03	1.91	1.63

Note: * See definition in Equation 10.4.

related to investment in R&D. Hence, this section will deal with the question of whether fast-growing sectors are high-tech. However, the growth of the various sectors over different time periods is also interesting *per se*.

Table 10.3 displays the technology intensities of the sectors, as well as the growth of the various sectors, expressed as the sum of the change of a sector's share of total OECD exports to the world, over two 9-year periods (the 1970s and the 1980s):

$$TG_{ij} = \sum_t \Delta y_{ij}. \tag{10.4}$$

Hence, TG_{ij} is the sum (over time) of the OECD growth (sectoral) vectors, as applied in the CMS analysis in the section above (see Equation 10.1, above). It should be noted that the trade growth columns are relative to each other; in other words the two columns (1973-81 and 1982-90 respectively) sum up to zero. From Table 10.3 the decline of some low-tech sectors in terms of exports is clearly displayed when using the TG_{ij}, as food, drink and tobacco; textiles, footwear and leather; as well as shipbuilding are losing relative importance at a relatively high pace. At the same time some high-tech sectors, such as electrical machinery; motor vehicles; aerospace; and instruments, are growing at a relatively high speed. Also some interesting differences between growth of different sectors, over time emerge, as e.g. the high speed of growth for the two ICT sectors (office machinery and computers; and communication equipment and semiconductors) in the 1980s as compared to the growth in the 1970s, is clearly evident. Also the effect of the stark fall of oil prices between the 1970s and the 1980s, is evident from Table 10.3, as well as the decline of the industrial chemical sector.

In addition, Table 10.3 contains calculations on annual growth rates, expressed relative to the average, across the 22 sectors (using the end years). It can be seen that the measure based on the CMS growth vectors (TG_{ij}), broadly corresponds to the calculations based on annual growth rates. However, there are some differences between the results, based on two measures. One such difference concerns e.g. 'wood cork and furniture', where the TG_{ij} measure indicates that the sector has grown more slowly than average over the 1980s, whereas the annual growth rate calculation points to a growth rate higher than the average. The difference is due to the fact that TG_{ij} takes into account the sector's importance for the overall *level* of exports. Hence, the negative TG_{ij} value is due to the fact that the sector has not grown much in terms of volume. The same phenomenon can be observed for 'office machines and computers', where the importance for overall exports was not so large in the 1970s, although

Table 10.4 Correlation matrix (Spearman) between trade growth and R&D intensities (n=22)

	Trade growth 82-90	R&D int. 1977	R&D int. 1986
Trade growth 1973-81	0.313	0.486	0.395
p-value	*0.156*	*0.022*	*0.069*
Trade growth 1982-90		0.584	0.566
p-value		*0.004*	*0.006*
RD int. 1977			0.971
p-value			*0.000*

the annual growth rate was a factor of 1.13 larger than the average growth rate.

Table 10.4 contains simple correlations, based on Table 10.3. First of all it can be seen that R&D intensities are very stable over time (ρ=0.971), while the growth of various sectors (measured as TG_{ij}) appears to be much more volatile over time (a non-significant ρ). Nevertheless, the most important observation coming out of Tables 10.3 and 10.4, is that *in general* fast-growing sectors are high-tech, as the Spearman rank correlations, in Table 10.4, display a positive and significant relationship between R&D intensities on the one hand, and relative trade growth on the other.

10.3. CONCLUSIONS

The aim of this chapter was to investigate empirically the proposition (k) that the growth rate of an economy depends, at least partly, on what the country is specialised in and how the specialisation pattern changes over time at the level of the country (17 OECD countries); that is, whether or not initial specialisation in, or a movement into fast-growing sectors, matters for economic growth.

The dependent variable was annual data on economic growth, in the period 1972-90. The independent variables were the four CMS effects, as well as the initial level of income relative to the US (a catching up variable); growth in terms of technology, based on number of US patents held by the firms of the country in question; and growth in terms of the capital stock.

The results displayed that the fixed effects model is the most appropriate technique, and that using this tool, the initial level of income (the catch up variable) was significant and had a negative sign as expected. The investment variable was also significant, while the technology variable was significant only through its interaction with the growth of the capital stock variable. The growth adaptation effect was the only significant variable (positive sign) of the CMS effects. Hence, it was concluded that a certain dynamism in terms of structural *change* is required by countries in order to achieve high levels of economic growth at the macro level. This finding is in line with proposition (k).

If the results of this chapter are compared to the empirical earlier findings, discussed in Section 10.1, the findings all point to the importance of economic structure for economic growth performance. However, some possible contradictions can be identified, although the empirical set-ups vary greatly amongst the studies. For instance, the finding of Chapter 9, at the sectoral level, stating that initial specialisation in certain types of activities matters for economic growth, could not be confirmed at the aggregate country level used in this chapter, as the 'structural effect' could not be shown to have any impact on economic growth. It can be noted that the insignificant effect of the 'structural effect' is in contrast to proposition (k). Furthermore, the finding by Meliciani and Simonetti (1998) showing that initial specialisation in fast-growing technological classes (based on patent data) has an impact on economic growth (although only for a certain period) could not be supported by the trade data applied in this chapter. Given these observations, it is an important task for future research to investigate whether the apparent contradictions between the studies are due to the different empirical set-ups, or whether the differences in terms of results are due to real world phenomena. Such a task should be fulfilled by applying the same methodology on the various types of data.

The final part of the chapter dealt with the question of whether the fast-growing sectors (as measured in the CMS analysis) are high-tech or not. Based on a comparison between the OECD growth vector from the CMS analysis, on the one hand, and R&D intensities in the 22 sectors (for the 1970s and for the 1980s), on the other, it was concluded that the fast-growing sectors are in general also high-tech sectors.

NOTES

1. We also wanted to include growth of the capital stock (investment) in a similar way to that of technology. Since investment figures are not available for all countries in 1963, this particular year was excluded.

2. Australia, Austria, Belgium, Canada, Denmark, Finland, France, Germany (West), Greece, Italy, Japan, the Netherlands, New Zealand, Norway, Spain, Sweden, the United Kingdom and the United States.

PART V

Conclusion

11. Retrospect and Prospect

This chapter will first summarise the findings of the book, and second discuss possible policy implications of these findings. Finally, in Section 11.2, we point to some potential directions of research, emerging out of the present work.

11.1. RETROSPECT

11.1.1. Findings

In Chapter 1, the subsequent general research question was posed: *How does Ricardian specialisation affect economic development in relatively advanced countries?* Accordingly, 'relatively advanced countries' was narrowed down to the OECD countries, and the question was split up into three sub-questions. These questions will be addressed separately, below, but we will return to the general question briefly, at the end of this sub-section.

The first question concerned the development of specialisation patterns over time: **A.** Do countries converge or diverge in terms of their specialisation patterns over time? In order to investigate this question, *Chapter 4* examined whether or not the group of OECD countries have been characterised by a high degree of stability of their *export* specialisation patterns at the country level. Furthermore it was tested whether the countries have become more or less specialised. In this context we distinguished between specialisation (or de-specialisation) in trade patterns on the one hand, and divergence (or convergence) on the other. A specialisation process refers to a process in which specialisation *intra-country* becomes more dispersed (and the opposite for de-specialisation). In contrast, a divergence process refers to a process in which countries become more different in terms of specialisation in a particular sector, *across countries* (and the opposite for convergence). Our results confirmed the hypothesis that the OECD catching up countries (Japan, Finland, Greece, Ireland, Italy, Portugal, Spain and Turkey) on average experienced the highest degree of structural change in their specialisation patterns, over the period in question. We examined the sensitivity for the level of aggregation, and we applied the analysis to a period of nearly three decades from 1965 to 1992. Twenty OECD countries were considered.

The *intra-country* results showed that the national specialisation patterns are rather sticky, although there was a tendency for countries to de-specialise in the medium to long term. The *sector-wise* results displayed convergence both in terms of β- and σ-convergence. In conclusion the results were discussed (de-specialisation in particular) in the context of economic integration.

As mentioned above, Chapter 4 showed that there was a general tendency for OECD countries to de-specialise in terms of export specialisation over the last 20-25 years. This finding is in contrast to findings made by other authors, working on technological specialisation. These authors found increasing technological specialisation from the late 1970s to the early 1980s measured as specialisation in US patents. Hence, the first aim of *Chapter 5* was to investigate whether these contradictory findings are due to a 'real world' phenomenon, or whether the explanation is purely technical, by comparing the development of export specialisation to specialisation in terms of US patents, using the same methodology, and level of aggregation. The second aim was to analyse the extent to which countries and sectors (in one single model) display stable specialisation patterns over time, also both in terms of exports and in terms of technology.

Chapter 5 confirmed that the OECD countries did in general de-specialise in terms of export specialisation. The evidence is less conclusive with regard to technological specialisation, as the results were mixed in the sense that just about half of the countries tend to increase in terms of the level of specialisation, while the other half tended to engage in de-specialisation. In terms of country and sectoral stability of specialisation patterns, it could be concluded that both trade specialisation and technological specialisation patterns were path-dependent in the sense that all country and sectoral patterns were correlated between seven three-year intervals, within the period in question. In comparison, however, trade specialisation patterns were more stable than were technological specialisation patterns.

Among the countries, Australia, Finland, France, West Germany, Greece, Italy, Portugal, Spain, Sweden and the United Kingdom displayed the highest degree of turbulence in the specialisation patterns, across sectors and time. The criteria concerned whether or not the hypothesis of an unchanged pattern could be rejected for both types of specialisation. Concerning the hypothesis of OECD catching up countries experiencing the highest degree of turbulence in the specialisation patterns, the results were not as clear-cut as they were in Chapter 4, although for the OECD 'catch-up countries' in the period in question (Finland, Greece, Italy, Spain, and Portugal) we did find that the specialisation patterns of these countries (Spain and Portugal in particular, given the low coefficients) belonged to the group of countries experiencing the highest degree of turbulence, both in terms of trade and technology specialisation patterns. The difference in the results has to do with the time periods considered, as Chapter 4 considers a period starting in 1965, while Chapter 5 starts in 1971. In this way it appears that e.g. Japan encountered a high degree of structural change in the

1960s, while this process stopped from the 1970s onwards.

After having dealt with the development of specialisations patterns over time, the next sequential step was to deal with the determinants of the direction of international trade specialisation in Part III, in order to address the second sub-question of the book: **B.** How does technology enter as an explanation of the direction of trade specialisation of countries? As a means of beginning to answer this question, *Chapter 6* took as its starting point that the importance of advanced users in home markets as an inducement to technological innovation is well recognised, providing an explanation for important parts of international export specialisation patterns. In this context, upstream-downstream interaction has been made the generic micro-foundation of theories of National Systems of Innovation. However, Chapter 6 argued that user-producer interaction is not the only (country-specific) inducement mechanism to innovation. Rather, the finding of Chapter 6 was in line with the proposition that when firms are science-based, linkages tend to be horizontal rather than vertical. The chapter mobilised historical and bibliometric methods to trace the long term development of technology in the Danish pharmaceutical company Novo Nordisk, and its links with the local (particularly university) environment.

Chapter 6 demonstrated the importance of science-based competencies in moving from natural resource based technologies to those of greater sophistication, thereby influencing trade specialisation of advanced countries.

Whereas Chapter 6 looked at inducement mechanisms to trade specialisation in a science based sector, *Chapter 7* took a more general approach in being a statistical analysis of several inducement mechanisms. Within the 'technology gap' approach there has been one tradition which has applied cumulativeness in technological change as an explanation for international trade specialisation, while another tradition has emphasised the role of inter-sectoral linkages (the so-called home market effect) in this context. However, given that the sources of innovation (inducements mechanisms) differ between firms according to principal sector of activity, different variables should not be expected to be of equal importance across industrial sectors. Thus, using the Pavitt taxonomy as a starting point, Chapter 7 statistically investigated the importance of a set of variables reflecting different inducement mechanisms, across 9 OECD countries.

The chapter concluded that the two types of technological activities, namely technological activities in the 'own' sector, and inter-sectoral linkages are both important in the determination of national export specialisation patterns. However, the importance differs according to the mode of innovation in each type of sector in the sense that inter-sectoral linkages were important for specialised supplier sectors as well as for scale intensive sectors, while the most important determinant was 'own' sector technological effort, in the case of science based sectors.

After having dealt with the direction of trade specialisation, Part IV looked at whether the direction of specialisation has any impact on the rate of economic development in order to take up the third sub-question of the book: **C.** Do international specialisation patterns (and changes therein) matter for growth? In order to approach this question, *Chapter 8* examined, using constant market share analysis, whether the degree to which countries expand their sectors (more than the average country) with above average technological opportunity had any impact on growth in aggregate market shares of exports. In this context, it was shown that there was a positive and significant relationship between trade performance and the individual countries' ability to move faster than the average country into technological sectors offering above average technological opportunity.

Chapter 9 moved on from the issue of trade performance dealt with in Chapter 8 to the question of to what extent the growth performance of an economy is determined by its external relations. Several types of theoretical literature on the topic of trade, growth and specialisation, including neoclassical approaches, post-Keynesian literature and some models in evolutionary economics, have shown that it is possible to enjoy higher rates of economic growth, given the presence of certain sectors in the economy, be they high-tech or fast-growing sectors. The chapter applied a data set on growth and trade in 11 manufacturing sectors, for the period 1965-88, for the OECD area (20 countries). The main novelty in the database was the assignment of these 75 products in the trade data to the 11 industrial sectors. The relationship between growth and specialisation was tested by running a regression with the sectoral growth of value added as the dependent variable, and several variables, including some measuring specialisation as well as other factors, as the independent variables.

The regression results presented in Chapter 9 seemed to indicate that specialisation does indeed matter for economic growth. However, this impact seemed to be gradually wearing off during the 1980s, as is the case for other factors included in the regression analysis.

Chapter 10 expanded on Chapter 9 by resting on the same theoretical discussion and by exploring a very similar research question, namely whether Ricardian specialisation matters for growth. However, whereas Chapter 9 examined whether intra-industry specialisation matters for growth at the level of the industry, Chapter 10 was an analysis of the effect of inter-industry specialisation on macro economic growth. Basically the idea was to conduct a constant market share (CMS) analysis (as in Chapter 8), and afterwards to include the obtained effects in regression models, using panel data techniques.

The dependent variable was annual data on economic growth (18 OECD countries), based on statistics over the period 1972-90. The independent variables were the CMS effects mentioned above, as well as initial level of income relative to the US (a catching up variable); growth in terms of technology, based on number of US patents held by the firms of the country in question; and growth in terms of capital stock.

The results displayed that the growth adaptation effect (measuring whether the country in question has actively [more than the average country] moved into slow or fast growing sectors) was the only significant variable (positive sign) of the CMS effects. Hence, it was concluded that a certain dynamism in terms of structural *change* is required by countries in order to achieve high levels of economic growth at the macro level. The final part of Chapter 10 dealt with the question of whether the fast-growing sectors (as measured in the CMS analysis) are high-tech or not. Based on a comparison between the OECD growth vector from the CMS analysis, on the one hand, and R&D intensities in the 22 sectors (for the 1970s and for the 1980s), on the other, it was concluded that the fast-growing sectors are in general also high-tech sectors.

Moving back to the general research question and on the basis of the findings of this book it is an obvious conclusion that Ricardian specialisation and structural change (i.e. change in specialisation patterns) is an integrated part of economic development processes. In Part II this conclusion was backed by the identification of regularities in of terms which countries and sectors adjust their specialisation patterns at the fastest rate, as well as by showing that the evolution of countries' specialisation patterns are path dependent over time. Part III made its contribution to the conclusion by showing regularities in how technology in various forms influences the direction of trade specialisation patterns. Part IV showed that the growth of market shares at the country level is related to the ability of countries to transform their specialisation patterns towards fast-growing sectors. It was also shown that inter-sectoral (industry) specialisation matters for growth, in terms of value added, at the level of the sector. Finally, it was shown that a (faster than the average country) movement into fast-growing sectors has a positive and significant effect on macro economic growth. Nevertheless, policy conclusions which at first seem tempting[1], given this finding, might turn out to be not so straightforward after all; this issue is to be dealt with in the next sub-section.

11.1.2. Policy Implications

Part III of the book found that the determinants of international trade specialisation are sector-specific, although certain regularities can be identified in terms of sectors being governed by certain technological regimes (or 'Pavitt-sectors') which transcend traditional sector boundaries. This conclusion has important policy implications. The prime policy implication is that generic technology policies might not lead to the desired results. If a policy maker wants to influence trade specialisation towards a higher technology level through innovation by means of a policy that gives support to specific sectors (e.g. in the form of support for corporate R&D), it is not likely to have any effect on firms situated in specialised supplier sectors. In that case support for upstream and downstream interaction, might be much more appropriate. On the other hand, such policies might not have the desired effect for firms situated in science-based sectors. Given these observations policy makers should take into account the given export specialisation profile of the country, when determining which portfolio of policies should be held.

Part IV of the book showed that being specialised in certain activities (or moving into such activities) matters both for competitiveness (measured in terms of export market shares), as well as for growth at the level of national sectors, as well as for growth at the level of the country. But where do the findings of Part IV of the book leave policy makers who want to 'steer' the economy into a high-growth specialisation path? First, it has to be noted that the opportunities for such policies are probably low. Chapter 4 found that, within the group of OECD countries, specialisation patterns tend to be sticky over the 1965-92 period. On the other hand, in terms of the 5-10 year periods that we have considered in Chapter 9, changes with regard to the sign of the impact of specialisation on growth are quite common. Thus, the relative stability of the factor loadings in Table A9.1 and other efforts to measure long term change of export specialisation patterns imply some degree of tension: the 'reaction speed' of specialisation patterns might simply be too low to allow for an active policy. In addition, as it is a 'stylised fact' that technological innovation involves fundamental uncertainty (Dosi, 1988), it might be difficult (if not impossible) to predict precisely which sectors are going to grow fastest *ex ante*. An indication of this problem was hinted in Chapter 10 (Sub-section 10.2.2), given the fact that the fast-growing sectors are different over time; in this case between the 1970s and the 1980s.

Our conclusion that both supply- and demand-side factors matter, calls for a cautious mix of different policies; e.g. technology policy aimed at increasing the rate of innovation and learning, industrial policies aimed at changing the specialisation patterns of the economy, and, within international rules, trade policies aimed at stimulating exports. It is obvious that if policies aimed at stimulating growth by specialising in the 'right' kind of activities are to be successful, policy makers must be prepared to aim at a high degree of interaction between their various instruments, as well as be willing to risk unsuccessful attempts, and admit these in an early enough stage. Enhancing growth by steering specialisation patterns seems a quite risky 'art' rather than a well-established 'science' without major uncertainty. Furthermore, it might be too late to catch up in a fast growing sector, when the sector has started to grow rapidly, if no technological competence is present at all. Hence, from the perspective of a policy-maker, it is probably wise to attempt to increase 'option values' (Mitchell and Hamilton, 1988) in terms of keeping doors open to the future, by means of non-committal support for emerging technologies. The basic proposition is to support research on a small scale in new areas, in order to monitor the areas, but also in order to support/secure a minimum of technological competence, should a field take off.

11.2. PROSPECT

As pointed out in the previous section, this book has a number of conclusions and implications. However, it also contains many implicit directions for future research in the field. This section will elaborate on a few of such possible directions.

In this way, Chapter 7 contains some promising directions for future research. One possibility is to change the set-up in such a way that the present static estimations become dynamic, or in other words to look at explaining change in specialisation and its determinant over time, rather than on the level of specialisation (and its determinants) as done in Chapter 7. However, an even more interesting idea might be to introduce the inter-sectoral linkages (or put differently; spillovers), in an empirical model of international market share dynamics. While the explanation of market share dynamics has been an important aspiration of a large part of the evolutionary empirical literature (e.g. Amendola, Dosi and Papagni, 1993; Amable and Verspagen, 1995; Verspagen and Wakelin, 1997), spillovers (or technological linkages) have to the mind of the present author not so far been incorporated in such a model. The set-up of the model could be similar to the one developed by Magnier and Toujas-Bernate (1994), and applied in Chapter 5 (Sub-section 5.1.3); i.e. a model allowing the slopes to differ in both the country and sector dimensions. Hence the estimations would aim at explaining market share dynamics by means of unit labour costs (as a reflection of production costs, or of skill levels, given a positive sign of the parameter for this variable), investment (an indicator of scale requirements), US patents (an indicator of the technological development), and then by adding a variable similar to the linkage variable we have constructed in Chapter 7, to see whether such linkages (or national spillovers) matter for gaining or losing market shares, over time. In fact it might also be possible to include international spillovers (given certain assumptions) as an explanatory factor, in such a model as well.

Another idea is to further extend on Part II of the book. In Chapters 4 and 5, the discussion of structural change in the specialisation patterns was phrased in a verbal way, *vis-à-vis* the economic growth performance of the various countries in the sample. However, while it is believed that structural change (measured as beta convergence/divergence) is an important part of growth processes, it could be modelled in a more rigorous way, so that the degree of structural change becomes an explanatory variable, in an empirical model (containing other more standard variables as well) explaining economic growth, possibly allowing for slopes to vary according to a taxonomy of countries (building on the taxonomy of countries found in Chapter 4), depending on the countries' size and level of economic development.

More generally the latter idea also points to the importance of a better *theoretical* understanding of structural change in catch up processes of countries. As pointed out in Chapter 4, at present the only theoretical explanation seems to be an exogenous change in the stock of human capital. In this context Beelen and Verspagen (1994) describes a process in which countries must change their production structure (and hence export structure), as well as their level of human capital as they catch up, in order to catch technology spillovers from the leading countries. In order to understand such processes, structural change should in the future be incorporated into formal models in an explicit way, based on the available empirical regularities on the topic.

Finally, the author would like to stress the importance of contrasting both formal trade and growth models, as well as econometric results to available historical evidence on the topic, and in this context discuss the importance of institutions in explaining various economic phenomena.

NOTES

1. It is obvious that such findings can be potentially abused as 'camouflage' for protectionist policies, hampering the benefits from free international trade (Krugman, 1996a).

References

Abernathy, W.J. and Utterback, J.M. (1975), 'A dynamic model of process and product innovation', *Omega*, **3** (6), 639-56.

Abramowitz, M. (1986), 'Catching up, forging ahead, and falling behind', *Journal of Economic History*, **XLVI** (2), 385-406.

Amable, B. (1997), 'The effect of foreign trade specialisation on growth: does specialisation in electronics foster growth?', paper presented at the Conference on Trade, Economic Integration and Social Coherence, Vienna, Austria, January.

Amable, B. and Verspagen, B. (1995), 'The role of technology in market shares dynamics', *Applied Economics*, **27** (2), 197-204.

Amendola, G., Dosi, G. and Papagni, E. (1993), 'The dynamics of international competitiveness', *Weltwirtschaftliches Archiv*, **129** (3), 451-71.

Amendola, G., Guerrieri, P. and Padoan, P.C. (1992), 'International patterns of technological accumulation and trade', *Journal of International and Comparative Economics*, **1**, 173-97.

Andersen, E.S. (1994), *Evolutionary Economics: Post-Schumpeterian Contributions*, London and New York: Pinter.

Andersen, E.S., Dalum, B. and Villumsen, G. (1981), 'The importance of the home market for the technological development and the export specialization of manufacturing industry', IKE Seminar, Aalborg University Press, Aalborg.

Aquino, A. (1981), 'Change over time in the pattern of comparative advantage in manufactured goods: an empirical analysis for the period 1972-1974', *European Economic Review*, **15** (1), 41-62.

Archibugi, D. and Pianta, M. (1992), *The Technological Specialisation of Advanced Countries. A Report to the EEC on International Science and Technology Activities*, Dortrecht: Kluwer Academic Publishers.

Archibugi, D. and Pianta, M. (1994), 'Aggregate convergence and sectoral specialization in innovation', *Journal of Evolutionary Economics*, **4** (1), 17-33.

Arthur, W.B. (1989), 'Competing technologies increasing returns and lock-in by historical events', *The Economic Journal*, **99** (March), 116-31.

Arundel, A., van de Paal, G. and Soete, L.L.G. (1995), 'Innovation strategies of Europe's largest industrial firms', PACE Report, MERIT, University of Limburg, Maastricht.

Bairam, E. (1988), 'Balance of payments, the Harrod foreign trade multiplier and economic growth: the European and North American experience',

Applied Economics, **20** (12), 1635-42.

Balassa, B. (1965), 'Trade liberalization and 'revealed' comparative advantage', *The Manchester School of Economic and Social Studies*, **32** (2), 99-123.

Ballance, R., Forstner, H. and Murray, T. (1985), 'On measuring revealed comparative advantage: a note on Bowen's indices', *Weltwirtschaftliches Arhiv*, **121** (2), 346-50.

Barro, R.J. and Sala-i-Martin, X. (1991), 'Convergence across states and regions', *Brooking Papers on Economic Activity* (1), 107-82.

Barro, R.J. and Sala-i-Martin, X. (1995), *Economic growth*, New York: McGraw-Hill.

Beelen, E. and Verspagen, B. (1994), 'The role of convergence in trade and sectoral growth', in J. Fagerberg, B. Verspagen and N.v. Tunzelmann (eds), *The Dynamics of Technology, Trade and Growth*, Aldershot, UK and Brookfield, US: Edward Elgar, pp. 75-98.

Bell, M. and Pavitt, K.L.R. (1993), 'accumulating technological capability in developing countries', in L.H. Summers and S. Shah (eds), *Proceedings of the World Bank Annual Conference on Development Economics, 1992: Supplement to The World Bank Economic Review and The World Bank Research Observer*, Washington D.C.: The World Bank, pp. 257-81.

Ben-David, D. (1991), 'Equalizing exchange: a study of the effects of trade liberalization', *NBER Working Paper* (3706).

Bergstrand, J. (1990), 'The Heckscher-Ohlin-Samuelson model, the Linder hypothesis and the determinants of bilateral intra-industry trade', *Economic Journal*, **100** (December), 1216-29.

Blanchard, O.J. and Katz, L.F. (1992), 'Regional evolutions', *Brookings Papers on Economic Activity*, **1**, 1-70.

Boggio, L. (1996), 'Growth and International competitiveness in a Kaldorian perspective', *Structural Change and Economic Dynamics*, **7** (3), 299-320.

Bowen, H.P. (1983), 'On the theoretical interpretation of trade intensity and revealed comparative advantage', *Weltwirtschaftliches Archiv*, **119** (3), 464-72.

Bowen, H.P., Leamer, E.E. and Sveikauskas, L. (1987), 'Multicountry, multifactor tests of the factor abundance theory', *The American Economic Review*, **77** (5), 791-809.

Cantwell, J. (1989), *Technological Innovation and Multinational Corporations*, Oxford: Blackwell.

Cantwell, J. (1991), 'Historical trends in international patterns of technological innovation', in J. Foreman-Peck (ed), *New perspectives on the late Victorian economy*, Cambridge: Cambridge University Press, pp. 37-72.

Cantwell, J. and Andersen, B. (1996), 'A statistical analysis of corporate technological leadership historically', *Economics of Innovation and New Technology*, **4** (3), 211-34.

Cantwell, J. and Janne, O. (1999), 'Technological globalisation and innovative centres: the role of corporate technological leadership and locational hierarchy', *Research Policy*, **28**, 119-44.

Carlsson, B. (1991), 'Flexible Manufacturing and U.S. Trade Performance', *Weltwirtschaftliches-Archiv*, **127** (2), 300-22.

Carlsson, B. and Stankiewicz, R. (1991), 'On the nature, function and composition of technological systems', *Journal of Evolutionary Economics*, **1**, 93-118.

CEPII (1983), *Economie Mondiale: la montée des tension*, Paris.

Cesaratto, S. and Mangano, S. (1993), 'Technological profiles and economic performance in the Italian manufacturing sector', *Economics of Innovation and New Technology*, **2** (3), 237-56.

Coe, D.T. and Helpman, E. (1995), 'International R&D spillovers', *European Economic Review*, **39** (5), 859-87.

Cohen, W.M. and Levinthal, D.A. (1989), 'Innovation and learning: the two faces of R & D', *The Economic Journal*, **99** (September), 569-96.

Crafts, N.F.R. and Thomas, M. (1986), 'Comparative advantage in UK manufacturing trade, 1910-1935', *Economic Journal*, **96** (September), 629-45.

Dalum, B., Laursen, K. and Verspagen, B. (1999), 'Does specialization matter for growth?', *Industrial and Corporate Change*, **8** (2), 267-88.

Dalum, B., Laursen, K. and Villumsen, G. (1998), 'Structural change in OECD export specialisation patterns: de-specialisation and "stickiness"', *International Review of Applied Economics*, **12** (3), 447-67.

David, P.A. (1985), 'Clio and the economics of QWERTY', *American Economic Review. Papers and Proceedings*, **75** (2), 332-7.

Dixit, A.K. and Stiglitz, J.E. (1977), 'Monopolistic competition and optimum product diversity', *American Economic Review*, **67** (3), 297-308.

Dixon, R.J. and Thirlwall, A.P. (1975), 'A model of regional growth-rate differences on Kaldorian lines', *Oxford Economic Papers*, **11** (2), 201-14.

Dollar, D. and Wolff, E.N. (1993), *Competitiveness, Convergence and International Specialisation*, Massachusetts: MIT Press.

Dosi, G. (1982), 'Technological paradigms and technological trajectories: a suggested interpretation of the determinants and directions of technical change', *Research Policy*, **11**, 147-62.

Dosi, G. (1988), 'Sources, procedures and microeconomic effects of innovation', *Journal of Economic Literature*, **26** (3), 1120-71.

Dosi, G., Fabiani, S., Aversi, R. and Meacci, M. (1994), 'The dynamics of international differentiation: a multi-country evolutionary model', *Industrial and Corporate Change*, **3**, 225-41.

Dosi, G., Pavitt, K.L.R. and Soete, L.L.G. (1990), *The Economics of Technical Change and International Trade*, Hemel Hempstead: Harvester Wheatsheaf.

Dosi, G. and Soete, L.L.G. (1988), 'Technical change and international trade', in G. Dosi, C. Freeman, R. Nelson, G. Silverberg and L. Soete (eds), *Technical Change and Economic Theory*, London: Harvester Wheatsheaf.

Dowrick, S. (1997), 'Innovation and growth: implications of the new theory and evidence', in J. Fagerberg, L. Lundberg, P. Hansson and A. Melchior (eds), *Technology and international trade*, Cheltenham, UK and Lyme, US: Edward Elgar, pp. 107-26.

Dunning, J.H. (1988), 'The eclectic paradigm of international production: an update and possible extensions', *Journal of International Business Studies*, **19**, 1-13.

Ethier, W.J. (1986), 'The multinational firm', *Quarterly Journal of Economics*, **101** (4), 805-34.

Fagerberg, J. (1988), 'International competitiveness', *Economic Journal*, **98** (June), 355-74.

Fagerberg, J. (1992), 'The home market hypothesis reexamined: the impact of domestic user-producer interaction on export specialisation', in B.-Å. Lundvall (ed), *National Systems of Innovation. Towards a Theory of Innovation and Interactive Learning*, London: Pinter Publishers, pp. 226-41.

Fagerberg, J. (1994), 'Technology and international differences in growth rates', *Journal of Economic Literature*, **32** (3), 1147-75.

Fagerberg, J. (1995), 'User-producer interaction, learning and comparative advantage', *Cambridge Journal of Economics*, **19** (1-4), 243-56.

Fagerberg, J. and Sollie, G. (1987), 'The method of constant-market-shares analysis reconsidered', *Applied Economics*, **19** (12), 1571-85.

Falvey, R. (1981), 'Commercial policy and intra industry trade', *Journal of International Economics*, **11** (4), 495-511.

Fikkert, B. (1997), 'The application of the Yale Technology Concordance to the construction of international spillovers: variables for India', *Economic Systems Research*, **9** (2), 193-204.

Flam, H. and Helpman, E. (1987), 'Vertical product differentiation and North-South trade', *American Economic Review*, **77** (5), 810-22.

Freeman, C. (1963), 'The plastics industry: a comparative study of research and innovation', *National Institute Economic Review* (26), 22-40.

Freeman, C. (1988), 'Japan: a new national system of innovation?', in G. Dosi, C. Freeman, R. Nelson, G. Silverberg and L.L.G. Soete (eds), *Technical Change and Economic Theory*, London: Pinter Publishers.

Geroski, P.A. (1990), 'Innovation, technological opportunity, and market structure', *Oxford Economic Papers*, **42** (3), 586-602.

Gibbons, M. and Johnston, R. (1974), 'The role of science in technological innovation', *Research Policy*, **3**, 220-42.

Granstrand, O., Oskarson, C., Sjöberg, N. and Sjölander, S. (1990), 'Business strategies for development/aquisition of new technologies: a comparison of Japan, Sweden and the US', paper prepared for the conference on Technology and Investment. Arranged by The Royal Swedish Academy of Engineering Sciences, Department of Industrial Management and Economics, Chalmers University of Technology, Göteborg.

Granstrand, O. and Sjölander, S. (1990), 'Managing innovation in multi-technology corporations', *Research Policy*, **19**, 35-60.

Griliches, Z. (1979), 'Issues in assessing the contribution of research and development to productivity growth', *The Bell Journal of Economics*, **10**, 92-116.

Grossman, G.M. (1992), 'A model of quality competition and dynamic comparative advantage', in G.M. Grossman (ed), *Imperfect Competition and International Trade*, Cambridge, Massachusetts: MIT Press, pp. 367-83.

Grossman, G.M. and Helpman, E. (1989), 'Product development and international trade', *Journal of Political Economy*, **97** (6), 1261-83.

Grossman, G.M. and Helpman, E. (1991a), *Innovation and Growth in the Global Economy*, Cambridge Massachusetts: MIT Press.

Grossman, G.M. and Helpman, E. (1991b), 'Quality ladders and product cycles', *The Quarterly Journal of Economics*, **106** (May), 557-86.

Grupp, H. (1994), 'The measurement of technical performance of innovations by technometrics and its impact on established technology indicators', *Research Policy*, **23** (2), 175-93.

Grupp, H. (1998), *Foundations of the Economics of Innovation*, Cheltenham, UK and Lyme, US: Edward Elgar.

Guerrieri, P. (1997). 'The changing world trade environment, technological capability and the competitiveness of the European Industry', paper presented at the Conference on Trade, Economic Integration and Social Coherence, Vienna, Austria, January.

Hall, S. (1988), *Invisible Frontiers: the race to synthesize a human gene*, London: Sidgwick and Jackson.

Hansen, J.D. (1997), 'Dynamic comparative advantage in a Ricardian model', in J. Fagerberg, L. Lundberg, P. Hansson and A. Melchior (eds), *Technology and international trade*, Cheltenham, UK and Lyme, US: Edward Elgar, pp. 91-106.

Hart, P.E. (1976), 'The dynamics of earnings, 1963-1973', *Economic Journal*,

86 (3), 541-65.

Hart, P.E. and Prais, S.J. (1956), 'The analysis of business concentration: a statistical approach', *Journal of the Royal Statistical Society (series 2)*, **119** (2), 150-91.

Hausman, J. (1978), 'Specification tests in econometrics', *Econometrica*, **46**, 1251-71.

Heckscher, E.F. (1949), 'The effect of foreign trade on the distribution of income', in H.S. Ellis and L.A. Metzler (eds), *Readings in the Theory of International Economics*, Homewood: Irwin.

Helpman, E. (1981), 'International trade in the presence of product differentiation, economies of scale and monopolistic competition: a Chamberlin-Heckscher-Ohlin Approach', *Journal of International Economics*, **11** (3), 305-40.

Hicks, D., Ishizuka, T., Keen, P. and Sweet, S. (1994), 'Japanese corporations, scientific research and globalization', *Research Policy*, **23** (4), 375-84.

Hirschman, A.O. (1958), 'Interdependence and industrialization', in , *The Strategy of Economic Development*, New Haven: Yale University Press.

Hirschman, A.O. (1961), *The Strategy of Economic Development*, paperback, New Haven, Conn.: Yale University Press.

Hirschman, A.O. (1977), 'A generalized linkage approach to development, with special reference to staples', *Economic Development and Cultural Change*, **25** (Supplement), 67-98.

Johnston (1991), *Econometric Methods*, 3rd. edn., New York: McGraw-Hill.

Kaldor, N. (1966), *Causes of the Slow Rate of Economic Growth of the United Kingdom*, Cambridge: Cambridge University Press.

Kaldor, N. (1970), 'The case for regional policies', *Scottish Journal of Political Economy*, **17** (November), 337-48.

Klevorick, A.K., Levin, R.C., Nelson, R.R. and Winter, S.G. (1995), 'On the sources and significance of interindustry differences in technological opportunities', *Research Policy*, **24**, 185-205.

Kol, J. and Mennes, L.B.M. (1985), 'Intra-industry specialization: Some observations on concepts and measurement', *International Journal of Economics*, **21** (1-2), 173-81.

Krugman, P. (1980), 'Scale economies, product differentiation, and the pattern of trade', *American Economic Review*, **70** (5), 950-9.

Krugman, P. (1981), 'Intra-industry specialization and the gains from trade', *Journal of Political Economy*, **89** (5), 959-73.

Krugman, P. (1985), 'A "technology gap" model of international trade', in K. Jungenfelt and D. Hague (eds), *Structural adjustment in Advanced Economies*, London: Macmillan.

Krugman, P. (1987), 'The narrow moving band, the dutch disease, and the competitive consequences of Mrs. Thatcher: notes on trade in the presence of dynamic scale economies', *Journal of Development Economics*, **27** (1-2), 41-55.

Krugman, P. (1989), 'Differences in income elasticities and trends in real exchange rates', *European Economic Review*, **33** (5), 1031-54.

Krugman, P. (1994), 'Competitiveness: a dangerous obsession', *Foreign Affairs*, **73** (March/April), 28-44.

Krugman, P. (1996a), *Pop Internationalism*, Cambridge Massachusetts: The MIT Press.

Krugman, P. (1996b), 'Technological change in international trade', in P. Stoneman (ed), *Handbook of the economics of innovation and technological change*, Oxford: Blackwell, pp. 342-65.

Lancaster, K. (1980), 'Intra-industry specialization under perfect monopolistic competition', *Journal of International Economics*, **10** (2), 151-75.

Laursen, K. (1996), 'Horizontal diversification in Danish national system of innovation: the case of pharmaceuticals', *Research Policy*, **25** (7), 1121-37.

Laursen, K. (1999), 'The impact of technological opportunity on the dynamics of trade performance', *Structural Change and Economic Dynamics*, **10** (3-4), 341-57.

Laursen, K. and Drejer, I. (1999), 'Do inter-sectoral linkages matter for international trade specialisation?', *The Economics of Innovation and New Technology*, **8**, 311-30.

Leamer, E.E. (1980), 'The Leontief Paradox, reconsidered', *Journal of Political Economy*, **88** (3), 495-503.

Leontief, W. (1953), 'Domestic production and foreign trade: the American position re-examined', *Proceedings of the American Philosophical Society*, **97**, 332-49.

Levin, R., Klevorick, A., Nelson, R.R. and Winter, S. (1987), 'Appropriating the returns from industrial Research and Development', *Brookings Papers on Economic Activity* (3), 783-820.

Levine, R. and Renelt, D. (1992), 'A sensitivity analysis of cross-country growth regressions', *American Economic Review*, **82** (4), 942-63.

Lim, K.T. (1997), 'Analysis of North Korea's foreign trade by revealed comparative advantage', *Journal of Economic Development*, **22** (2), 97-117.

Linder, S.B. (1961), *An Essay on Trade and Transformation*, Stockholm: Almquist and Wiksell.

Los, B. (1996), 'A review of industry technology spillover measurement methods in productivity studies', paper presented at the MERIT/METEOR Conference on Innovation, Evolution and Technology, August 25-27,

Faculty of Public Administration and Public Policy, Twente.

Lucas, R.E.B. (1988), 'On the mechanisms of economic development', *Journal of Monetary Economics*, **22** (1), 3-42.

Lundvall, B.-Å. (1988), 'Innovation as an interactive process - from user-producer interaction to national systems of innovation', in G. Dosi, C. Freeman, R. Nelson, G. Silverberg and L.L.G. Soete (eds), *Technical Change and Economic Theory*, London: Pinter Publishers, pp. 349-67.

Lundvall, B.-Å., (ed) (1992), *National Systems of Innovation. Towards a Theory of Innovation and Interactive Learning*, London: Pinter Publishers.

Lundvall, B.-Å., Olesen, N.M. and Aaen, I. (1984), 'Det landbrugsindustrielle kompleks (The agro-industrial complex)', Serie om industriel udvikling, Aalborg University Press, Aalborg.

Magnier, A. and Toujas-Bernate, J. (1994), 'Technology and trade: empirical evidence for the major five industrialized countries', *Weltwirtshaftliches Archiv*, **130** (3), 494-520.

Malerba, F. and Orsenigo, L. (1990), 'Technological regimes and patterns of innovation: a theoretical and empirical investigation of the Italian case', in A. Heertje and M. Perlman (eds), *Evolving technologies and market structure*, Cambridge: Cambridge University Press, pp. 283-305.

Mansfield, E., Schwartz, M. and Wagner, S. (1981), 'Imitation costs and patents: an empirical study', *Economic Journal*, **91** (December), 907-18.

Markusen, J.R. (1984), 'Multinationals, multi-plant economies, and the gains from trade', *Journal of International Economics*, **16** (3-4), 205-26.

Marshall, A. (1890), *Principles of Economics*, edition (1961), London: Macmillan.

Martin, B.R. (1994), 'British Science in the 1980s - has the relative decline continued?', *Scientometrics*, **29**, 27-57.

McCombie, J.S.L. and Thirlwall, A.P. (1995), *Economic Growth and the Balance-of-Payments Constraint*, New York: St. Martin's Press.

Meliciani, V. and Simonetti, R. (1998), 'Specialisation in areas of strong technological opportunity and economic growth', in G. Eliasson, C. Green and C. McCann (eds), *Microfoundations of Economic Growth*, Ann Arbor: University of Michigan Press, pp. 70-93.

Michaely, M. (1962/67), *Concentration in International Trade*, Contributions to Economic Analysis, Amsterdam: North-Holland Publishing Company.

Mitchell, G. and Hamilton, W. (1988), 'Managing R&D as a strategic option', *Research Technology Management*, **31** (May-June), 15-22.

Narin, F. and Olivastro, D. (1992), 'Status report: linkage between technology and science', *Research Policy*, **21**, 237-49.

Nelson, R.R., (ed) (1993), *National Innovation Systems: A Comparative*

Analysis, New York: Oxford University Press.

Nelson, R.R. and Winter, S. (1982), *An Evolutionary Theory of Economic Change*, Cambridge, Massachusetts: Harvard University Press.

Nelson, R.R. and Wolff, E.N. (1997), 'Factors behind cross-industry differences in technical progress', *Structural Change and Economic Dynamics*, **8** (2), 205-20.

Nørretranders, T. and Haaland, T. (1990), 'Dansk dynamit: Dansk forsknings internationale status vurderet ud fra bibliometriske indikatorer (Danish Dynamite. The international status of Danish scientific research, based on bibliometric indicators)', Forskningspolitik, Forskningspolitisk Råd, Copenhagen.

OECD (1992), *Industrial Policy in OECD Countries: Annual Review*, Paris: OECD.

OECD (1997), *Science, Technology and Industry: Scoreboard of Indicators*, Paris, OECD.

Ohlin, B. (1933), *Interregional and International Trade*, Cambridge: Harvard University Press.

Padoan, P.C. and Pericoli, M. (1993), 'The single market and Eastern Europe: specialization patterns and prospects for integration', *Economic Systems*, **17** (4), 279-99.

Papagni, E. (1992), 'High-technology exports of EEC countries: persistence and diversity of specialization patterns', *Applied Economics*, **24** (8), 925-33.

Pasinetti, L.L. (1981), *Structural Change and Economic Growth*, Cambridge: Cambridge University Press.

Patel, P. and Pavitt, K.L.R. (1991), 'Large firms in the production of the world's technology: an important case of non-globalisation', *Journal of International Business Studies*, **22**, 1-21.

Patel, P. and Pavitt, K.L.R. (1993), 'National systems of innovation: why they are important and how they might be defined, compared and assessed', paper prepared for the book *Interacting Systems of Innovation: the Sources of Growth?*, P. Bianci, & M. Quere (*eds*), SPRU, University of Sussex, Brighton.

Patel, P. and Pavitt, K.L.R. (1994a), 'The nature and economic importance of national innovation systems', *STI Review* (14), 9-32.

Patel, P. and Pavitt, K.L.R. (1994b), 'Technological competencies in the world's largest firms: characteristics, constraints and scope for managerial choice', mimeo, SPRU, University of Sussex, Brighton.

Patel, P. and Pavitt, K.L.R. (1994c), 'Uneven (and divergent) technological accumulation among advanced countries: evidence and a framework for exploration', *Industrial and Corporate Change*, **3** (4), 759-85.

Patel, P. and Pavitt, K.L.R. (1997), 'The technological competencies of the world's largest firms: complex and path dependent, but not much variety', *Research Policy*, **26** (2), 141-56.

Pavitt, K.L.R. (1984), 'Sectoral patterns of technical change: towards a taxonomy and a theory', *Research Policy*, **13** (6), 343-73.

Pavitt, K.L.R. (1988), 'Uses and abuses of patent statistics', in A.J.F. van Raan (ed), *Handbook in Quantitative Studies of Science and Technology*, Amsterdam: Elsevier Science Publishers.

Pavitt, K.L.R. (1989), 'International patterns of technological accumulation', in N. Hood and J.E. Vahlne (eds), *Strategies in Global Competetion*, London: Croom Helm.

Pavitt, K.L.R. (1993), 'What do firms learn from basic research?', in D. Foray and C. Freeman (eds), *Technology and the Wealth of Nations: the Dynamics of Constructed Advantage*, London: Pinter Publishers, pp. 29-40.

Porter, M.E. (1990), *The Comparative Advantage of Nations*, New York: Free Press.

Posner, M.V. (1961), 'International trade and technical change', *Oxford Economic Papers*, **13**, 323-41.

Proudman, J. and Redding, S. (1997), 'Persistence and mobility in international trade', Bank of England Working Paper, Bank of England, London.

Ricardo, D. (1817), *Principles of Political Economy and Taxation*, reprinted in P. Sraffa (ed) (1951), The Works and Correspondence of David Ricardo, Vol. 1, Cambridge: Cambridge University Press.

Richter-Friis, H. (1991), *Livet på Novo (Life at Novo)*, Copenhagen: Gyldendal.

Rivera-Batiz, L. and Xie, D. (1993), 'Integration among unequals', *Regional Science and Urban Economics*, **23** (3), 337-54.

Rivera-Batiz, L.A. and Romer, P.M. (1991), 'International Trade and Endogenous Technological Change', *European Economic Review*, **35** (4), 971-1004.

Romer, P.M. (1990), 'Endogeneous technological change', *Journal of Political Economy*, **98** (5), 71-102.

Rosenberg, N. (1976), *Perspectives on Technology*, Cambridge: Cambridge University Press.

Rothwell, R., Freeman, C., Jervis, P., Robertson, A. and Townsend, J. (1974), 'SAPPHO updated - project SAPPHO phase 2.', *Research Policy*, **3** (3), 258-91.

Rumelt, R. (1974), *Strategy, Structure and Economic Performance*, Cambridge, Massachusetts: Harvard University Press.

Schmookler, J. (1966), *Invention and Economic Growth*, Cambridge, Massachusetts and London: Harvard University Press.

Schubert, A., Gläzel, W. and Braun, T. (1989), 'World flash on basic research. Scientometric data-files: a comprehensive set of indicators on 2649 journals and 96 countries in all major science fields and subfields 1981-1985', *Scientometrics*, **16** (1-6), 3-478.

Schumpeter, J.A. (1912), *The Theory of Economic Development: An Inquiry into Profits, Capital, Credit, Interest and the Business Cycle*, translated by R. Opie (1934), London: Oxford University Press.

Schumpeter, J.A. (1942), *Capitalism, Socialism and Democracy*, paperback edition (1996), introduction by Richard Swedberg, London: Routledge.

Soete, L.L.G. (1981), 'A general test of the technological gap trade theory', *Weltwirtschaftliches Archiv*, **117** (4), 638-66.

Soete, L.L.G. and Verspagen, B. (1992), 'Competing for growth: the dynamics of technology gaps', in L.L. Pasinetti and R.M. Solow (eds), *Economic Growth and the Structure of Long-Term Development*, London: Macmillan, pp. 272-99.

Solow, R.M. (1956), 'A contribution to the theory of economic growth', *Quarterly Journal of Economics*, **70**, 65-94.

Stone, J.A. and Lee, H.-H. (1995), 'Determinants of intra-industry trade: a longitudal, cross-country analysis', *Weltwirtschaftliches Archiv*, **131** (1), 67-84.

Teece, D. (1988), 'Technological change and the nature of the firm', in G. Dosi, C. Freeman, R. Nelson, G. Silverberg and L. Soete (eds), *Technical Change and Economic Theory*, London: Pinter Publishers, pp. 256-81.

Thirlwall, A.P. (1979), 'The balance of payments constraint as an explanation of international growth rate differences', *Banca Nazionale del Lavoro Quarterly Review*, **32** (March), 45-53.

Tidd, J., Bessant, J. and Pavitt, K.L.R. (1997), *Managing Innovation: Integrating Technological, Market and Organisational Change*, Chichester: John Wiley & Sons.

Tinbergen, J. (1943), 'Zur Theorie der Langfristigen Wirtschaftsentwicklung', *Weltwirtschaftliches Archiv*, **55**, 511-49.

Trefler, D. (1995), 'The case of the missing trade and other mysteries', *American Economic Review*, **85** (5), 1029-46.

UNIDO (1986), 'International comparative advantage in manufacturing: Changing profiles of resources and trade', Unido publication sales no. E86 II B9, United Nations Industrial Development Organization, Vienna.

van Hulst, N., Mulder, R. and Soete, L.L.G. (1991), 'Exports and technology in manufacturing industry', *Weltwirtschaftliches Archiv*, **127** (2), 246-64.

Vanek, J. (1968), 'The factor proportions theory: the N-Factor case', *Kyklos*, **21** (4), 749-55.

Vernon, R. (1966), 'International investment and international trade in the product cycle', *Quarterly Journal of Economics*, **80**, 190-207.

Verspagen, B. (1993), *Uneven Growth Between Interdependent Economies*, Aldershot, UK and Brookfield, US: Edward Elgar.

Verspagen, B. (1995), 'R&D and productivity: a broad cross-section cross-country look', *The Journal of Productivity Analysis*, **6** (2), 117-35.

Verspagen, B. (1997), 'Estimating international technology spillovers using technology flow matrices', *Weltwirtshaftliches Arhiv*, **133** (2), 226-48.

Verspagen, B. and Wakelin, K. (1997), 'Trade and technology from a Schumpeterian perspective', *International Review of Applied Economics*, **11** (2), 181-94.

Vollrath, T.L. (1991), 'A theoretical evaluation of alternative trade intensity measures of revealed comparative advantage', *Weltwirtschaftliches Archiv*, **127** (2), 265-80.

von Hippel, E. (1988), *The Sources of Innovation*, New York and Oxford: Oxford University Press.

Wakelin, K. (1997), *Trade and Innovation:Theory and Evidence*, Cheltenham, UK and Lyme, US: Edward Elgar.

Webster, A. and Gilroy, M. (1995), 'Labour skills and the UK's comparative advantage with its European union partners', *Applied Economics*, **27** (4), 327-42.

World Bank (1994), 'China: foreign trade reform', Country Study Series, World Bank, Washington D.C.

Yeats, A.J. (1985), 'On the appropriate interpretation of the revealed comparative advantage index: implications of a methodology based on industry sector analysis', *Weltwirtschaftliches Archiv*, **121** (1), 61-73.

Young, A. (1991), 'Learning by doing and the dynamic effects of international trade', *Quarterly Journal of Economics*, **106** (2), 369-405.

Young, A.A. (1928), 'Increasing returns and economic progress', *Economic Journal*, **38** (December), 527-42.

Index